A *partial indulgence* is granted the Christian faithful who on the day of the liturgical feast of any Saint recite in that Saint's honor the prayer taken from the Missal or another prayer approved by legitimate authority.

(*Handbook of Indulgences*, no. 54)

Lives of the Saints

This edition is dedicated to
SAINT JOSEPH
Patron of the Universal Church

Lives . . .
of the Saints

FOR EVERY DAY OF THE YEAR

In Accord with the Norms and Principles of the New Roman Calendar

Revision of the Original Edition of
REV. HUGO HOEVER, S.O.Cist., Ph.D.

Illustrated

CATHOLIC BOOK PUBLISHING CORP.
New Jersey

PREFACE

"THE Church has always believed that the Apostles and Christ's Martyrs who had given the supreme witness of faith and charity by the shedding of their blood are closely joined with us in Christ, and she has always venerated them with special devotion, together with the Blessed Virgin Mary and the holy Angels. The Church has piously implored the aid of their intercession. To these were soon added also those who had more closely imitated Christ's virginity and poverty, and finally others whom the outstanding practice of the Christian virtues and the divine charisms recommended to the pious devotion and imitation of the faithful.

"When we look at the lives of those who have faithfully followed Christ, we are inspired with a new reason for seeking the City that is to come and at the same time we are shown a most safe path by which among the vicissitudes of this world, in keeping with the state in life and condition proper to each of us, we will be able to arrive at perfect union with Christ, that is, perfect holiness. In the lives of those who, sharing in our humanity, are however more perfectly transformed into the image of Christ, God vividly manifests His presence and His face to men. He speaks to us in

Nihil Obstat: James T. O'Connor, S.T.D., Censor Librorum

Imprimatur: Patrick J. Sheridan, D.D., Vicar General, Archdiocese of N.Y.

The Nihil Obstat and Imprimatur are official declarations that a book or pamphlet is free of doctrinal or moral error. No implication is contained therein that those who have granted the Nihil Obstat and Imprimatur agree with the contents, opinions or statements expressed.

ISBN 978-0-89942-870-3 24 RD 16

Note: The dates for the saints who do not form part of the General Liturgical Calendar are in the main based on the newly revised calendar drawn up by the National Liturgical Commission of France. This lists a saint for for each day of the year in accord with the new principles and was endorsed by "Notitiae," the official publication of the Congregation for Divine Worship.

them, and gives us a sign of His Kingdom, to which we are strongly drawn, having so great a cloud of witnesses over us and such a witness to the truth of the Gospel.

"Nor is it by the title of example only that we cherish the memory of those in heaven, but still more in order that the union of the whole Church may be strengthened in the Spirit by the practice of fraternal charity. For just as Christian communion among wayfarers brings us closer to Christ, so our companionship with the Saints joins us to Christ, from Whom as from its Fountain and Head issues every grace and the very life of the people of God.

"It is supremely fitting, therefore, that we love those friends and coheirs of Jesus Christ, who are also our brothers and extraordinary benefactors, that we render due thanks to God for them and 'suppliantly invoke them and have recourse to their prayers, their power and help in obtaining benefits from God through His Son, Jesus Christ, Who is our Redeemer and Savior.' For every genuine testimony of love shown by us to those in heaven by its very nature tends toward and terminates in Christ Who is the 'crown of all Saints,' and through Him, in God Who is wonderful in His Saints and is magnified in them. . . .

"The authentic cult of the Saints consists not so much in the multiplying of external acts, but rather in the greater intensity of our love, whereby, for our own greater good and that of the whole Church, we seek from the Saints 'example in their way of life, fellowship in their communion, and aid by their intercession.' "

(Vatican Council II: *Constitution on the Church*, no. 50)

CONTENTS

SOLEMNITY OF MARY, MOTHER OF GOD

January 1

FROM all eternity God thought of the Virgin of Nazareth as the future Mother of His Son. At the Annunciation, Mary became the Mother of God. This is her most exalted title, the source of all her other privileges. On Calvary, Christ gave His Mother to all men to be their spiritual Mother, so that through her they might come to God as through her He came to them.

This feast takes the place of the Maternity of Mary formerly kept on October 11, which was instituted by Pope Pius XI in 1931, as a commemoration of the 15th centenary of the Council of Ephesus in 431.

PRAYER God, through the fruitful virginity of Mary You bestowed the blessings of eternal salvation on mankind. Grant that we may enjoy her intercession, for through her we received Your Son, the Author of Life. Amen.

STS. BASIL THE GREAT AND GREGORY NAZIANZEN,

Bishops and Doctors of the Church

January 2

IN the revision of the calendar the Church has seen fit to honor these two great Doctors of the Church and fast friends on the same day.

St. Basil

St. Basil the Great was born at Caesarea of Cappadocia in 330. Both of his parents and several of his brothers and sisters are honored among the Saints. He attended school in Caesarea, as well as Constantinople and Athens, where he became acquainted with St. Gregory Nazianzen in 352. A little later, he opened a school of oratory in Caesarea and practiced law.

Eventually he decided to become a monk and founded a monastery in Pontus which he directed for five years. He wrote a famous monastic rule which has proved the most lasting of those in the East. After founding several other monasteries, he was ordained and, in 370, made Bishop of Caesarea. In this post (until his death in 379) he continued to be a man of vast learning and constant activity, genuine eloquence and immense charity. This earned for him the title of "Great" during his life and Doctor of the Church after his death.

ST. Gregory was born at Arianzen in Cappadocia of parents who are both honored among the saints. He studied at Caesarea, Alexandria, and Athens, in which latter city he had as fellow pupils St. Basil and Julian the Apostate. On his return to Nazianzen he was baptized by his father and began to lead a most holy life. In 358, he joined St. Basil in the solitude of Pontus and remained until his father (who was Bishop of Nazianzen) recalled him shortly after and ordained him a priest, much against his wishes. He was appointed Bishop of Sasima, a small town, in 372 by St. Basil.

St. Gregory preferred a life of quiet solitude and reflection, but circumstances always conspired to call him away from it. In 379, he was made Bishop of Constantinople and remained there until 381 when he was finally able to resign and return to his solitude up to his death in 389. The depth of his theological knowledge and the vastness of his eloquence have made him one of the greatest Doctors of the Greek Church.

PRAYER Lord God, You desired to enlighten Your Church by the life and teachings of Sts. Basil and Gregory. Grant that we may learn Your truth with humility and faithfully put it into practice with love. Amen.

ST. GENEVIEVE, Virgin

January 3—*Patroness of Paris*

ST. GENEVIEVE was born about the year 422, at Nanterre near Paris. She was seven years old when St. Germain of Auxerre came to her native village on his way to Great Britain to combat the heresy of Pelagius. The child stood in the midst of a crowd gathered around the man of God, who singled her out and foretold her future sanctity. At her desire the holy Bishop led her to a church, accompanied by all the faithful, and consecrated her to God as a virgin.

When Attila was reported to be marching on Paris, the inhabitants of the city prepared to evacuate, but St. Genevieve persuaded them to avert the scourge by fasting and prayer, assuring them of the protection of Heaven. The event verified the prediction, for the barbarian suddenly changed the course of his march.

The life of St. Genevieve was one of great austerity, constant prayer, and works of charity. She died in the year 512.

PRAYER Lord God, You showered heavenly gifts on St. Genevieve the Virgin. Help us to imitate her virtues during our earthly life and enjoy eternal happiness with her in heaven. Amen.

ST. ELIZABETH ANN SETON, Widow

January 4

ELIZABETH SETON was born in 1774, of a wealthy and distinguished Episcopalian family, probably at Trinity Church in New York, and was a faithful, fervent adherent of the Episcopal Church until her conversion to Catholicism.

In 1794, Elizabeth married William Seton, and they reared five children in the midst of suffering and sickness. Elizabeth and her sick husband traveled to Leghorn, Italy, and there William died. While in Italy, Elizabeth became acquainted with Catholicism and in 1805 she made her Profession of Faith in the Catholic Church.

She established her first Catholic school in Baltimore in 1808; in 1809 she established a religious community in Emmitsburg, Maryland.

Mother Seton saw her small community of teaching sisters grow and expand from Emmitsburg (1809) to New York (1814), Cincinnati (1829), Halifax (1849), New Jersey (1859), Greensburg (1870), and St. Louis (1909). She died on January 4, 1821. She was beatified in 1963 and canonized on September 14, 1975 by Pope Paul VI.

PRAYER God, You raised up St. Elizabeth in Your Church so that she might instruct others in the way of salvation. Grant us so to follow Christ after her example that we may reach You in the company of our brothers. Amen.

ST. JOHN NEPOMUCENE NEUMANN,
Bishop

January 5

JOHN NEUMANN was born in Bohemia on March 28, 1811. Since he had a great desire to dedicate himself to the American missions, he came to the United States as a cleric and was ordained in New York in 1836 by Bishop Dubois.

On January 16, 1842, he made his profession as a Redemptorist, the first to do so in America. He labored in Ohio, Pennsylvania, and Maryland. In 1852, he was consecrated Bishop of Philadelphia. There he worked hard for the establishment of parish schools and for the erection of many parishes, especially national parishes for the numerous immigrants. He was also the first Bishop of the United States to prescribe the Forty Hours Devotion in his diocese.

Bishop Neumann died on January 5, 1860, and was canonized on June 19, 1977 by Pope Paul VI.

PRAYER God, Light and Shepherd of souls, You established Blessed John as Bishop in Your Church to feed Your flock by his word and form it by his example. Help us through his intercession to keep the Faith he taught by his word and follow the way he showed by his example. Amen.

THE EPIPHANY OF THE LORD

Sunday between January 2 - January 8

THE feast of the Epiphany is one of the oldest in the Church and one of the greatest in the ecclesiastical year. The word *Epiphany* is a Greek term which signifies a manifestation or revelation. During the first three centuries the manifestation of Christ to the chosen people, and His manifestation as the Savior of all races and nations, were celebrated on the same day, but since the 4th century, December 25 has been the feast of the Nativity, or Christmas, and January 6 the feast of the Epiphany, or the feast of the Three Wise Men. It is so called because the Gospel of the day tells us that *Magi* (now considered to be astrologers) came from the East to Jerusalem saying: "Where is the newborn King of the Jews? We saw His star at its rising and have come pay Him homage."

They may have come from Arabia, Chaldea or Persia. Tradition says that there were three, Gaspar, Melchior, and Balthasar. The prophecy that "a star shall rise out of Jacob," and the teaching of the prophet Daniel at Babylon, had spread throughout the East. When the mysterious star appeared, learned men recognized it as a sign that the coming of the Messiah was at hand and that He would be born in Judea. Following the star they reached Bethlehem. On entering the house, they found the child with Mary, His Mother. They prostrated themselves and did Him homage. Then they opened their coffers and presented Him with gifts of gold, frankincense, and myrrh.

PRAYER God, this day You revealed Your only Son to the Gentiles. Grant that we who already know You by faith may one day contemplate Your sublime beauty. Amen.

ST. ANDRÉ BESSETTE, Religious

January 6

BORN near Quebec in 1845, André worked in the United States for a few years. Returning to Canada, he entered the Congregation of the Holy Cross as a Brother. Because of poor health as a child, André had been unable to attend school regularly and could not read or write. He was assigned as a doorkeeper at the College of Notre Dame in Montreal and remained in that capacity for over forty years. He also performed the tasks of janitor, infirmarian, barber, gardener, and lamplighter. His piety and willingness to help others charmed the students and their parents.

André also developed a great devotion to St. Joseph. People flocked to his cell to ask for his opinion and his prayers for some favor or some cure, and André complied, while entrusting all to St. Joseph, the Spouse of the Virgin Mother of God and foster-father of the Divine Infant. In time, he was able to have a chapel built to St. Joseph. After his death on January 6, 1937, the shrine grew into the great basilica of St. Joseph's Oratory in Montreal, which is visited by pilgrims from all over the world. He was canonized in 2010 by Pope Benedict XVI.

PRAYER O God, friend of the humble, You inspired Brother André with great devotion to St. Joseph and singular dedication to the poor and afflicted. Grant us, through his intercession, to follow his example of prayer and charity, so that with him we may attain the splendor of Your glory. Amen.

ST. RAYMOND OF PENYAFORT, Priest

January 7—*Patron of Canonists*

BORN of a noble family in 1175, at the castle of Penyafort in Catalonia, St. Raymond was allied to the King of Aragon. At the age of twenty he taught philosophy at Barcelona. Requiring no remuneration for his services, he endeavored to form the heart as well as the intellect of his students. At the age of thirty he went to Bologna to perfect himself in the study of canon and civil law, and received the degree of doctor. On his return to Barcelona in 1219, the Bishop made him canon, archdeacon, and vicar-general. A few years later, in 1222, he entered the Order of St. Dominic, eight months after the death of its holy founder.

He labored zealously for the conversion of the Moors and the Jews, and in the composition of a treatise for the instruction of confessors. Pope Gregory IX summoned him to Rome, appointing him auditor at the apostolic palace, penitentiary, and confessor to himself. During this period he composed his work of canon law, known as the "Five Decretals." On his return to his own country he was elected general of the Dominican Order to succeed Jordan of Saxony, who had been the immediate successor of St. Dominic. After arranging and explaining the constitutions of the Order he resigned the office, and began again to apply himself to the exercises of an apostolic life. He died in 1275, at one hundred years of age.

PRAYER God, You endowed Your Priest, St. Raymond, with the gift of showing mercy to sinners and prisoners. Help us by his intercession to be freed from slavery to sin and with clear consciences to practice those things that are pleasing to You. Amen.

ST. APOLLINARIS, Bishop

January 8

ST. APOLLINARIS was one of the most illustrious Bishops of the 2nd century. Eusebius, St. Jerome, Theodoret, and others speak of him in the highest terms, and they furnish us with the few facts that are known of him.

He addressed an "apology," that is, a defense, of the Christian religion to the Emperor Marcus Aurelius, who, shortly before, had obtained a signal victory over the Quadi, a people inhabiting the country now called Moravia. One of his legions, the twelfth, was composed chiefly of Christians. When the army was perishing for want of water, the soldiers of this legion fell upon their knees and invoked the assistance of God. The result was sudden, for a copious rain fell, and, aided by the storm, they conquered the Germans. The emperor gave this legion the name "Thundering Legion" and mitigated his persecution.

It was to protect his flock against persecution that St. Apollinaris, who was Bishop of Hierapolis in Phrygia, addressed his apology to the Emperor to implore his protection and to remind him of the favor he had received from God through the prayers of the Christians. The date of the death of St. Apollinaris is not known, but it probably occurred before that of Marcus Aurelius, about the year 175.

PRAYER God, You made St. Apollinaris an outstanding exemplar of Divine love and the Faith that conquers the world, and added him to the roll of saintly Pastors. Grant by his intercession that we may persevere in Faith and love and become sharers of his glory. Amen.

ST. ADRIAN OF CANTERBURY, Abbot

January 9

A NATIVE of Africa, this learned and saintly man became Abbot of a monastery near Monte Cassino, Italy. Pope St. Vitalian judged him to be the best person to fill the vacant post of Archbishop of Canterbury, for his talents were most suitable for instructing and nurturing a nation still young in the Faith. But St. Adrian, deeming himself unworthy, suggested St. Theodore of Tarsus in his place. The Pope agreed but sent him along to be the assistant and adviser of the Archbishop.

Setting out in 668, the two holy men proceeded by way of France. There, St. Adrian was arrested by Ebroin, Mayor of Neustria, as an agent of the Eastern Emperor; and St. Theodore alone was able to go on. When St. Adrian was finally able to reach England, he found St. Theodore already confirmed in his See, and was named Abbot of the monastery of Sts. Peter and Paul at Canterbury.

Under St. Adrian's administration, this monastic school attracted students from all over and had a far-reaching influence. The Saint himself was learned in the Scriptures, well-versed in the Fathers of the Church, and a fine Greek and Latin scholar. All these subjects were taught there, as well as poetry, astronomy, and calendar calculation. St. Adrian died on January 9, 710.

PRAYER Lord, amid the things of this world, let us be wholeheartedly committed to heavenly things in imitation of the example of evangelical perfection You have given us in St. Adrian the Abbot. Amen.

ST. WILLIAM, Bishop

January 10

ST. WILLIAM was a descendant of the family of the ancient Counts of Nevers. He was educated under the care of Peter, Archdeacon of Soissons, his maternal uncle. At an early age he learned to despise the vanities of the world and to give himself with ardor to exercises of piety and to the acquisition of knowledge. On entering the ecclesiastical state he became Canon of Soissons and of Paris. Later he resolved to abandon the world and enter the Order of Grammont. He lived in this Order for some time and practiced great austerities. Dissensions arose between the fathers and lay brothers, which caused him to pass over to the austere Order of Citeaux that had recently been founded.

He took the habit at Pontigny, and after some time became Abbot, first of Fontaine Jean, and later of Chaalis near Senlis.

He had a special devotion to the Blessed Sacrament and loved to spend much of his time at the foot of the altar. In the year 1200 the clergy of the Church of Bourges elected him to succeed Henry de Sully, their Archbishop; but the news overwhelmed him with grief, and only a double command from his general, the Abbot of Citeaux, and from the Pope could move him to accept the dignity. In his new office he redoubled his austerities; he constantly wore a hair shirt and never ate flesh meat.

He was preparing for a mission among the Albigenses when he died kneeling at prayer in 1209. As he had requested, he was buried in ashes wearing a hair shirt and was canonized in 1217 by Pope Honorius III.

PRAYER Almighty and ever-living God, You willed to make Bishop William rule over Your people. Grant by his interceding merits that we may receive the grace of Your mercy. Amen.

ST. PAULINUS, Patriarch of Aquileia

January 11

ST. PAULINUS was born about 726 on a country farm near Friuli, Italy. He spent his youth tilling the soil for his struggling family, but also found time to engage in scholarly pursuits. So adept did he become at these pursuits that he gained a reputation as a grammarian and professor, and was invited by Charlemagne to come to his court, around 776. Here he met the noted Alcuin of York, and the two became fast friends.

In 787, the Emperor appointed Paulinus Patriarch of Aquileia near his birthplace in northern Italy, and he gave great luster to that church by his outstanding zeal, solid piety, and extraordinary talents. He attended all the great councils which were convoked in his day, and he himself called a synod at Friuli in 791 (or 796) to combat the errors then circulating against the mystery of the Incarnation. He even wrote two tracts against the more serious of these errors, Adoptionism, which maintained that Christ as man is only the adoptive Son of God. He also wrote hymns, poems, and other works.

When Pepin conquered the Avars, St. Paulinus immediately dispatched missionaries to convert these pagans who were now accessible to the Faith. However, he vigorously condemned the practice then in vogue of baptizing uninstructed converts or imposing the Faith by force on unwilling ones. On January 11, 804, the earthly life of this holy man came to an end.

PRAYER God, You made St. Paulinus an outstanding exemplar of Divine love and the Faith that conquers the world, and added him to the roll of saintly Pastors. Grant by his intercession that we may persevere in Faith and love and become sharers of his glory. Amen.

ST. BENEDICT BISCOP (BENNET), Abbot

January 12

ST. BENEDICT, or Bennet as he is commonly called, was of noble birth and an officer of the court of Oswi, the religious king of Northumberland, England, in the 7th century. At the age of twenty-five he left the world, made a journey of devotion to Rome, and on his return applied himself to the study of Scripture and the practice of pious exercises. After spending two years at the renowned monastery of Lerins and receiving the habit there, he accompanied St. Theodorus, Archbishop of Canterbury, and St. Aidan to England at the request of Pope Vitalian.

He returned to Rome a few more times to study the various religious disciplines and collect books and pictures of the Saints. After serving under Theodorus and Aidan, he was given a grant by the King of Northumberland and built the famous monastery of Weremouth, bringing over from France stonemasons and glaziers to construct it according to the Roman models he had seen. He also built another monastery six miles away at Jarrow, and ruled both since they were regarded as one.

In his zeal to make his monastery as close to the Roman models as possible, Benedict prevailed upon Pope Agatho to let him take back to England the precentor of St. Peter's in Rome to teach the monks Gregorian Chant. After suffering from a severe illness for three years, this holy and zealous worker for God died in January, 690.

PRAYER Lord, amid the things of this world, let us be wholeheartedly committed to heavenly things in imitation of the example of evangelical perfection You have given us in St. Benedict the Abbot. Amen.

ST. HILARY,

Bishop and Doctor of the Church

January 13—*Patron against Snake Bites*

ST. HILARY was born at Poitiers, France, of one of the most noble families of Gaul. He was brought up as a pagan. His own philosophic inquiries and the reading of the Bible led him to the knowledge of the true Faith and the reception of the Sacrament of Baptism. He then regulated his life according to the rules of the Faith he had embraced, and, though a layman, zealously endeavored to confirm others in true Christianity.

His wife, to whom he had been married before his conversion and by whom he had a daughter named Apra, was still living when he was chosen Bishop of Poitiers, about the year 353. According to the practice which then existed, married men were sometimes promoted to the episcopacy, but as St. Jerome clearly testifies, they ever after lived in continence.

The Arian heresy principally occupied his pen, and he became one of the most strenuous defenders of the Divinity of Jesus Christ. At the Council of Seleucia, in 360, he bravely defended the decrees of Nicaea, and then retired to Constantinople.

St. Hilary died at Poitiers in the year 398. He was the mildest of men, full of condescension and affability to all, but against Emperor Constantius, who showed himself an enemy of the

Church, he used the severest language. He is invoked against snake bites.

PRAYER Lord God, You endowed St. Hilary with heavenly doctrine. Through his help, may we faithfully keep that teaching and profess it in our conduct. Amen.

ST. SAVA, Bishop

January 14—*Patron of the Serbian Peoples*

THE younger son of Stephen I, who founded the Nemanydes dynasty and the independent state of Serbia, St. Sava was born in 1175 and became a monk of Mt. Athos in 1191. In 1219, he became Bishop of the Serbs and in 1222 Archbishop.

This saintly man organized the Serbian Church properly, using monks to do pastoral and missionary work among the neglected people. By unremitting efforts he consolidated Christianity among the Serbians and established Serbian Bishops. He also took an active part in secular affairs, contributing to the integration of the Serbian kingdom under his brother Stephen II. He died in 1235.

PRAYER God, Light and Shepherd of souls, You established St. Sava as Bishop in Your Church to feed Your flock by his word and form it by his example. Help us through his intercession to keep the Faith he taught by his word and follow the way he showed by his example. Amen.

ST. ITA (IDA), Virgin

January 15

ST. ITA was born in County Waterford toward the end of the 6th century. Though she came from a noble family she decided early in life to dedicate herself to God. She organized a convent in Killeedy, County Limerick, where she remained all her life, and which became famous as a training school for little boys.

Her counsel was sought by bishops and she was instrumental in training two boys who went on to become saints: Brendan and Mochoemoc. One day Brendan asked her what three things God loved in a special way, and her reply was: "True faith in God with a pure heart, a simple life with a religious spirit, and an open hand inspired by charity." Asked which three things God especially abhorred, she responded: "A scowling face, obstinacy in wrongdoing, and arrogant trust in the power of money."

St. Ita died on January 15, 570 and is known as the second Brigid. They are the most glorious women saints of the Celtic Church.

PRAYER Lord God, You showered heavenly gifts on St. Ita the Virgin. Help us to imitate her virtues during our earthly life and enjoy eternal happiness with her in heaven. Amen.

ST. MARCELLUS, Pope

January 16

ST. MARCELLUS was elected Pope in 307, the last year of the persecution of the Church by Diocletian. He undertook the ecclesiastical reorganization of the Church and was most merciful to those who repented after having denied their Faith.

When certain people known as the Lapsi refused to do penance for their apostasy and thus were not pardoned by St. Marcellus, the tyrant Emperor Maxentius sent St. Marcellus into exile, where he died in 309 as a result of privations.

PRAYER Almighty and eternal God, You willed to set St. Marcellus over Your entire people and to go before them in word and example. By his intercession keep the pastors of Your Church together with their flocks and guide them in the way of eternal salvation. Amen.

ST. BERARD AND COMPANIONS, Martyrs

***The Same Day*—January 16**

WHEN southern Spain was ruled by the Moors, St. Francis of Assisi sent five Franciscan friars, Berard, Peter, Accursius, Adjutus, and Otto, to preach to the Moors. They went to Seville and then to Morocco, where the Sultan, annoyed by their preaching, cut off their heads with his scimitar, about the year 1226. A young Canon Regular of Coimbra was so inflamed by these protomartyrs of the Friars Minor that he joined the Franciscans and went on to become the great St. Anthony of Padua. On hearing of their death, St. Francis exclaimed: "Now I can truly say that I have five brothers."

PRAYER O God, You sanctified the beginnings of the Order of Friars Minor by the glorious combat of Your Martyrs Berard, Peter, Accursius, Adjutus, and Otto. Help us to imitate their virtues as we rejoice in their triumph. Amen.

ST. ANTHONY, Founder of Monasticism

January 17—*Patron of Gravediggers*

ST. ANTHONY was born at Coma, Upper Egypt, in 251, of rich and virtuous Christian parents. After dividing all his possessions among the poor while still a young man, he retired into the desert. Here he lived the life of a hermit for many years, practicing heroic mortifications and devoting himself to silence, prayer, and manual labor.

After a severe probation of twenty years in spiritual trials and assaults of the devil, the fame of his sanctity and miracles, and the power of his example and word, drew to him hundreds of followers, to whom he gave guidance and a rule of life. In 305 he founded a religious community of cenobites who lived in detached cells. He died in 356, at the age of 105.

PRAYER Lord God, You gave St. Anthony the Abbot the grace of serving in the desert in prayer with You. Aided by his intercession, may we practice self-denial and hence always love You above all things. Amen.

STS. VOLUSIAN, Bishop, AND DEICOLUS, Abbot

January 18

ACCORDING to tradition, St. Volusian was of senatorial rank. He served as Bishop of Tours from 488 to 496. What little information exists about him concerns the last year of his life. As a result of his rank, he was continually involved with the politics of his day and finally he was driven from his episcopate by the Goths. The latter adopted this course of action because of their belief that the Bishop was planning to form an alliance with the Franks against them.

St. Volusian made good his escape from Tours and traveled to Spain where he went into exile. He died in that same year of 496. According to some historians, St. Volusian was followed into Spain by the Goths who captured him and cut off his head. This possible martyrdom was probably the basis for his canonization as a saint.

St. Deicolus, also known as St. Desle, left his native land of Ireland in the company of St. Columban, and both men settled at Luxeuil. St. Deicolus established the abbey of Lure, where he remained for the rest of his life as a hermit.

Despite his hardships, his contentment was always clearly evident. When St. Columban once asked him, "Deicolus, why are you always smiling?" this saintly soul simply replied: "Because no one can take God from me." The time of his death is recorded as having been about 625.

PRAYER Lord, may the intercession of Sts. Volusian and Deicolus commend us to You, so that by their patronage we may obtain what we do not deserve by any merits of ours. Amen.

ST. WULSTAN, Bishop

January 19

ST. Wulstan, a Benedictine monk, was one of the most outstanding figures in the religious history of England. Born about 1009, he spent twenty-five years in a monastery at Worcester where he became highly regarded for his asceticism and humility. In 1062 he reluctantly accepted the office of Bishop of Worcester and went on to administer it with great effectiveness till his death in 1095.

Together with Archbishop Lanfranc of Canterbury, he succeeded in putting to an end the slave trade that flourished between England and Ireland. In the secular struggles of the time, this saintly man assisted William I against the Barons and William II against the Welsh, and refused to resign in the face of William the Conqueror. He inaugurated the custom of pastoral visitations in England.

PRAYER God, Light and Shepherd of souls, You established St. Wulstan as Bishop in Your Church to feed Your flock by his word and form it by his example. Help us through his intercession to keep the Faith he taught by his word and follow the way he showed by his example. Amen.

ST. FABIAN, Pope and Martyr

January 20

ST. FABIAN was Pope from 236 to 250, succeeding St. Anterus. He sent St. Dionysius and other preachers of the Gospel into Gaul, and condemned Privatus, the originator of a new heresy in Africa. St. Cyprian, who relates this latter fact, calls St. Fabian an incomparable man. He suffered martyrdom in the year 250, in the seventh general persecution under the Emperor Decius.

PRAYER Lord God, You are the glory of priests. Through the prayers of the Martyr St. Fabian may we make progress in Faith and in fitting service. Amen.

ST. SEBASTIAN, Martyr

The Same Day, January 20—*Patron of Athletes*

ST. SEBASTIAN was born at Narbonne in Gaul, educated at Milan, and martyred at Rome about the year 284.

According to an account of the 5th century and now considered unhistorical, he entered the army at Rome under the Emperor Carinus, about the year 283, in order to render assistance to the martyrs. When Diocletian left for the East, St. Sebastian continued to enjoy the esteem of Maximian, his coadjutor in the Empire.

St. Sebastian had prudently concealed his religion, but he was at last detected and accused before Diocletian, who condemned him to be shot to death by arrow. The sentence was executed to the extent that he was left for dead.

Restored to health by the care of a pious widow, he boldly appeared before the Emperor and reproached him for his injustice against the Christians. The Emperor, recovering from his surprise at beholding St. Sebastian alive, commanded that he be beaten to death with clubs. His body was thrown into a sewer; but a pious lady had it privately removed, and buried it in the catacombs.

PRAYER Lord, grant us a spirit of strength. Taught by the glorious example of Your Martyr St. Sebastian, may we learn how to obey You rather than men. Amen.

ST. AGNES, Virgin and Martyr

January 21—*Patroness of the Children of Mary*

ST. AGNES suffered martyrdom during the bloody persecution of the Emperor Diocletian around 304 at the age of thirteen and became one of the best known and most highly regarded of the Roman martyrs. Her name is still retained in the First Eucharistic Prayer for Holy Mass.

The Acts of her Passion, which date back only to the 5th century, are considered to be not entirely reliable but they do tell us something about her. The young noblemen of Rome, attracted by her wealth and beauty, vied with one another in endeavoring to obtain her hand in marriage, but she refused them all, saying that she had chosen a Spouse who could not be seen with mortal eyes. Her suitors, in hope of shaking her constancy, accused her of being a Christian.

She was brought before a judge and remained unswayed by either his kindness or his threats. Fires were kindled, instruments of torture were placed before her eyes, but, immovable in her constancy, she surveyed them with heroic calmness. She was sent to a house of prostitution, but the sight of her inspired such awe that not one of the wicked youths of the city dared approach her. One, bolder than the others, was suddenly struck with blindness and he fell trembling.

The youthful Saint came forth from this den of infamy uncontaminated in mind and body, and still a pure spouse of Christ. Her most prominent suitor was so enraged that he incited the judge still more against her. The heroic Virgin was condemned to be beheaded. "She went to the place of execution," says St. Ambrose, "more cheerfully than others go to their wedding."

Amid the tears of the spectators the instrument of death fell, and she went to meet the Immortal Spouse whom she had loved better than her life. She was buried on the Via Nomentana, and Constantine erected a church in her honor.

PRAYER All-powerful and ever-living God, You choose the weak in this world to confound the powerful. As we celebrate the anniversary of the martyrdom of St. Agnes, may we like her remain constant in faith. Amen.

ST. VINCENT OF SARAGOSSA,
Deacon and Martyr

January 22—*Patron of Winegrowers*

ST. VINCENT, the protomartyr of Spain, was a deacon of the 3rd century. Together with his bishop, Valerius of Saragossa, he was apprehended during a persecution of Dacian the governor of Spain.

Valerius was banished but Vincent was subjected to fierce tortures before ultimately dying from his wounds. According to details of his death (which seem to have been considerably developed later on), his flesh was pierced with iron hooks, he was bound upon a red-hot gridiron and roasted, and he was cast into a prison and laid on a floor strewn with broken pottery. But through it all his constancy remained unmoved (leading to his jailer's conversion) and he survived until his friends were allowed to see him and prepare a bed for him on which he died.

The Saint's fame spread rapidly throughout Gaul and Africa—there survive several sermons of St. Augustine given on his feast day.

PRAYER Almighty and ever-living God, graciously pour out Your Spirit upon us. Let our hearts be filled with that true love which enabled Your holy Martyr St. Vincent to overcome all bodily torments. Amen.

ST. VINCENT PALLOTTI, Priest

***The Same Day*—January 22**

BORN in Rome in 1795, St. Vincent became a priest and dedicated himself completely to God and the care of souls. He dreamed of gaining for Christ all non-Catholics, especially the Mohammedans. Thus he inaugurated a revolutionary program which envisaged the collaboration of the laity in the apostolate of the clergy.

But St. Vincent was also well aware of the many deprivations in the natural sphere that hindered the spread of the Faith. He thus obtained and spent huge sums for the poor and underprivileged. He founded guilds for workers, agricultural schools, loan associations, orphanages and homes for girls—all of which made him the pioneer and precursor of Catholic Action.

His greatest legacy was the congregation which he founded for urban mission work, known as the "Society for Catholic Action." This indefatigable laborer for Christ died in 1850 from a severe cold which he most likely caught on a rainy night after giving his cloak to a beggar. He was canonized in 1963 by Pope St. John XXIII.

PRAYER God, You taught Your Church to observe all the heavenly commandments in the love of God and neighbor. Help us to practice works of charity in imitation of Your Priest St. Vincent and merit to be numbered among the blessed in Your Kingdom. Amen.

ST. ILDEFONSUS, Bishop

January 23

ST. ILDEFONSUS is highly regarded in Spain and closely associated with devotion to the Blessed Virgin which he fostered by his famous work concerning her perpetual virginity. Born around 607, Ildefonsus came from a noble family and was probably a pupil of St. Isidore of Seville. While still quite young, he entered the Benedictine monastery of Agalia near Toledo and went on to become its abbot. In that capacity he attended the Councils of Toledo in 653 and 655.

In 657 the clergy and people elected this holy man to succeed his uncle, St. Eugenius, as Archbishop of Toledo. He performed his episcopal duties with diligence and sanctity until his death in 667. This Saint was a favorite subject for medieval artists, especially in connection with the legend of Our Lady's appearance to present him with a chalice.

St. Ildefonsus was a prolific writer, but unfortunately only four of his works have survived. Among these are the one already mentioned and an important document of the history of the Spanish Church during the first two-thirds of the 7th century, entitled *Concerning Famous Men.*

PRAYER God, Light and Shepherd of souls, You established St. Ildefonsus as Bishop in Your Church to feed Your flock by his word and form it by his example. Help us through his intercession to keep the Faith he taught by his word and follow the way he showed by his example. Amen.

ST. FRANCIS DE SALES,

Bishop and Doctor of the Church

January 24—*Patron of Writers*

ST. FRANCIS, son of the Count de Sales, was born near Annecy in Savoy, in 1567. Showing an early inclination for the ecclesiastical state he received tonsure at eleven years of age. Soon afterward, he was sent to Paris to study philosophy and theology. He went on to the University of Padua where he was honored with a doctorate in both canon and civil law.

On his return home, with the reluctant consent of his parents who had envisioned other things for him, Francis entered the priesthood. A little later, he took upon himself the arduous mission of Chablais, where Calvinism had obtained a stronghold. In the midst of the most enormous difficulties, he pursued his labors with apostolic heroism, and was rewarded with the most wonderful fruits of conversion. While engaged in this work he received his appointment as coadjutor to the Bishop of Geneva, whom he succeeded as Bishop in 1602.

He now began to labor zealously in his diocese for the clergy and people, and extended his labors elsewhere, preaching the Lenten sermons at various places outside of the diocese. He also composed several instructive works for the edification of the faithful. In 1610 he founded the Order of the Visitation, with the help of the Baroness de Chantal, now St. Jane Frances.

In the midst of his constant pastoral work Francis found time to write the book that has made him known to succeeding ages: *Introduction to a Devout Life* (1609). It shows how ordinary life can be sanctified; no problem is too small for its author: dress, entertainments, flirtations, etc. His one concern is how to lead the reader to the love of God and the imitation of Christ.

In an age when fanaticism was the rule in controversies, Francis manifested an exceptional restraint and meekness. His pastoral zeal, which was anxious for the sanctification of the laity and the adaptation of the religious life to the new needs, marks a turning point in the history of spirituality. He died in 1622 with the word

"Jesus" on his lips, and was canonized in 1665 by Pope Alexander VII.

PRAYER Father in heaven, You prompted St. Francis de Sales to become all things to all for the salvation of all. May his example inspire us to dedicated love in the service of our brothers and sisters. Amen.

THE CONVERSION OF ST. PAUL, Apostle

January 25

ST. PAUL was born at Tarsus, Cilicia, of Jewish parents who were descended from the tribe of Benjamin. He was a Roman citizen from birth. As he was "a young man" at the stoning of St. Stephen and "an old man" when writing to Philemon, about the year 63, he was probably born around the beginning of the Christian era.

To complete his schooling, St. Paul was sent to Jerusalem, where he sat at the feet of the learned Gamaliel and was educated in the strict observance of the ancestral Law. Here he also acquired a good knowledge of exegesis and was trained in the practice of disputation. As a zealous Pharisee, he returned to Tarsus before the public life of Christ opened in Palestine.

Some time after the death of Our Lord, St. Paul returned to Palestine. His profound conviction and emotional character made his zeal develop into a religious fanaticism against the infant Church. He took part in the stoning of the first martyr, St. Stephen, and in the fierce persecution of the Christians that followed.

Entrusted with a formal mission from the high priest, he departed for Damascus to arrest the Christians there and bring them bound to Jerusalem. As he was nearing Damascus, about noon, a light from heaven suddenly blazed round him. Jesus with His glorified body appeared to him and addressed him, turning him away from his apparently successful career. An immediate transformation was wrought in the soul of St. Paul. He was suddenly converted to the Christian Faith and became an Apostle. *(See also p. 262.)*

PRAYER Lord God, You taught the whole world through the preaching of the Apostle St. Paul. As we celebrate his Conversion grant that, following his example, we may be witnesses to Your truth in this world. Amen.

STS. TIMOTHY AND TITUS, Bishops

January 26 — (St. Timothy) ***Patron against Stomach Disorders***

ST. TIMOTHY was from Lystra in Lycaonia, born of a Greek father and a Jewish mother. He was educated in the assiduous reading of the Scriptures. His mother, Eunice, and his grandmother, Lois, as well as St. Timothy himself, probably embraced the Faith during St. Paul's first stay at Lystra. On St. Paul's return there during the second missionary journey, St. Timothy was highly recommended by the Christians. Accordingly the Apostle chose him as a missionary companion and sent him on difficult, confidential missions.

During the first imprisonment of the Apostle at Rome, St. Timothy was with his master. After this imprisonment he accompanied the Apostle on his last missionary journey and was left at Ephesus to take charge of the Church there. The Apostle, shortly before his death, wrote St. Timothy to come to him before the winter. According to tradition St. Timothy spent the rest of his life at Ephesus as its Bishop. He was martyred during the winter of the year 97.

ST. TITUS was the friend and disciple of St. Paul, who ordained him Bishop of Crete. About the year 56 St. Paul sent him on a mission to Corinth to reform the Church there. He is said to have been the most cherished disciple of St. Paul, who, in the year 64, addressed one of his epistles to him instructing him in the care of his flock. St. Titus accompanied St. Paul and St. Barnabas to the Council of Jerusalem. He was uncircumcised, and although at the Council Judaizers insisted that he submit to this rite, St. Paul refused to permit it. According to tradition he returned to Crete to exercise his episcopal office, and died there about the year 96.

PRAYER Lord God, You filled Sts. Timothy and Titus with apostolic virtues. Through their intercession may we live good and religious lives here on earth and thus be worthy of our heavenly home. Amen.

ST. ANGELA MERICI, Virgin

January 27

BORN in 1474 at Desenzano on the shore of Lake Garda, Italy, St. Angela Merici became a tertiary of St. Francis at fifteen years of age. In a vision God revealed to her that she would establish a "company" to promote the welfare of souls. At Desenzano she established a school for the instruction of young girls and a second school at Brescia. She gathered around her twelve religious companions and founded the Ursulines at Brescia.

St. Angela was of a reflective bent and possibly the first to grasp the changed role of women in the society transformed by the Renaissance. She envisaged that those who joined her would remain in the world but devote themselves to every type of corporal and spiritual work of mercy, with special emphasis on education.

However, her idea of education was very different from that of a convent school. She preferred to send her followers to teach girls in their own families. Through this she hoped to effect an improvement in social conditions. For it was her belief that "disorder in society is the result of disorder in the family." Her idea of a religious order of women without distinctive habit and without solemn vows and enclosure was also in advance of her times—although her Order was obliged to adopt the canonical safeguards then required of all nuns.

On November 25, 1535, the solemn canonical institution of the company of St. Ursula took place in the Oratory of the Piazza del Duomo. As a patron, St. Angela chose St. Ursula because ever since her martyrdom, St. Ursula was regarded as the ideal type of Christian virginity.

In the year of her death, 1540, it was estimated that at least half the town of Brescia was Lutheran or Calvinist. However, the schools of the Ursulines did their share in strengthening and extending Catholicism and in safeguarding Italy from what we now term "modern unbelief." She was canonized in 1807 by Pope Pius VII.

PRAYER Lord, let St. Angela never cease commending us to Your kindness. By always imitating her charity and prudence may we succeed in keeping Your teachings and preserving good morals. Amen.

ST. THOMAS AQUINAS,

Priest and Doctor of the Church

January 28—*Patron of Schools*

ST. THOMAS, born toward the end of 1226, was the son of Landulph, Count of Aquino, who, when St. Thomas was five years old, placed him under the care of the Benedictines of Monte Casino. His teachers were surprised at the progress he made, for he surpassed all his fellow pupils in learning as well as in the practice of virtue.

When he became of age to choose his state of life, St. Thomas renounced the things of this

world and resolved to enter the Order of St. Dominic in spite of the opposition of his family. In 1243, at the age of seventeen, he joined the Dominicans of Naples. Some members of his family resorted to all manner of means over a two-year period to break his constancy. They even went so far as to send an impure woman to tempt him. But all their efforts were in vain and St. Thomas persevered in his vocation. As a reward for his fidelity, God conferred upon him the gift of perfect chastity, which has merited for him the title of the *Angelic Doctor.*

After making his profession at Naples, he studied at Cologne under the celebrated St. Albert the Great. Here he was nicknamed the "Dumb Ox" because of his silent ways and huge size, but he was really a brilliant student. At the age of twenty-two, he was appointed to teach in the same city. At the same time he also began to publish his first works. After four years he was sent to Paris. The Saint was then a priest. At the age of thirty-one he received his doctorate.

At Paris he was honored with the friendship of the King, St. Louis, with whom he frequently dined. In 1261 Urban IV called him to Rome, where he was appointed to teach, but he positively declined to accept any ecclesiastical dignity. St. Thomas not only wrote (his writings fill twenty hefty tomes characterized by brilliance of thought and lucidity of language), but he preached often and with the greatest fruit. Clement IV offered him the Archbishopric of Naples which he also refused.

He left the great monument of his learning, the *Summa Theologica*, unfinished, for on his way to the Second Council of Lyons, ordered there by Gregory X, he fell sick, and died at the Cistercian monastery of Fossa Nuova in 1274. He was canonized in 1323 by Pope John XXII.

PRAYER Father of wisdom, You inspired St. Thomas Aquinas with an ardent desire for holiness and study of sacred doctrine. Help us, we pray, to understand what he taught and to imitate what he lived. Amen.

ST. GILDAS THE WISE, Abbot

January 29

BORN about 500 in the Valley of the Clyde, St. Gildas was a celebrated teacher and the first British historian. The facts of his life are uncertain. According to the earliest version we possess, he was forced to flee to Wales, where he married and, after his wife's death, became a pupil of St. Illtyd. After spending some time in Ireland, he made a pilgrimage to Rome about 520 and founded a religious house at Ruys in Brittany on his way back, reaching Wales in 527. Later he visited Ruys and Ireland again and died at Ruys on January 29, 570, surrounded by his disciples.

St. Gildas wrote a famous history condemning British vice, which is the only history of the Celts. It covers the period from the coming of the Romans to Gildas' own time, but its purpose is more hortatory than strictly historical. Hence, it may have taken an exaggerated view of the evils of its times. St. Gildas also wrote some penitential canons.

PRAYER Lord, amid the things of this world, let us be wholeheartedly committed to heavenly things in imitation of the example of evangelical perfection which You have given us in St. Gildas. Amen.

ST. BATHILDIS, Widow

January 30

ST. BATHILDIS was an English girl of the 7th century captured by pirates and sold in 641 as a slave to the household of the mayor of the palace at Paris. She was constrained to marry King Clovis II, a foolish and debauched man, and at his death became regent. In this capacity, she struggled against simony and the slave traffic, and also brought about other changes for the good of the people.

She founded the abbey of Corbie and the nunnery of Chelles. In 665 she withdrew to the latter and led a life of prayer and self-denial until her death in 680.

PRAYER God, You inspired St. Bathildis to strive for perfect charity and so attain Your Kingdom at the end of her pilgrimage on earth. Strengthen us through her intercession that we may advance rejoicing in the way of love. Amen.

ST. JOHN BOSCO, Priest

January 31—*Patron of Editors*

ST. JOHN BOSCO was born on a poor farm near Turin, Italy, in 1815. At an age when the modern child would be enjoying the pastime of a kindergarten education, he was out on the hillside tending sheep. At about his ninth year, when he expressed the desire to become a priest, it was found possible to let him commence his education by walking more than four miles daily for half a year. The other half, in Spring and Summer, was spent in the fields.

The day before he entered the seminary, his mother, laying her hands on his shoulders as he stood robed in his clerical dress, said: "To see you dressed in this manner fills my heart with joy. But remember that it is not the dress that gives honor to the state, but the practice of virtue. If at any time you come to doubt your vo-

cation, I beseech you, lay it aside at once. I would rather have a poor peasant for my son than a negligent priest. When you came into the world I consecrated you to Our Lady; when you began to study I bade you honor her and have recourse to her in all your difficulties; now I beg you to take her for your Queen."

Today the motto on the Salesian coat of arms: *Da mihi animas cetera tolle tibi*—"Give me only souls and keep all the rest"—bears witness to the fidelity of Don Bosco to the words of a truly Christian mother.

This admirable "Apostle of Youth" is almost our contemporary. He founded the Salesian Society of St. Francis de Sales and the Daughters of

Mary Help of Christians. His life's work was consecrated to the care of young boys and girls. He died in 1888, and was canonized in 1934 by Pope Pius XI.

PRAYER God of mercy, You called St. John Bosco to be a father and teacher of the young. Grant that inspired by his ardent charity we may serve You alone and never tire of bringing others to Your Kingdom. Amen.

ST. BRIDGID (BRIDE) OF IRELAND, Virgin

February 1—*Patroness of Dairy Workers*

ST. BRIDGID is known as the second Patron of Ireland and "the Mary of the Gael." Born in County Louth near Dundalk about 450, of parents baptized by St. Patrick, she showed signs of sanctity from her youth. According to a legend, she asked God to take away her beauty in order to escape marriage and pursue her religious vocation. And when she received the veil from St. Mel, her beauty which had given way to deformity returned.

She founded the first convent in Ireland at "Cil-Dara" (the Church of the Oak), now Kildare, over which she presided many years. She also established communities in other parts of Ireland and by her prayers and miracles exercised a potent influence on the growth of the early Irish Church.

St. Bridgid was generous and joyful, vehement and energetic. Her one desire was to aid the poor and needy and relieve those in distress. One of her friends once brought her a basket of choice apples and saw her distribute them to the crowd of sick people thronging about her. The friend could not refrain from exclaiming: "They were for you, not for them." St. Bridgid simply said: "What is mine is theirs." She died in 523 and was buried in Downpatrick in the same grave as Sts. Patrick and Columba.

PRAYER Lord, our God, grant that Your faithful spouse, St. Bridgid, may kindle the flame of Divine love in us for the everlasting glory of Your Church. Amen.

PRESENTATION OF THE LORD

February 2

THE second day in February is the feast of the Presentation of the Child Jesus in the Temple, which is also called the feast of the Purification of the Blessed Virgin. Another name for this popular feast is Candlemas Day.

Forty days after His birth, Mary and Joseph brought Jesus to the Temple of Jerusalem to present Him to the Lord as the law of Moses prescribed. They carried with them the usual offering of the poor, a pair of turtledoves. The law of Moses commanded that the first-born male child should be offered to God in thanksgiving for the sparing, by the exterminating Angel, of the Israelites in Egypt.

The law also prescribed that on the fortieth day after the birth of her child a mother should offer a sacrifice of purification from legal stain: namely, a lamb and a young pigeon, or, should she be poor, a pair of young pigeons or turtledoves.

At the time of the presentation and purification there was in the Temple a just and God-fearing man named Simeon, who recognized the infant Messiah, and taking Him in his arms declared Him the Savior, the Light of the Gentiles and the Glory of Israel.

On this feast candles are blessed and carried in procession with appropriate prayers and ceremonies. The blessed beeswax candles typify the humanity which God the Son assumed, and signify that Jesus Christ is the True Light of the world by His doctrine, grace, and example. They also represent the ardent faith, hope, and charity with which the Christian should follow Christ by humble obedience to His Gospel and imitation of His virtues.

Blessed candles are lighted at Mass and other church services; at the administration of all the Sacraments except Penance; in imparting blessings, in processions, and in other liturgical ceremonies. There should be at least two blessed candles in every Catholic home for use when the

Sacraments are administered to the sick, and at times of any special danger, blessing, or family devotion.

PRAYER Almighty and ever-living God, on this day Your only Son was presented in the Temple as sharing our human nature. We humbly ask that we too may be presented to You with purified intentions. Amen.

ST. BLASE, Bishop and Martyr

February 3—*Patron of Those with Throat Diseases*

THE blessing of throats, invoking the intercession of St. Blase, has become a very popular devotion. St. Blase devoted the early years of his life to the study of philosophy and afterward became a physician. He was ordained to the priesthood and made Bishop of Sebaste in Armenia, where he was seized and carried off to prison by Agricolous, the Governor.

On his way to prison, a distracted mother whose child was suffering from a disease of the throat implored his aid. At his intercession the child was cured, and since that time his aid has often been solicited in cases of a similar disease. After cruel tortures the Saint was beheaded in the year 316. Through his intercession many have been cured of throat diseases or protected from them.

The priest in giving the blessing of St. Blase holds two candles in the form of a cross touching the throat, and prays that through the merits and intercession of St. Blase the person blessed may be delivered from throat diseases and from every other evil. The priest says: "Through the intercession of St. Blase, Bishop and Martyr, may God deliver you from every disease of the throat, and from every other illness. In the name of the Father, and of the Son, and of the Holy Spirit." The person responds: "Amen."

PRAYER Lord, hear Your people through the intercession of St. Blase. Help us to enjoy peace in this life and find a lasting refuge in the next. Amen.

ST. ANSGAR, Bishop

The Same Day, February 3—*Patron of Scandinavia*

KNOWN as the "Apostle of the North" and specifically of Denmark and Sweden, St. Ansgar was born (801) near Amiens of a noble family. He was educated from childhood at the Benedictine monastery of Old Corbie in Picardy and later became a monk there and abbot of New Corbie in Westphalia.

On fire with love for God and eager to spread the Faith, he went to Denmark whose king had been newly converted. After establishing a school at Schleswig, he was expelled by the local pagans. Journeying to Sweden, the holy man of God built the first Christian Church there. In 832 he was made Bishop of Hamburg and in 848 Archbishop of Bremen. In 854 he was entrusted with the organization of the hierarchy in the Nordic countries. In 854 he returned to Denmark, converted Erik, King of Jutland, and helped mitigate the horrors of the slave trade. He died in 865.

PRAYER God, You willed to send St. Ansgar to enlighten many peoples. Through his intercession, grant that we may walk in the light of Your truth. Amen.

ST. VERONICA

February 4—*Patroness of Dressmakers and Photographers*

ST. VERONICA, a pious matron of Jerusalem, accompanied Christ to Calvary and offered HIm a towel on which He left the imprint of His face. This event is commemorated in the Sixth Station of the Cross.

An Italian legend records that St. Veronica cured Emperor Tiberius with this image called Veronica's Veil and later left it in the care of Pope Clement and his successors. A French legend records that she married Zacheus, a convert, in France; accompanied him to Rome; left him as a hermit at Rocamadour; assisted Martial and brought relics of the Blessed Virgin Mary to Soulac, where she died. Some identify her with "the woman with an issue of blood" who was cured by Jesus.

The story told of this Saint has had a wide appeal to Christians over the centuries. For it vividly illustrates a truth that is relevant for all time and all peoples: the theme of compassion for Christ in His sufferings.

PRAYER Lord God, You showered heavenly gifts on St. Veronica. Help us to imitate her during our earthly life and enjoy eternal happiness with her in heaven. Amen.

ST. AGATHA, Virgin and Martyr

February 5—*Patroness of Nurses*

ST. AGATHA, an illustrious Sicilian virgin, noble of birth, but more so for her heroic virtue, was martyred (at Catania in 251 during the Decian persecution) for refusing the solicitations of a Roman senator.

Her martyrdom and early cult are historically certain but the details are legendary. According to a legend of the 6th century, the Roman senator, whose name was Quintanius, had St. Agatha subjected to various cruel tortures including cutting off her breasts. When she continued to resist, she was thrown upon red-hot coals. At this point a violent earthquake shook the town. Quintanius, fearing that the people would rise up in protest, had Agatha returned to prison, where she died of her tortures.

In addition to being patroness of nurses, St. Agatha is invoked against earthquakes and diseases of the breast. Her name is contained in Eucharistic Prayer I at Mass.

PRAYER Lord God, St. Agatha always pleased You by her chastity and in the end by her martyrdom. May she obtain for us merciful pardon for our sins. Amen.

STS. PAUL MIKI and COMPANIONS, Martyrs

February 6

IN 1597, forty-five years after St. Francis Xavier had evangelized much of Japan, St. Paul Miki and twenty-five others were martyred for the Faith after being led to the place of execution near Nagasaki by a spectacular journey intended to impress the population. The martyrdom was spurred on by a Spanish captain's statement that the missionaries were paving the way for the Spanish and Portuguese conquest of Japan.

Among those martyred were three Japanese Jesuits: Paul Miki, John Goto, James Kisai; six Franciscans, four of whom were Spanish: Peter Baptist, Martin de Aguirre, Francis Blanco, Francis-of-St.-Michael; one Mexican: Philip de las Casas; and one Indian: Gonsalo Garcia; the other seventeen were Japanese: lay people including a soldier, physician, and altar boys. All were pierced with a lance like their Savior. With their canonization in 1862 by Pope Pius IX, they became the protomartyrs of the whole Far East.

PRAYER Lord God, You are the strength of all the Saints. You called Sts. Paul Miki and Companions to eternal life through the Cross. Grant us, through their intercession, perfect fidelity to keep the Faith until our death. Amen.

ST. RICHARD OF LUCCA, King

February 7

ST. RICHARD was a prince of the West Saxons in the 8th century but he was accorded the title of King by his people who held him in great veneration. We know little about him, but the most telling point is the sainthood of his three children: Willibald, Wunibald, and Walburga.

Taking his two sons, Willibald who was a Benedictine monk at the monastery of Waltham, and Wunibald, this saintly man undertook a pilgrimage to Rome. After staying at Rouen for some time, they continued through France and northern Italy despite severe hardships. On the way they visited churches and shrines and nourished their faith and devotion. Exhausted by the lengthy and difficult journey, St. Richard died at Lucca in Italy in 722 and enjoys great veneration there.

His sons helped their uncle, St. Boniface, the apostle of Germany, to evangelize the Franks. His daughter became abbess of Heidenheim and ran a school for the children of Frankish nobles.

PRAYER Lord God, You alone are holy and no one is good without You. Through the intercession of St. Richard help us to live in such a way that we may not be deprived of a share in Your glory. Amen.

ST. JEROME EMILIANI, Priest

February 8—*Patron of Orphans*

BORN in 1481, St. Jerome was a Venetian nobleman who joined the army and was taken prisoner. After a miraculous liberation, attributed to the intercession of the Blessed Virgin, he decided to begin a new life entirely devoted to charity toward the poor, especially orphans.

He was ordained at thirty-seven and plunged into his real life's work. Around 1530, he founded the first known orphanage of modern times and in the ensuing years he founded many more, as well as hospitals and institutes for fallen women. In 1532 he established the congregation of Clerks Regular of Somascha, which looked after the education of youth in colleges, academies, and seminaries. He was the first to teach children the Faith by using questions and answers. St. Jerome died in 1537, a victim of an epidemic then raging, while ministering to those stricken by it. He was canonized in 1767 by Pope Clement XIII.

PRAYER God, Father of mercies, You made St. Jerome the helper and father of orphans. By his intercession help us to preserve that spirit of adoption by which we are called, and really are, Your children. Amen.

ST. APOLLONIA, Virgin and Martyr

February 9—*Patroness of Dentists*

ST. APOLLONIA was a deaconess of advanced age and noted sanctity who suffered martyrdom during the persecution of Decius about 248-249. After a life spent in self-sacrifice and works of charity, this holy woman fell prey to a howling mob venting its fury on any Christians it could find. Enraged at her courageous refusal to sacrifice to idols, some in the mob struck out at her and knocked out all her teeth.

St. Apollonia was then threatened with being burnt alive in a fire that was enkindled. She asked for a few moments to think things over. Then, so anxious was she to embrace martyrdom that she tore free from the hands of her tormentors and, prompted by the Holy Spirit, leapt into the fire before they were ready. And the pagans remained amazed to see a weak woman more anxious to die for Christ than the cruel pagans were to torment her. She is invoked against toothaches and dental diseases.

PRAYER Lord God, You showered heavenly gifts on St. Apollonia. Help us to imitate her virtue during our earthly life and enjoy eternal happiness with her in heaven. Amen.

ST. SCHOLASTICA, Virgin

February 10—*Patroness of Convulsive Children*

ST. SCHOLASTICA, sister of St. Benedict, consecrated her life to God from her earliest youth. After her brother went to Monte Cassino, where he established his famous monastery, she took up her abode in the neighborhood at Plombariola, where she founded and governed a monastery of nuns, about five miles from that of St. Benedict, who, it appears, also directed his sister and her nuns. She visited her brother once a year, and as she was not allowed to enter his monastery he went in company with some of his brethren to meet her at a house some distance away. These visits were spent in conferring together on spiritual matters.

On one occasion they had passed the time as usual in prayer and pious conversation and in the evening they sat down to take their refection. St. Scholastica begged her brother to remain until the next day. St. Benedict refused to spend the night outside his monastery. She had recourse to prayer and a furious thunderstorm burst upon them so that neither St. Benedict nor any of his companions could return home. They spent the night in spiritual conferences. The next morning they parted to meet no more on earth.

Three days later St. Scholastica died, and her holy brother beheld her soul in a vision as it ascended into heaven. He sent his brethren to bring her body to his monastery and laid it in the tomb he had prepared for himself. She died about the year 543, and St. Benedict followed her soon after.

PRAYER God our Father, today we celebrate the memory of St. Scholastica. Grant that, following her example, we may serve You with perfect love and rejoice in experiencing Your goodness. Amen.

OUR LADY OF LOURDES

February 11

THE first of the eighteen apparitions of the Blessed Virgin Mary to the humble Bernadette took place at Lourdes on February 11, 1858. On March 25, when Bernadette asked the Beautiful Lady her name, she replied: "I am the Immaculate Conception."

The devotion of people all over the world to Our Lady of Lourdes, together with the countless miracles that have been wrought through her intercession, has caused one of the most marvelous regenerations in the history of the Church.

PRAYER Merciful God, come to the aid of our frailty. May we who keep the memory of the immaculate Mother of God rise from our iniquities with the help of her intercession. Amen.

ST. SATURNINUS AND COMPANIONS,

Martyrs

February 12

ABOUT the year 304, during the persecution of Diocletian, a priest from Abitina in Africa and forty-eight other Christian men, women, and children from the same city were arrested during the Sunday assembly for refusing to hand over the Sacred Scriptures. They included the four children of Saturninus, of whom the two elder were lectors, Mary was a virgin consecrated to God, and Hilary was a young boy.

These dedicated Christians were sent to Carthage for trial and brought before the proconsul Anulinus. After some of them were tortured, all appeared before Anulinus, February 11, 304, and strongly defended their Faith before being sent back to prison. We do not know for certain whether these faithful followers of Christ were executed on the next day or whether the proconsul let them die of hunger.

PRAYER Lord, we devoutly recall the sufferings of St. Saturninus and his companions. Give success to our joyful prayers and grant us also constancy in our Faith. Amen.

ST. CATHERINE DE RICCI, Virgin

February 13

ST. CATHERINE DE RICCI was born in Florence in 1522. Her baptismal name was Alexandrina, but she took the name of Catherine upon entering religion. From her earliest infancy she manifested a great love of prayer, and in her sixth year her father placed her in the convent of Monticelli in Florence, where her aunt, Louisa de Ricci, was a nun. After a brief return home, she entered the convent of the Dominican nuns at Prat in Tuscany, in her fourteenth year.

While very young, she was chosen mistress of novices, then subprioress, and at twenty-five years of age she became perpetual prioress. The reputation of her sanctity drew to her side many illustrious personages, among whom three later sat in the chair of Peter, namely, Cervini, Aldobrandini, and Alexander de Medici, later called Marcellus II, Clement VIII, and Leo XI respectively. She corresponded with St. Philip Neri and, while still living, she appeared to him in Rome in a miraculous manner.

She is famous for the "Ecstasy of the Passion" which she experienced every Thursday from noon until Friday at 4 P.M. for twelve years. After a long illness she passed away in 1589.

PRAYER Lord God, You showered heavenly gifts on St. Catherine. Help us to imitate her virtues during our earthly life and enjoy eternal happiness with her in heaven. Amen.

STS. CYRIL, Monk, AND METHODIUS, Bishop

February 14—*Patrons of the Unity of the Eastern and Western Churches*

THE two brothers, Sts. Cyril and Methodius, Apostles of the Slavs, were born in Thessalonica, 826 and 827, and educated at Constantinople. After St. Cyril had preached in southern Russia, they were sent by the Patriarch St. Ignatius as missionaries to the Bulgarians, whom they soon converted to Christianity (861-865). Then they extended their work into Moravia and Dalmatia.

When they came to Rome to render an account of their mission, they were consecrated Bishops by Pope Hadrian II. St. Cyril died in

Rome in 869, leaving St. Methodius to continue the apostolate alone, which he did with success in Moravia, Bohemia, Poland, and the neighboring countries. To him is attributed the Slav alphabet, into which tongue he translated Holy Scripture. He died in Moravia, April 6, 883, worn out by his heroic labors and long struggles with enemies that never ceased to antagonize him. The relics of the two brothers are venerated in the church of St. Clement in Rome.

PRAYER Merciful God, You have enlightened the Slavonic nations by the teaching of the brothers Cyril and Methodius. Help us to assimilate the teachings of Your doctrine and perfect us as a people united in the true Faith and its expansion. Amen.

ST. VALENTINE, Priest and Martyr

The Same Day,* February 14 — *Patron of Greetings

ST. VALENTINE, a Roman priest, together with St. Marius and his family, assisted the martyrs who suffered during the reign of Emperor Claudius II in the 3rd century. Being apprehended, he was sent to the Prefect of Rome, who commanded that he be beaten with clubs and afterward beheaded. He suffered martyrdom about the year 270.

The custom of sending valentines on this day is the revival of an ancient pagan practice, which consisted in boys drawing the names of girls in honor of their goddess, Februata Juno, on February 15. To abolish this practice names of Saints were substituted on billets drawn upon this day.

PRAYER God of power and mercy, through Your help St. Valentine has overcome the tortures of his passion. Help us who celebrate his triumph to remain victorious over the wiles of our enemies. Amen.

ST. CLAUDE DE LA COLOMBIERE, Priest

February 15

BORN in 1641, St. Claude entered the Society of Jesus in Lyons, France, and gained widespread fame as an orator and educator in Paris. He had great devotion to the Sacred Heart of Jesus and, on a visit to the Visitation convent in Paray-le-Monial, met St. Margaret Mary Alacoque and learned of the visions she had been privileged to receive. He spent eighteen months at Paray-le-Monial acting as her spiritual director and encouraging her to spread the devotion as she had been commanded by Our Lord.

Father Claude himself became a zealous apostle of the devotion to the Sacred Heart, regarding it as the means of revitalizing the Faith among the people. He continued to promote the devotion when he was sent to London to preach to the Duchess of York, and succeeded in converting the Duke of York as well as other Protestants. Because of the intense hostility against Catholics at the time, his efforts earned a death sentence.

Father Claude received a commutation of his death sentence and returned to France in ill health. He died at Paray-le-Monial in 1682. He was beatified in 1929 by Pope Pius XI and canonized on May 31, 1992, by Pope St. John Paul II.

PRAYER Lord, our God, You spoke to St. Claude in the depths of his heart that he might bear witness to Your boundless love. May his gifts of grace illumine and comfort Your Church. Amen.

ST. ONESIMUS, Martyr

February 16—*Patron of Servants*

ST. ONESIMUS was a native of Phrygia. He robbed his master and fled to Rome, where he met St. Paul who was then a prisoner. The Apostle converted him to Christianity, baptized him, and sent him back to Colossae with a letter to Philemon, his former master, beseeching his pardon. This letter written by the hand of St. Paul himself had the desired effect. St. Onesimus obtained pardon of Philemon and returned to St. Paul, whom he afterward faithfully served.

He was later sent to Colossae with Tychicus as the bearer of the Epistle to the Colossians.

PRAYER Almighty, ever-living God, You enabled St. Onesimus to fight to the death for justice. Through his intercession enable us to bear all adversity and with all our strength hasten to You Who alone are life. Amen.

SEVEN FOUNDERS OF THE ORDER OF SERVITES

February 17

ON THE feast of the Assumption in 1233, seven members of a Florentine Confraternity devoted to the Holy Mother of God were gathered in prayer: Buonfiglio Monaldo, Alexis Falconieri, Benedict dell'Antella, Bartholomew Amidei, Ricovera Uguccione, Gerardino Sostegni, and John Buonagiunta. The Blessed Virgin appeared to the young men, exhorting them to devote themselves to her service in retirement from the world.

With the approval of their Bishop, these zealous Christians who had once been prominent businessmen of Florence retired to Monte Senario, near Florence. They founded a new Order which, in recognition of the special manner of venerating the Seven Sorrows of Our Lady, was called "Servants of Mary," or "Servites."

PRAYER Lord, infuse in us the piety of these blessed brothers by which they devoutly venerated the Mother of God and led Your people toward You. Amen.

ST. MARIE BERNADETTE SOUBIROUS,

Virgin

February 18

ST. MARIE Bernadette Soubirous was born at Lourdes in 1844. At fourteen years of age she

witnessed eighteen apparitions of Our Blessed Lady at Lourdes, instructing her to make known the miraculous healing powers which the Blessed Virgin, by her presence, would give to the waters at Lourdes.

In 1866 St. Marie Bernadette Soubirous joined the Sisters of Charity at Nevers, taking her perpetual vows in 1878. Her contemporaries admired her humility and the authentic character of her testimony about the appearance of the Blessed Virgin.

Nevertheless she had to endure many severe trials during her religious life and exhibited heroic patience in sickness. She realized that the healing spring was not for her, and was fond of saying: "The Blessed Virgin used me as a broom to remove dust. When the work is finished, the broom is placed behind the door and left there."

She died in 1879 at the age of thirty-five and was canonized in 1933 by Pope Pius XI.

PRAYER Lord God, You showered heavenly gifts on St. Bernadette. Help us to imitate her virtues during our earthly life and enjoy eternal happiness with her in heaven. Amen.

ST. CONRAD OF PIACENZA, Hermit

February 19

BORN into a noble family of Piacenza, Italy, in 1290, St. Conrad married a nobleman's daughter in his youth. While on a hunting party, he had some brush set afire to flush a quarry; the fire spread and destroyed an entire grain field and a neighboring forest.

Unable to put out the flames, Conrad and his men fled to the city, and an innocent peasant was apprehended, tortured, and condemned to death as the perpetrator of the deed. When Conrad saw the doomed man on the way to being executed, he was horrified and publicly confessed his responsibility for the disaster. He and his wife sacrificed their wealth to make restitution.

This event inspired the two of them to enter religious life. Conrad, then twenty-five years old, joined a group of Third Order Franciscan hermits and his wife entered the Poor Clares. In quest of more solitude, Conrad retired to a hermitage in the Noto Valley near Syracuse, Sicily, where for the next thirty-six years he lived a life of prayer and severe penance, spending a great part of his time caring for the sick in a nearby hospital. He died in 1351.

PRAYER Lord God, You alone are holy and no one is good without You. Through the intercession of St. Conrad help us to live in such a way that we may not be deprived of a share in Your glory. Amen.

ST. EUCHERIUS, Bishop

February 20

ST. EUCHERIUS was born in Orlèans, France. His meditations on the Epistles of St. Paul influenced him to abandon the world in 714. He retired to the Abbey of Jumiège in the diocese of Rouen. He soon acquired a reputation for sanctity and when his uncle, Suaveric, Bishop of Orlèans, died, the people named St. Eucherius to take his place. Charles Martel, mayor of the palace, who practically governed France, granted their request, despite his own lack of favor toward the Saint. Thus, St. Eucherius left his beloved solitude to assume the episcopal dignity in 721.

His apostolic zeal was tempered with such meekness that he was beloved by all who knew him. After being sent into exile by Charles Martel, St. Eucherius retired to the monastery of St. Tron, where he spent the remainder of his life in prayer and contemplation. He died there in 743.

PRAYER God, Light and Shepherd of souls, You established St. Eucherius as Bishop in Your Church to feed Your flock by his word and form it by his example. Help us through his intercession to keep the Faith he taught by his word and follow the way he showed by his example. Amen.

ST. PETER DAMIAN,

Bishop and Doctor of the Church

February 21—*Patron of Headache Sufferers*

A DEVOTED collaborator of Pope St. Gregory VII and, like him, a Benedictine, St. Peter Damian was one of the most glorious lights of the Church in the 11th century. Born in Ravenna in 1007, he became a Camaldolese monk at the monastery of Fonte Avellana, of which he became Abbot. He later became Cardinal and Bishop of Ostia and Velletri.

St. Peter Damian worked zealously for the internal reform of the Church by fighting against such abuses as simony and incontinence. He wrote many works on ascetical theology. He is numbered as one of the Doctors of the Church and died at Faenza in 1072.

PRAYER Almighty God, help us to follow the teachings and example of St. Peter. Placing Christ above all things, may we be ever active in the service of Your Church and attain the joys of eternal light. Amen.

CHAIR OF ST. PETER THE APOSTLE

February 22

CHURCH historians affirm positively that St. Peter founded the See of Antioch before he went to Rome. Antioch was then the capital of the East. St. Gregory the Great states that the Prince of the Apostles was Bishop of that city for seven years. It is also a fact, based upon the unanimous consent of Christian antiquity, that St. Peter was at Rome and founded the Church there. However, his sojourn in the capital of the Roman Empire was not continuous, as he was often absent when performing his apostolic functions in other countries.

This feast, which commemorates St. Peter's pontifical authority, formerly was celebrated on two different days: on January 18, in honor of his Pontificate at Rome, and on February 22, in honor of his Pontificate at Antioch.

PRAYER Almighty God, grant that those of us whom You have firmly rooted with a strong foundation in the apostolic profession may not be shaken by the hesitations of this world. Amen.

ST. POLYCARP, Bishop and Martyr

February 23

WE ARE acquainted with the life of this Saint from his Acts, composed by the Church of Smyrna, and abridged by Eusebius. They form a very authentic document of Christian antiquity.

St. Polycarp embraced Christianity while very young, about the year 80, and became a disciple of St. John the Evangelist who made him Bishop of Smyrna, probably before his exile to Patmos in 96. He governed that See for seventy years, and among his disciples were St. Irenaeus and the writer Papias. The former has recorded that his master knew St. John and others who had seen Jesus.

From Eusebius, St. Irenaeus, and St. Jerome we learn that about the year 158 St. Polycarp went to Rome to consult Pope Anicetus regarding the date of the Easter celebration, as there was a difference between the East and the West. It was agreed that both might follow their own custom. In the fourth general persecution, under the Emperors Lucius Verus and Marcus Aurelius, the Saint was apprehended and brought before the proconsul. Refusing to deny Christ, he was condemned to be burned.

The authors of the Acts tell us that they were witnesses of the fact that the flames did not touch him, but formed an arch over his head. Thereupon, he was pierced with a sword; such a great amount of blood issued from the wound that it extinguished the fire. The death of the Saint occurred about the year 166. His body was burned, but his bones are preserved in the Church of San Ambrogio in Rome.

PRAYER God of all creation, You led St. Polycarp into the company of the Martyrs. Through his intercession we ask that, as we share in

Christ's cup of suffering, we may some day rise to eternal life. Amen.

ST. ETHELBERT, King of Kent

February 24

ST. ETHELBERT was a descendant of Hengist, the legendary ancestor of the Jutish House of Kent. He became King in 560 and extended his power to all England south of the Humber. He married a Christian princess, Bertha, who was the daughter of the Frankish King Charibert. This resulted in the first introduction of Christianity into Anglo-Saxon England, since her father insisted that his daughter should be free to practice her Faith in England.

When St. Augustine of Canterbury arrived in England in 597 with his Roman mission, he was accorded a pleasant welcome by Ethelbert who was himself still a heathen. Inspired by the example of his wife's Faith as well as St. Augustine's zeal, Ethelbert was converted and baptized on Pentecost in 597. He thus became the first Christian English King and thereafter gave his full support to the cause of Christ in his realm.

St. Ethelbert was constantly concerned to promote the welfare of his people. He enacted wholesome laws which were held in esteem in succeeding ages in England. He abolished the worship of idols throughout his kingdom and turned their temples into churches or shut them down. He was also instrumental in converting

Sebert, King of the East Saxons, with his people, and Redwald, King of the East Angles. He died in 616 after reigning fifty-six years.

PRAYER Lord God, You alone are holy and no one is good without You. Through the intercession of St. Ethelbert help us to live in such a way that we may not be deprived of a share in Your glory. Amen.

ST. TARASIUS, Bishop

February 25

ST. TARASIUS was a subject of the Byzantine Empire. He was raised to the highest honors in the Empire as Consul, and later became first secretary to the Emperor Constantine and his mother, Irene. On being elected Patriarch of Constantinople, he consented to accept the dignity offered to him only on condition that a General Council should be summoned to resolve the disputes concerning the veneration of sacred images, for Constantinople had been separated from the Holy See on account of the war between the Emperors.

The Council was held in the Church of the Holy Apostles at Constantinople in 786; it met again the following year at Nicaea and its decrees were approved by the Pope.

The holy Patriarch incurred the enmity of the Emperor by his persistent refusal to sanction his divorce from his lawful wife. He witnessed the death of Constantine, which was occasioned by his own mother; he beheld the reign and the downfall of Irene and the usurpation of Nicephorus.

St. Tarasius' whole life in the episcopacy was one of penance and prayer, and of hard labor to reform his clergy and people. He occupied the See of Constantinople twenty-one years and two months. His charity toward the poor was one of the characteristic virtues of his life. He visited in person all the houses and hospitals in Constantinople, so that no indigent person might be overlooked in the distribution of alms. This saintly Bishop was called to his eternal reward in 806.

PRAYER God, Light and Shepherd of souls, You established St. Tarasius as Bishop in Your Church to feed Your flock by his word and form it by his example. Help us through his intercession to keep the Faith he taught by his word and follow the way he showed by his example. Amen.

ST. PORPHYRIUS, Bishop

February 26

ST. PORPHYRIUS was born at Thessalonica in Macedonia. In 378, at the age of twenty-five, he left home and friends to consecrate himself to God among the monks of Scete in Egypt. After five years spent there in monastic exercises, he went to Palestine to visit the holy places of Jerusalem, and then took up his abode in a cave near the Jordan, where he passed five more years.

One day while praying on Mount Calvary St. Porphyrius was miraculously cured of an illness; not a trace of the disease was left. In 393 the Bishop of Jerusalem, much against the wishes of the Saint, ordained him priest and committed to him the keeping of the Holy Cross. In 396 John, Archbishop of Caesarea, employed a ruse to make him Bishop of Gaza. He sent for him on the plea of wishing to consult him, and when he had him in his power he imposed upon him episcopal consecration.

St. Porphyrius died on February 26, 420. His life, written by his faithful disciple and companion Mark, is an important source of information about paganism in the Christian East.

PRAYER God, You made St. Porphyrius an outstanding exemplar of Divine love and the Faith that conquers the world, and added him to the roll of saintly pastors. Grant by his intercession that we may persevere in Faith and love and become sharers of his glory. Amen.

ST. GABRIEL OF OUR LADY OF SORROWS,
Cleric

February 27—*Patron of Clerics*

BORN in 1838, this Saint of modern times was originally named Francis after the great Saint of his native city Assisi. He attended the Jesuit college of Spoleto, where he was a great favorite with his fellow students and professors. Fastidious in manner and dress, he was fond of literature and the theater. However, he decided to leave the world after being miraculously cured from two bouts of illness.

He was guided by Our Lady into the Passionist Institute, where he took the name Gabriel and became a veritable Apostle of her Sorrows. At twenty-four years of age he died of tuberculosis, having already attained to a heroic degree of sanctity by a life of self-denial and great devotion to Our Lord's Passion. He was canonized in 1920 by Pope Benedict XV and is the patron of youth, especially of young religious.

His life was without any miraculous event; after his death (in 1862) many miracles occurred at his tomb in Isola di Gran Sasso, Italy.

PRAYER God, You inspired St. Gabriel to strive for perfect charity and so attain Your Kingdom at the end of his pilgrimage on earth. Strengthen us through his intercession that we may advance rejoicing in the way of love. Amen.

ST. ROMANUS, Abbot

February 28

ST. ROMANUS, at the age of thirty-five, left his family and entered a monastery at Lyons. Here he remained a short time before taking with him the constitutions and conferences of the celebrated monastic author, Cassian, to retire to a spot in the solitude of Mount Jura. His occupations consisted in prayer, reading, and manual labor. Later his brother Lupicinus and some others joined him. These were followed by such a large number that it became necessary to erect two monasteries, as well as one for women.

The two brothers governed their monasteries in great harmony. The abstinence they prescribed for their monks was milder than that observed by the Orientals and by the monks of Lerins. The principal reason for this was that the physical constitution of the Gauls required more nourishment. However, they always abstained from every kind of meat, and only used milk and eggs in time of sickness.

St. Romanus died in 460 on his return from a pilgrimage. Lupicinus toiled for twenty more years on earth and also achieved the crown of sanctity—his feast is on March 21.

PRAYER Lord, amid the things of this world, let us be wholeheartedly committed to heavenly things in imitation of the example of evangelical perfection You have given us in St. Romanus. Amen.

ST. OSWALD, Bishop

February 29

A DANE by birth, St. Oswald studied in the household of his uncle, Archbishop Odo of Canterbury and became a priest of Winchester. He went to Fleury, France, where he took the monastic habit. Returning to England in 959, he was later made Bishop of Worcester (962) by St. Dunstan. In this office, he worked hard to eliminate abuses and built many monasteries, including the famous abbey of Ramsey in Huntingdonshire.

In 972, St. Oswald became Archbishop of York, although he also retained the See of Worcester in order to promote his monastic reforms which were under attack by Elfhere, King of Mercia. In addition to striving to improve the morals of his clergy, thie Saint also labored to increase their theological knowledge—he himself wrote two treatises and several synodal decrees.

St. Oswald was associated for most of his public life with St. Dunstan and St. Ethelwold and when he died in 992 popular veneration joined his name to theirs. He has been revered ever since as one of the three saints who revived English monasticism.

PRAYER God, You made St. Oswald an outstanding exemplar of Divine love and the Faith that conquers the world, and added him to the role of saintly pastors. Grant by his intercession that we may persevere in Faith and love and become sharers of his glory. Amen.

ST. ALBINUS, Bishop

March 1

ST. ALBINUS was born of a noble family of Brittany. In his early youth he was fervent in the practice of piety and embraced the monastic state at Cincillae, near Angers. In 504, at thirty-five years of age, he was chosen Abbot, which office he filled for twenty-five years, until he became Bishop of Angers. He governed his diocese until his death, which occurred in 549.

As a monk, St. Albinus was a perfect model of virtue, especially of prayer, mortification of the senses, and obedience. He was entirely dead to himself, living only for Christ. As Bishop, he governed his church with zeal, restoring discipline everywhere, while in his private conduct he lived the same life of sanctity as he had lived when a monk. His humility equaled his other virtues, so that he looked on himself as the most unprofitable among the servants of God.

PRAYER God, Light and Shepherd of souls, You established St. Albinus as Bishop in Your Church to feed Your flock by his word and form it by his example. Help us through his intercession to keep the Faith he taught by his word and follow the way he showed by his example. Amen.

BLESSED CHARLES THE GOOD, Martyr

March 2

IN 1086, St. Canute, king of Denmark and father of Blessed Charles the Good, was slain in St. Alban's Church, Odense. Charles who was only five years old was taken by his mother to the court of Robert, Count of Flanders, his maternal grandfather. When he grew up, he became a knight and accompanied Robert in a crusade to the Holy Land where he distinguished himself; on their return, Charles also fought against the English with his uncle.

On Robert's death, his son Baldwin succeeded him and designated Charles as his heir. At the same time, he arranged for Charles' marriage to the daughter of the Count of Clermont. During Baldwin's rule, Charles was closely associated with him, and the people came to have a high regard for his wise and beneficent ways as well as his personal holiness. At Baldwin's death, in 1119, the people made his cousin their ruler.

Charles ruled his people with wisdom, diligence, and compassion; he made sure that times of truce were respected and fought against black marketers who hoarded food and were waiting to sell it at astronomical prices to the people. This incurred their undying wrath and one day (in 1127) as Charles was praying in the church of St. Donatian they set upon him and killed him.

PRAYER Almighty, ever-living God, You enabled Blessed Charles to fight to the death for justice. Through his intercession enable us to bear all adversity and with all our strength hasten to You Who alone are life. Amen.

ST. KATHARINE DREXEL, Virgin

March 3

BORN in 1858, into a prominent Philadelphia family, Katharine became imbued with love for God and neighbor. She took an avid interest in the material and spiritual well-being of black and native Americans. She began by donating money but soon concluded that more was needed—the lacking ingredient was people.

Katharine founded the Sisters of the Blessed Sacrament for Indians and Colored People, whose members would work for the betterment of those they were called to serve. From the age of 33 until her death in 1955, she dedicated her life and a fortune of 20 million dollars to this work.

In 1894, Mother Drexel took part in opening the first mission school for Indians, in Santa Fe, New Mexico. Other schools quickly followed—for native Americans west of the Mississippi River and for blacks in the southern part of the United States. In 1915 she also founded Xavier University in New Orleans. At her death there were more than 500 Sisters teaching in 63 schools throughout the country. Katharine was canonized by Pope St. John Paul II on October 1, 2000.

PRAYER God, let St. Katharine never cease commending us to Your kindness. By imitating her charity and prudence may we succeed in keeping Your teachings and preserving good morals. Amen.

ST. CUNEGUNDES, Empress

The Same Day,* March 3—*Patroness of Lithuania

THE father of St. Cunegundes was Sigfrid, first Count of Luxemburg. After a pious education, she was married to St. Henry, Duke of

Bavaria, who, upon the death of Emperor Otho III, was chosen King of the Romans. St. Cunegundes was crowned at Paderborn in 1002.

In 1014 she went with her husband to Rome and became Empress, receiving together with him the imperial crown from the hands of Pope Benedict VIII. Though married, she lived in continence, for, with her husband's consent, she had made a vow of virginity before her marriage.

Calumniators accused her of scandalous conduct, but her innocence was signally vindicated by Divine Providence, as she walked over pieces of flaming iron without injury, to the great joy of the Emperor. Her husband, Henry II, died in 1024, leaving his widow comparatively poor, for she had given away nearly all her wealth in charitable works.

In 1025, on the anniversary of his death, and on the occasion of the dedication of a monastery which she had built for Benedictine nuns at Kaffungen, she clothed herself with a poor habit, adopted the veil, which she received from the hands of the Bishop, and entered that same monastery. Her occupations consisted in prayer, reading, and manual labor, and thus she spent the last fifteen years of her life. She died in 1040, and her body was carried to Bamberg, where it was laid near that of her husband, St. Henry.

PRAYER God, You inspired St. Cunegundes to strive for perfect charity and so attain Your Kingdom at the end of her pilgrimage on earth.

Strengthen us through her intercession that we may advance rejoicing in the way of love. Amen.

ST. CASIMIR

March 4—*Patron of Poland*

ST. CASIMIR was the third among the thirteen children of Casimir III, King of Poland. He was born on October 5, 1458. Although educated in a royal court, he had a horror of luxury and practiced many mortifications in secret. Under the care of the holy canon, John Dugloss, he grew up in singular innocence. One of his principal devotions was to the Blessed Virgin, in whose honor he composed, or at least frequently recited, the well-known "Hymn of St. Casimir."

When the crown of Hungary was offered to him, St. Casimir marched at the head of an army of 20,000 men to the frontier, to comply with his father's will. The reigning King of Hungary whom the people wished to dethrone was Matthias Corvinus. On reaching the frontier and learning that the differences between King and people had been adjusted, St. Casimir gladly returned home. Realizing afterward the injustice of the attempt against the King of Hungary, he could never be prevailed upon to assume the crown when the Hungarians again offered it to him.

To the end of his life St. Casimir preserved untainted his purity of soul and body, nor could he ever be induced to enter the state of matrimony.

A lingering tuberculosis ended his brief career, which was brought to a close at Vilna, the capital of Lithuania, in 1482, at twenty-four years of age.

PRAYER Almighty God, to serve You is to reign. By the interceding prayers of St. Casimir help us ever to serve You in sanctity and justice. Amen.

ST. JOHN JOSEPH OF THE CROSS, Priest

March 5

ST. JOHN JOSEPH of the Cross was born about the middle of the 17th century on the beautiful island of Ischia, near Naples. From his childhood he was a model of virtue, and in his sixteenth year he entered the Franciscan Order of the Strictest Observance, or Reform of St. Peter of Alcantara. Such was the edification he gave in his Order that within three years after his profession he was sent to found a monastery in Piedmont. He became a priest out of obedience, and obtained, as it seemed, an inspired knowledge of moral theology.

With his superiors' permission he built another monastery and drew up rules for that community, which were confirmed by the Holy See. He afterward became master of novices. Some time later he was made provincial of the province of Naples, erected in the beginning of the 18th century by Clement XI.

He labored hard to establish in Italy that branch of his Order which the Sovereign Pontiff had separated from the one in Spain. In his work he suffered much, and became the victim of numerous calumnies. However, the Saint succeeded in his labors, endeavoring to instill in the hearts of his subjects the double spirit of contemplation and penance bequeathed to his Reform by St. Peter of Alcantara.

St. John Joseph exemplified the most sublime virtues, especially humility and religious discipline. He also possessed numerous gifts in the supernatural order, such as those of prophecy and miracles. Finally, consumed by labors for the glory of God, he was called to his reward. Stricken with apoplexy, he died an octogenarian in his monastery at Naples, March 5, 1734 and was canonized in 1839 by Pope Gregory XVI.

PRAYER God, You inspired St. Joseph to strive for perfect charity and so attain Your Kingdom at the end of his pilgrimage on earth. Strengthen us through his intercession that we may advance rejoicing in the way of love. Amen.

ST. COLETTE, Virgin

March 6

ST. COLETTE was born at Corbie, France, in 1381 of humble and aged parents. When she was twenty-two, her parents died and she began life as an anchoress according to the Rule of the Third Order of St. Francis. After four years of this life, she was inspired in 1406 to introduce the strict observance of St. Clare, which was only observed in a modified form at her time.

Entrusted with the reform of the Third Order by Pope Benedict XIII, St. Colette traveled the length and breadth of France and Flanders, founding or reforming convents; and in doing so she is said to have met St. Joan of Arc at Moulins in 1429. Over the course of forty years, she surmounted many spiritual and physical obstacles to establish fifteen communities of reformed Poor Clares. One branch of the Order is still called the Colettines after her.

This holy and indefatigable worker for God died in 1447 at the community she had founded in Ghent.

PRAYER Lord, our God, grant that Your faithful spouse, St. Colette, may enkindle in us the flame of Divine love which she enkindled in other virgins for the everlasting glory of Your Church. Amen.

STS. PERPETUA AND FELICITY, Martyrs

March 7

STS. PERPETUA and Felicity and the friends who died with them at Carthage are in a special class among the primitive martyrs since we possess authentic detailed records which give us a vivid picture of their experiences and personalities. There is a diary of St. Perpetua herself, a page by another martyr, and a concluding account by a first-hand witness who is thought to have been Tertullian.

St. Perpetua was a twenty-two-year-old noble lady of Carthage with a baby son and St. Felicity was a married slave who was pregnant. They were arrested under the anti-Christian edict of 202 along with three fellow Christians, Saturninus, Secundulus, and Revocatus. All had been converted by a layman, Saturus, who joined them voluntarily in the dungeon in which they were imprisoned for refusing to sacrifice to the gods.

St. Perpetua yielded her nursing child to her pagan father but remained firm in her Faith in spite of his pleas. St. Felicity gave birth to a child in prison and also remained steadfast in the Faith when the child was taken from her.

The martyrs were condemned to death and mauled by beasts in the amphitheater before finally being beheaded in the year 203. So shaken was the executioner by St. Perpetua's commanding aristocratic appearance that she herself had to guide his blade to her neck.

Their martyrdom became known throughout the Church—St. Augustine preached in their honor at least three times. St. Perpetua is mentioned in the Roman Canon or Eucharistic Prayer I, but the Felicity mentioned with her is probably the Roman Martyr of 162.

PRAYER God, inspired by Your love, Sts. Perpetua and Felicity were able to disregard persecution and overcome the torment of death. Aided by their prayers, may we make constant progress in our love for You. Amen.

ST. JOHN OF GOD,
Religious
March 8

Patron of Booksellers

ST. JOHN was born in Portugal in 1495 of humble but virtuous parents. His early years were spent as a shepherd, in great innocence and virtue; but in 1522 he enlisted in a military company and served against the French and, later, the Turks in Hungary, while Charles V was King of Spain. Evil associations caused his spirit of piety to decline, but in 1536 he left the army and entered the service of a lady near Seville as a shepherd.

At about forty years of age he resolved upon an entire change of life and began to devote himself to the service of God. After some vicissitudes he settled in Granada in 1538 and opened a shop. The sermons of St. John of Avila impressed him to such a degree that in order to draw humiliations upon himself, he acted as a madman. He desisted from this extraordinary conduct by the command of the holy preacher.

In 1540 St. John hired a house to harbor sick persons, and thus laid the foundations of a new Order, the Brothers Hospitallers of St. John of God. He devoted himself with unremitting zeal to the care of the sick. After ten years of hard labor his health deteriorated. His last illness, as the latter portion of his life had been, was most edifying. He expired on his knees before the altar, March 8, 1550 and was canonized in 1690 by Pope Alexander VIII.

PRAYER God, You filled St. John with the spirit of compassion. Grant that by practicing works of charity we may deserve to be numbered among the elect in Your Kingdom. Amen.

ST. FRANCES OF ROME, Religious

March 9—*Patroness of Widows and Motorists*

ST. FRANCES was born in Rome of a noble family in 1384. She wished to enter a monastery, but in obedience to her parents, at the age of twelve, she married a wealthy nobleman named Lawrence Ponziani.

In the matrimonial state she led a very pious life, though she never allowed her spiritual exercises to interfere with her domestic duties. She had to endure many trials, particularly during the great schism, when her husband was banished; but she suffered all with exemplary patience, blessing the holy will of God.

After the schism her husband recovered his estates. In 1425 she founded the Oblate Congregation of Tor di Specchi, to which she gave the Rule of St. Benedict. After the death of her husband she received the habit in this community in 1437, and began to live as though she were the lowest of the sisters. Soon after, she was chosen superior. God conferred upon her numerous favors in the supernatural order. She died March 9, 1440, at the age of fifty-six and was canonized in 1608 by Pope Paul V.

PRAYER God, in St. Frances You have given us a singular example of both the monastic and the conjugal way of life. Help us to persevere in serving You so that in all the vicissitudes of life we may both look to You and follow You. Amen.

ST. DOMINIC SAVIO

The Same Day,* March 9—*Patron of Choristers

BORN at Riva, Italy, in 1842, St. Dominic Savio was only fifteen when he died but he had already attained a high degree of sanctity. A pupil of the great St. John Bosco who loved him like a son, St. Dominic organized the Company of the Immaculate Conception to help St. John in running the Oratory. Though St. Dominic's life was one of poverty, work, and suffering, it was filled with the cheerfulness and joy of sanctity. This model for youths once wrote to a friend: "Here we make sanctity consist in being joyful all the time and in faithfully performing our duties."

PRAYER Lord God, You alone are holy and no one is good without You. Through the intercession of St. Dominic help us to live in such a way that we may not be deprived of a share in Your glory. Amen.

ST. MACARIUS, Bishop

March 10

ST. MACARIUS was Bishop of Jerusalem from about 313 till his death about 334. He was a lifelong and staunch opponent of Arianism and fought strenuously against this pernicious heresy. He was present at the Council of Nicaea in 325 and played a large role in drafting the Creed.

Soon after the Council, together with St. Helena he miraculously discovered the true Cross in Jerusalem, and he was commissioned by her son, Emperor Constantine, to build the Church of the Holy Sepulcher. Later, he and his fellow Bishops of Palestine received another letter from Constantine to construct a church at Mamre.

PRAYER God, Light and Shepherd of souls, You established St. Macarius as Bishop in Your Church to feed Your flock by his word and form it by his example. Help us through his interces-

sion to keep the Faith he taught by his word and follow the way he showed by his example. Amen.

ST. EULOGIUS, Martyr

March 11

ST. EULOGIUS belonged to a noble family of Cordova, which was then the capital of the Moors in Spain. Ordained to the priesthood, he was placed at the head of the most important ecclesiastical school in Spain, which then flourished at Cordova. His virtues, to which he joined assiduous fasting and prayer, gained for him universal esteem.

In the year 850, a violent persecution broke out against the Christians. As one who encouraged the martyrs, St. Eulogius was cast into prison together with his Bishop and many priests. He wrote an *Exhortation to Martyrdom* for the virgins Flora and Mary, who were then beheaded on November 24, 851. These two Saints promised to pray for their companions, and six days after their death Eulogius and the others were freed.

The persecution continued and St. Eulogius became the support of the dispersed flock, encouraging a group of other martyrs who were martyred in 853. He wrote their history, entitled *Memorial of the Saints*, which is permeated by an ardent zeal and spirit of martyrdom.

In 858, it became St. Eulogius' turn to suffer for his Faith. A virgin named Leocritia (or Lucretia) of a noble family of the Moors was converted and sought his protection against her irate parents. He hid her among friends for a time but eventually they were all discovered and condemned to death. St. Eulogius was beheaded on March 11, 859, and St. Leocritia four days later.

PRAYER God of power and mercy, through Your help St. Eulogius has overcome the tortures of his passion. Help us who celebrate his triumph to remain victorious over the wiles of our enemies. Amen.

ST. THEOPHANES THE CHRONICLER

March 12

MEN seemed to be constantly obstructing all the personal aspirations of this holy man, who was born in Samothrace, Greece, about 759. Possessed of wealth and worldly influence, he was first obliged to marry in spite of his reservations. When his wife entered a convent, with his complete accord, he left the court of Constantine V, and retired to live in solitude. But he was soon involved in founding two monasteries and constrained to act as Abbot of the one on Mount Sigriana.

He turned his hand to research and wrote a chronography or history of the world. But even here he ran into obstacles. His studies were interrupted by the persecution of Leo the Armenian over the Iconoclast controversy concerning ikons. Because of his constancy in the Faith, this saintly scholar was imprisoned and sent into exile, and he ultimately died from the mistreatment he incurred.

Throughout all these contradictions and trials, St. Theophanes maintained his love for God, and the Lord made everything work out for his good.

PRAYER *Lord, we devoutly recall the sufferings of St. Theophanes. Give success to our joyful prayers and grant us also constancy in our Faith. Amen.*

ST. RODERICK, Martyr

March 13

RODERICK (or Rodriguez) was a priest living in 9th century Spain at the time of the Moorish domination and persecution. He had two brothers—one had become a Moslem and the other had practically abandoned the Faith. One day, while trying to break up a violent quarrel between the two, Roderick was beaten senseless by both of them. His Moslem brother then carried him through the streets, publicly proclaiming that Roderick had renounced Christ and wished to die a Moslem. Roderick, too ill to speak out, suffered in silence, but as soon as he got well he escaped from his brother's hands.

His brother sought him out and had him brought before the kadi or judge on the charge of having returned to the Christian Faith after embracing Mohammedanism. The Saint protested fiercely, declaring that he had never himself denied the Faith; but the judge refused to believe him and relegated him to one of the worst dungeons in the city of Cordova.

While in the dungeon, Roderick befriended Solomon, another Christian charged with the same offense. The two dedicated followers of Christ encouraged one another during the lengthy imprisonment which had been designed to shake their constancy. Seeing that his original stratagem did not work, the judge had them set apart for a time; but when this also failed to achieve the desired retractions, he condemned both of them to be beheaded, in 857. St. Eulogius (who was eventually martyred during that same persecution: see March 11) witnessed their bodies lying near a river, and saw the soldiers throwing the stones reddened by the Saints' blood into the river to make sure that the Christians could not make relics of them.

PRAYER Almighty, ever-living God, You enabled St. Roderick to fight to the death for justice. Through his intercession enable us to bear all adversity and with all our strength hasten to You Who alone are life. Amen.

ST. MATHILDA, Queen

March 14—*Patroness of Queens*

ST. MATHILDA was the daughter of Theodoric, a Saxon Count. At an early age she was placed in the monastery of Erfurt under the care of Maud, her grandmother, who was

Abbess of the monastery which she had entered after the death of her husband. Here St. Mathilda learned needlework and acquired the love of labor, prayer, and spiritual reading. She remained in the convent until her parents gave her in marriage, in 913, to Henry "the Fowler," so-called from his fondness for hawking. He became Duke in 916 on the death of his father, and in 919 he was chosen to succeed Conrad as King of Germany.

The pious Queen adorned the throne by her many virtues. She visited and comforted the sick and the afflicted, instructed the ignorant, succored prisoners, and endeavored to convert sinners, and her husband concurred with her in her pious undertakings. After twenty-three years of married life King Henry died, in 936. No sooner had he expired than she had a Mass offered up for the repose of his soul, and from that moment she renounced all worldly pomp.

Of her three sons, Otho afterward became Emperor, Henry was Duke of Bavaria, and St. Bruno edified the Church as Archbishop of Cologne. Otho became King of Germany in 937, and in 962 he was crowned Emperor at Rome. In the contest between her two sons, Otho and Henry, for the crown which was elective, the Queen favored the former, a fault she expiated by great suffering, for both these sons subjected her to a long and cruel persecution. She died in 968.

PRAYER *God, You gladden us each year by the feast of St. Mathilda. Grant that as we honor her in such festivities we may also imitate her example in our conduct. Amen.*

ST. LOUISE DE MARILLAC, Widow

March 15—*Patroness of Social Workers*

ST. LOUISE DE MARILLAC was born on August 15, 1591. In 1613 she married Antoine Le Gras, who died thirteen years later, leaving Louise with a young son. She became a nun, and in 1625 chose St. Vincent de Paul, then known as Monsieur Vincent, as her spiritual director.

With the help of Monsieur Vincent, she established the Daughters of Charity, Servants of the

Sick Poor, dedicated to the corporal and spiritual service of the poor in their homes. She died in 1660, and was canonized in 1934 by Pope Pius XI.

PRAYER God, You inspired St. Louise to strive for perfect charity and so attain Your kingdom at the end of her pilgrimage on earth. Strengthen us through her intercession that we may advance rejoicing in the way of love. Amen.

ST. HERIBERT (HERBERT), Bishop

March 16—*Invoked in Time of Drought*

ST. HERIBERT was born at Worms in Germany about 970 and educated at the Abbey of Gorze in Lorraine. He wanted to enter the Benedictine Order there, but his father recalled him to Worms and obtained a canonry for him. As a young priest, Heribert became a trusted counsellor of the youthful Emperor Otto III, chancellor of the diocese, and finally Archbishop of Cologne in 998.

In that same year he accompanied the Emperor to Rome and assisted him in his last moments before his death in 1002. In the ensuing skirmishing for the post of Emperor, St. Heribert at first was opposed to St. Henry II through a mutual misunderstanding. But in time the two Saints, Archbishop and Emperor, were publicly reconciled and labored together for the good of the people.

St. Heribert was practically a model of what a Bishop should be. He was a peaceful man but a firm disciplinarian; a holy man but one who knew the value of money and saw to it that his was always divided among the poor. He was a man of prayer, and in a time of drought it was in answer to his prayers that a torrential rain fell, saving the harvest and delivering the people from famine. He died in 1021 and is invoked in time of drought.

PRAYER God, Light and Shepherd of souls, You established St. Heribert as Bishop in Your Church to feed Your flock by his word and form it by his example. Help us through his intercession to keep the Faith he taught by his word. Amen.

ST. PATRICK, Bishop, Apostle of Ireland

March 17—*Patron of Ireland*

THE date and place of St. Patrick's birth are uncertain. He was born about the year 389, the son of Calpurnius, a Roman-British deacon, and Conchessa. When he was sixteen, he was carried as a captive into Ireland and obliged to serve a heathen master as a herdsman. Despite the harshness of the life there, he not only held on to his Faith but also learned the science of prayer and contemplation.

After six years he effected a miraculous escape and returned home. In a dream, he was told to go back and Christianize Ireland. St. Patrick prepared for his task by studying in the

monastery of Lerins from about 412-415 and was ordained at Auxerre by St. Amator about 417.

In 431, after a period during which his vocation to Ireland was tested by the hesitancy of his superiors in entrusting such a mission to him, St. Patrick was sent to assist Bishop Paladius in Ireland. On the death of the latter, St. Patrick was consecrated Bishop by St. Germanus (432) after receiving the approbation of Pope Celestine I. He traveled the length and breadth of Ireland, planting the Faith everywhere despite the hostility of the Druids, and succeeded in converting several members of the royal family.

On a visit to Rome in 442, he was commissioned by Pope Leo the Great to organize the Church of Ireland and on his return made Armagh the primatial See and established Bishops in various places.

In winning a pagan nation for Christ, St. Patrick established many monasteries for men and women and made it famous for its seats of piety and learning. In the ensuing centuries Irish monks carried the Faith to England, France, and Switzerland.

After living a completely apostolic life of labor and prayer, St. Patrick died on March 17, 461, in the monastery of Saul, in Down in Ulster, leaving behind his *Confessions* which give a vivid picture of a great man of God.

PRAYER God, You sent Patrick to preach Your glory to the Irish people. Through his merits and intercession grant that we who have the honor of bearing the name of Christian may constantly proclaim Your wonderful designs to others. Amen.

ST. CYRIL OF JERUSALEM,

Bishop and Doctor of the Church

March 18

ST. CYRIL was born in the vicinity of Jerusalem about the year 315. Having made great progress in the knowledge of the pagan philosophers and the Fathers of the Church, but above all in the Sacred Scriptures, he was ordained priest about the year 345 by Maximus, Bishop of Jerusalem.

About the end of the year 350 he succeeded Maximus in the See of Jerusalem. St. Cyril entered upon his episcopal office at a time when the Church was distracted by the Arian heresy. A difference arose between him and Acacius, the Arian Bishop of Caesarea, who claimed jurisdiction over the Church of Jerusalem, a claim to which St. Cyril did not submit. He was forced to take refuge at Tarsus for a time. At the death of Constantius and the accession of Julian, he was restored to his See.

St. Cyril witnessed the vain attempt of Julian the Apostate to rebuild the temple of Jerusalem with the concomitant miraculous circumstances that accompanied it. It is said that Julian had determined to put an end to the life of the holy man after his Persian expedition, but death prevented the execution of his design.

St. Cyril was once more driven from his See in 367 by the Arian Emperor Valens, but he returned to it in 378 at the accession of Gratian. In 381 he assisted at the General Council of Constantinople and formally accepted the full Nicene Creed. He died in the year 386.

PRAYER God, through St. Cyril You miraculously unified Your Church that she might more fully grasp the mysteries of salvation. Through his intercession help us to acknowledge Your Son and so obtain more abundant life. Amen.

ST. JOSEPH,
Husband of Mary

March 19—*Patron of the Universal Church*

ST. JOSEPH, the pure spouse of the Blessed Virgin Mary and foster-father of our Blessed Lord, was descended from the royal house of David. He is the "just man" of the New Testament, the lowly village carpenter of Nazareth, who among all men of the world was the one chosen by God to be the husband and protector of the Virgin Mother of Jesus Christ, God Incarnate. To his faithful, loving care was entrusted the childhood and youth of the Redeemer of the world.

After the Mother of God, not one of the children of men was ever so gifted and adorned with natural and supernatural virtues as was St. Joseph, her spouse. In purity of heart, in chastity of life, in humility, patience, fortitude, gentleness, and manliness of character, he reveals to us the perfect type and model of the true Christian.

Poor and obscure in this world's possessions and honors, he was rich in grace and merit, and eminent before God in the nobility and beauty of holiness. Because St. Joseph was the representative of the Eternal Father on earth, the divinely appointed head of the Holy Family, which was the beginning of the great Family of God, the Church of Christ, on December 8, 1870, the Vicar of Jesus Christ, Pope Pius IX, solemnly proclaimed the foster-father of Jesus as Patron of the Universal Church, and from that time his feast has been celebrated on March 19 as one of high rank. In some places it is observed as a holy day of obligation.

Devotion to St. Joseph, fervent in the East from the early ages, has in later times spread and increased in such a marvelous way that in our day the Catholics of all nations vie with one another in honoring him. Besides the feast of March 19 there is another feast, that of St. Joseph the Worker, Spouse of the Blessed Virgin Mary (May 1). Promulgated in 1955, it replaced the older "Solemnity of St. Joseph" which had been celebrated since 1847—first as the "Patronage of St. Joseph" on the third Sunday after Easter and after 1913 as the "Solemnity of St.

Joseph" on the Wednesday before the third Sunday after Easter. John XXIII inserted the name of St. Joseph in the Roman Canon or Eucharistic Prayer I.

From his throne of glory in heaven, St. Joseph watches over and protects the Church militant, and no one who calls on him in need ever calls in vain. He is the model of a perfect Christian life and the patron of a happy death. His patronage extends over the Mystical Body of Christ, over the Christian family, the Christian school, and all individuals who in their need appeal to his charity and powerful intercession, especially in the hour of death; for he who, when dying, received the affectionate ministry of his foster-Son, Jesus, and his Virgin spouse, Mary, may well be trusted to obtain for us the mercy of God and the grace of a peaceful and holy death.

PRAYER Almighty God, You entrusted to the faithful care of Joseph the beginnings of the mysteries of man's salvation. Through his intercession may Your Church always be faithful in her service so that Your designs will be fulfilled. Amen.

ST. WULFRAN, Bishop

March 20

THE father of this Saint was an officer of King Dagobert. St. Wulfran spent some years in the court of King Clotaire III, practicing virtue in spite of the seductions of the world.

In 682, he was chosen and consecrated Archbishop of Sens, and governed that diocese for two and one-half years. The example of the English missionaries among the idolatrous Frisians moved this holy man to resign his Bishopric. After a retreat in the Abbey of Fontenelle he went to Friesland as a missionary. He was very successful and baptized a number of idolaters.

After his labors in Friesland, St. Wulfran again retired to Fontenelle to prepare himself for his death, which occurred in 720.

PRAYER God, Light and Shepherd of souls, You established St. Wulfran as Bishop in Your Church to feed Your flock by his word and form it by his example. Help us through his intercession to keep the Faith he taught by his word and follow the way he showed by his example. Amen.

ST. NICHOLAS OF FLUE, Hermit

March 21—*Patron of Switzerland*

THIS great Saint and Father of his country was born in the Canon of Unterwalden on the Lake of Lucerne, Switzerland, in 1417. At the age of thirty or so, he married a farmer's daughter, Dorothy Wiss, who bore him ten children. He also proved to be a capable farmer, military leader, member of the assembly, councillor, judge, and a person of complete moral integrity.

At the same time, St. Nicholas led a life of contemplative prayer and rigorous fasting. After twenty years of married life, he received God's call to leave the world and his family and become a hermit. Thus in 1467 with the heroic consent of his wife he settled in a hermitage at Ranft within a few miles of his home. It is said that for nineteen years he lived there without benefit of food or drink, taking only the Eucharist. His reputation for sanctity grew and many came from all parts of Europe to seek his advice.

The enormous influence of this holy man of God exhibited itself in 1481 when a dispute arose between the delegates of the Swiss confederates at Stans and there was a real and imminent threat of civil war. An appeal was made to St. Nicholas who worked through the night and came up with a set of proposals that all could agree on. Switzerland had been saved.

St. Nicholas died six years later (March 21, 1487), surrounded by his wife and children. He is honored by Swiss Protestants and venerated by Swiss Catholics.

PRAYER Lord God, You alone are holy and no one is good without You. Through the intercession of St. Nicholas help us to live in such a way that we may not be deprived of a share in Your glory. Amen.

ST. LEA, Widow

March 22

A letter which St. Jerome wrote to St. Marcella provides the only information we have about St. Lea, a devout 4th century widow. Upon the death of her husband, she retired to a Roman monastery and ultimately became its superior. Since his correspondent was acquainted with the details of St. Lea's life, St. Jerome omitted these in his letter. He concentrated instead on the fate of St. Lea in comparison with that of a consul who had recently died.

"Who will praise the blessed Lea as she deserves? She renounced painting her face and adorning her head with shining pearls. She exchanged her rich attire for sackcloth, and ceased to command others in order to obey all. She dwelt in a corner with a few bits of furniture; she spent her nights in prayer, and instructed her companions through her example rather than through protests and speeches. And she looked forward to her arrival in heaven in order to receive her recompense for the virtues which she practiced on earth.

"So it is that thenceforth she enjoyed perfect happiness. From Abraham's bosom, where she resides with Lazarus, she sees our consul who was once decked out in purple now vested in a shameful robe, vainly begging for a drop of water to quench his thirst. Although he went up to the capital to the plaudits of the people, and his death occasioned widespread grief, it is futile for the wife to assert that he has gone to heaven and possesses a great mansion there. The fact is that he is plunged into the darkness outside, whereas Lea who was willing to be considered a fool on earth has been received into the house of the Father, at the wedding feast of the Lamb.

"Hence, I tearfully beg you to refrain from seeking the favors of the world and to renounce all that is carnal. It is impossible to follow both the world and Jesus. Let us live a life of renunciation, for our bodies will soon be dust and nothing else will last any longer."

PRAYER Lord, amid the things of this world, let us wholeheartedly be committed to heavenly things in imitation of the example of evangelical perfection You have given us in St. Lea. Amen.

ST. TURIBIUS DE MOGROVEJO, Bishop

March 23

BORN in 1538 at Majorca, Spain, St. Turibius became a Professor of Law at the University of Salamanca and was appointed president of the court of the Inquisition at Granada. In 1581, while still a layman he was appointed to the See of Lima, Peru—a most difficult charge both religiously and geographically.

For the next twenty-five years, this saintly man wore himself out in the service of his flock. He traversed his entire diocese on foot, willingly exposing himself to the steaming climate, wild animals, tropical maladies, and other dangers in order to reform the clergy and instruct the people in the Faith. He founded the first seminary on the American continent, and baptized and confirmed close to a million people.

His work was aided because he took pains to learn the Indian languages of the people (in which he was associated with St. Francis Solano) and opposed all attempts to justify their mistreatment by the Spanish. Thus, he exerted a great influence on other South American countries also.

St. Turibius was ever solicitous of the feelings of the poor and unstinting in his charities toward them. In the course of his ministrations he also befriended and confirmed St. Rose of Lima. In 1606, at the age of sixty-eight, he received Viaticum and passed on to his heavenly reward.

PRAYER God, You increased Your Church by means of the apostolic care and zeal for truth of St. Turibius, Your Bishop. Grant that the people who have been consecrated to You may experience a new increase of Faith and holiness. Amen.

ST. CATHERINE OF SWEDEN, Virgin

March 24—*Invoked against Miscarriages*

ST. CATHERINE was the daughter of Ulfo Gudmarsson, Prince of Nericia, Sweden, and of St. Bridget. She was educated at the direction of the Abbess of the convent. When she had reached the age of thirteen, her father gave her in marriage to Egard, a young German nobleman of great virtue. However, by her prayers and discourses the holy virgin persuaded her husband to join with her in making a mutual vow of perpetual chastity, thereby foregoing their lawful marital rights for the love of God. Thus they encouraged each other to mortification, prayer, and works of charity.

After the death of her father, St. Catherine joined her mother, St. Bridget, in a pilgrimage to Rome in 1349, out of devotion to the Passion of Christ and to the relics of the Roman martyrs. In 1373, St. Bridget died at Rome and St. Catherine returned to Sweden with her mother's body.

In 1375, she returned to Rome to promote her mother's canonization and to obtain the confirmation of the Brigittines or Order of St. Savior. She died as the Abbess of Vadzstena, Sweden, on March 24, 1381.

During the last twenty-five years of her life, St. Catherine lived in mortification and penance. Each day she purified her soul from sin by the Sacrament of Penance. She was canonized in 1484 by Pope Pius II.

The Order of St. Savior or the Brigittines, founded by St. Catherine of Sweden, was approved by Urban V and affiliated to the Augustinians. This Order has for its purpose literary work, especially the translation of religious works.

PRAYER Lord God, You showered heavenly gifts on St. Catherine the Virgin. Help us to imitate her virtues during our earthly life and enjoy eternal happiness with her in heaven. Amen.

THE ANNUNCIATION OF OUR LORD

March 25

THE feast of the Annunciation falls on March 25. On this day the Church commemorates the coming of the Archangel Gabriel to announce to the Blessed Virgin that she was to be the Mother of the promised Redeemer. On this same day, God the Son, the Second Person of the Blessed Trinity, by the power of the Holy Spirit, assumed a human body and a human soul, and became the Son of Mary.

This date is, therefore, a double feast, the Annunciation of the maternity of the Blessed Virgin, and the Incarnation of the Son of God. The Angel of the Incarnation was sent to that maiden of Nazareth who, deeming herself least worthy among the daughters of Zion, had been chosen by her Creator to be the most blessed among women.

"The Angel Gabriel was sent from God to a town of Galilee named Nazareth, to a virgin betrothed to a man named Joseph, of the house of David. The virgin's name was Mary. Upon arriving, the Angel said to her: 'Hail, full of grace. The Lord is with you. Blessed are you among women.' She was deeply troubled by his words, and wondered what his greeting meant. The Angel went on to say to her: 'Do not fear, Mary. You have found favor with God. You shall conceive and bear a son and give him the name Jesus. . . . The Holy Spirit will come upon you

"Hail, full of grace."

and the power of the Most High will overshadow you; hence, the holy offspring to be born will be called Son of God. . . .' Mary said: 'I am the maid-servant of the Lord. Let it be done to me as you say' " (Luke 1:28-38).

Mary bowed her head and will to the Divine decree, and at that instant the great fact of the Incarnation was accomplished. A Virgin of the House of David had become the Mother of God. The Second Person of the Blessed Trinity had become Man, man like unto us in all things save sin. The fact of the Incarnation proves that Mary is the Mother of God. He Who was born Man of her is God, and Mary is His Mother. She is the Mother of the Divine Redeemer of the world; she is the Mother of our Divine Lord and Master; she is the Mother of the Savior and our Perfect Friend; she is the Mother of the Savior Who shed His Precious Blood for us on Calvary.

Next after His Heavenly Father and the Holy Spirit, there was no one whom Jesus venerated and loved as He venerated and loved His Blessed Mother. He who has not love and veneration for the Mother of Jesus is unlike our Divine Savior in that particular perfection of His character which comes next after His piety toward the Eternal Father and the Holy Spirit. But, besides all this, love and veneration are due to Mary for her own sake, because she is the Mother of mankind; because above all other mere creatures she has been sanctified by the Holy Spirit; and because in being chosen the Mother of the Incarnate Son, she is the Mother of us all.

"As soon as man receives into his heart the full meaning of the Annunciation and the full light of the Incarnation, two self-evident truths arise upon his reason: the one, the presence of Jesus in the Blessed Sacrament; the other, the love and veneration of His Blessed Mother" (Cardinal Manning).

PRAYER God, You willed that Your Word should truly become Man in the womb of the Virgin Mary. We confess that our Redeemer is both God and Man. Grant that we may deserve to be made like Him in His Divine Nature. Amen.

ST. MARGARET CLITHEROW, Martyr

March 26

MARGARET CLITHEROW was born at Middleton, England, in 1555, of Protestant parents. Possessed of good looks and full of wit and merriment, she was a charming personality. In 1571, she married John Clitherow, a well-to-do grazier and butcher (to whom she bore two children), and a few years later she entered the Catholic Church. Her zeal led her to harbor fugitive priests, for which she was arrested and imprisoned by the authorities.

Recourse was had to every means in an attempt to make her deny her Faith, but the holy woman stood firm. Finally, she was condemned to be pressed to death on March 25, 1586. She was stretched out on the ground with a sharp rock on her back and crushed under a door overladen with unbearable weights. Her bones were broken and she died within fifteen minutes.

The humanity and holiness of this servant of God can be readily glimpsed in her words to a friend when she learned of her condemnation: "The sheriffs have said that I am going to die this coming Friday; and I feel the weakness of my flesh which is troubled at this news, but my spirit rejoices greatly. For the love of God, pray for me and ask all good people to do likewise." She was canonized in 1970 by Pope St. Paul VI.

PRAYER God, by Your gift virtue is perfected in weakness. Grant to all who recall the glory of St. Margaret that she who obtained strength from You to triumph may also ever obtain from You the grace to enable us to triumph. Amen.

ST. RUPERT OF SALZBURG, Bishop

March 27

ST. RUPERT, a Frank by nationality, was Bishop of Worms until the last years of the 7th century (697) when he became a missionary to Regensburg in Bavaria. After converting and baptizing Duke Theodo, without whose permission nothing could take place in the territory, St. Rupert and his followers converted many of the nobles and encountered no serious opposition to their work of evangelization among the people.

Meeting with conspicuous success at Regensburg, the zealous Bishop went on to Altotting and then extended his activities over a wide area along the Danube—always with great success. As his center, he took the old ruined town of Juvavum, which he renamed Salzburg, and rebuilt.

In addition to Christianizing the people and building churches and monasteries for them, this holy man also civilized his converts and promoted the development of the salt mines of Salzburg. He thus contributed to the bodies and souls of his flock. The Lord called this devoted servant to his reward on Easter Sunday about the year 710.

PRAYER God, You built up Your Church by means of the religious zeal and apostolic care of St. Rupert. Grant by his intercession that she may ever experience a new increase of Faith and holiness. Amen.

ST. GUNTRAMNUS (GONTRAN), King

March 28

ST. GUNTRAMNUS, fourth son of Clovis, was King of Burgundy and part of Aquitaine from 561 to 592. He was very popular with his subjects who honored him as a Saint after his death. This honor was well deserved, for despite the fact that the King had at times given way to human weakness (he divorced one wife and had the unsuccessful physician of another executed), he did much penance and displayed great zeal for religion.

When his estates were ravaged by a contagious disease known as "St. Anthony's fire," he saw to it that the most unfortunate of his subjects were cared for, imposed rigorous fasts on himself, and offered himself as a victim to Divine Justice for the good of his people.

St. Guntramnus was a just ruler and an enthusiastic promoter of religious works. He encouraged the holding of three synods to improve the discipline of the clergy, and endowed churches and monasteries.

PRAYER God, You transferred St. Guntramnus from the care of an earthly reign to the glory of a heavenly Kingdom. Through his intercession, grant that we may seek Your eternal Kingdom in the earthly tasks which we fulfill. Amen.

ST. JOSEPH OF ARIMATHEA

March 29—*Patron of Funeral Directors*

ST. JOSEPH OF ARIMATHEA was a just and devout man who was looking for the Kingdom of God. Although during Our Lord's public life he was afraid to show himself openly as His disciple, after the crucifixion he had the courage to seek out Pilate and ask for the Body of Jesus. Aided by Nicodemus, he took the Body of the Savior from the Cross, bound it up in wrappings of cloth with perfumed oil, and laid it in his own new tomb which had been hewn from a formation of rock (Jn 19:38-42).

PRAYER God, You alone are holy and without You no one is good. Through the intercession of St. Joseph, grant that we may so live as not to be deprived of Your glory. Amen.

ST. JOHN CLIMACUS, Abbot

March 30

ST. JOHN, called Climacus from his book *The Ladder (Climax) of Paradise*, was born about the year 525. At the age of sixteen he renounced all worldly goods to dedicate himself to God in the religious state. For forty years he lived as a solitary in his hermitage at the foot of Mount Sinai. In the year 600 he was chosen Abbot of Mount Sinai and superior-general of all the monks and hermits in that country. Such was his reputation that St. Gregory the Great, who was then Pope, wrote to him recommending himself to his prayers and sent him gifts for his hospital near Mount Sinai.

St. John never sought either glory or fame; on the contrary, he endeavored to hide the natural and supernatural gifts with which he was endowed, in order the better to practice humility.

His famous work, the *Climax*, was written only in deference to the will of another. It is a spiritual treatise consisting of concise sentences, and affording several examples that illustrate the monastic life of that period. He governed the monastery of Mount Sinai for four years, sighing constantly under the weight of his dignity, which he resigned shortly before his death. Heavenly contemplation and the continual exercise of divine love and praise were his delight and comfort in his earthly pilgrimage.

On March 30, 605, the blessed life of this great Saint came to an end in the hermitage that had witnessed his uninterrupted communing with God. From the time he entered the monastic state, St. John had earnestly applied himself to root out of his heart self-complacency in his actions; he practiced silence as a means of acquiring humility, and he made it a rule never to contradict, never to dispute with anyone. He appeared to have no will of his own, so great was his submission.

PRAYER Lord, amid the things of this world, let us be wholeheartedly committed to heavenly things in imitation of the example of evangelical perfection You have given us in St. John the Abbot. Amen.

ST. BENJAMIN, Deacon and Martyr

March 31

THE Christians in Persia had enjoyed twelve years of peace during the reign of Isdegerd, son of Sapor III, when in 420 it was disturbed by the indiscreet zeal of Abdas, a Christian Bishop who burned the Temple of Fire, the great sanctuary of the Persians. King Isdegerd threatened to destroy all the churches of the Christians unless the Bishop would rebuild it.

As Abdas refused to comply, the threat was executed; the churches were demolished, Abdas himself was put to death, and a general persecution began which lasted forty years. Isdegerd died in 421, but his son and successor, Varanes, carried on the persecution with greater fury. The Christians were submitted to the most cruel tortures.

Among those who suffered was St. Benjamin, a deacon, who had been imprisoned a year for his Faith. At the end of this period, an ambassador of the Emperor of Constantinople obtained his release on condition that he would never speak to any of the courtiers about religion.

St. Benjamin, however, declared that it was his duty to preach Christ and that he could not be silent. Although he had been liberated on the agreement made between the ambassador and the Persian authorities, he would not acquiesce in it, and neglected no opportunity of preaching. After untold suffering and tortures, St. Benjamin died a Martyr about the year 424.

PRAYER Almighty, ever-living God, You enabled St. Benjamin to fight for justice even unto death. Through his help, grant that we may tolerate all adversity and hasten with all our might to You Who alone are life. Amen.

ST. HUGH, Bishop of Grenoble

April 1

ST. HUGH was born at Chateauneuf, in the territory of Valence in Dauphine in 1053, and from the cradle he appeared to be a child of benediction. He embraced the ecclesiastical state, and accepted a canonry in the cathedral of Valence. His virtues rendered him the ornament of that church. Hugh, Bishop of Die, later Archbishop of Lyons and Cardinal Legate of the Holy See, was so pleased with him that he took him into his own household and employed him in numerous affairs of importance.

At a Council held at Avignon in 1080, he was forced to accept the See of Grenoble, which had fallen into a deplorable condition. The legate took St. Hugh with him to Rome, where he received episcopal consecration at the hands of Pope Gregory VII. Returning home, the Saint at once began to labor hard for the reformation of his diocese, and soon had the satisfaction of beholding a wonderful change for the better, effected through his zeal.

After two years, presuming the permission of the Holy See, he privately resigned his Bishopric and entered the novitiate of the Benedictine Order of Cluny; but the Pope commanded him to resume his pastoral charge. It was to St. Hugh that St. Bruno and his six companions addressed themselves in their design of forsaking the world, and the holy Bishop directed them to the desert of Chartreuse, where they founded the Carthusian Order. The long and penitential life of St. Hugh came to a close April 1, 1132, after a lingering illness and he was canonized in 1134 by Pope Innocent II.

PRAYER God, Light and Shepherd of souls, You established St. Hugh as Bishop in Your Church to feed Your flock by his word and form it by his example. Help us through his intercession to keep the Faith he taught by his word and follow the way he showed by his example. Amen.

ST. FRANCIS OF PAOLA, Hermit

April 2—*Patron of Mariners*

ST. FRANCIS was born about the year 1416, at Paola, a small city in Calabria. His parents were very poor, but virtuous. He learned to read in the Franciscan convent at St. Mark's, a town in the same province. After spending a year with the Franciscans, he took up his abode in solitude about half a mile from Paola in 1432.

Before he was twenty, two others joined him to share in his devout exercises. The neighbors built them three cells and a chapel, in which a priest from the parish church said Mass for them. This is looked upon as the beginning of the Order of Minims, the foundation of which is placed in 1436.

The Order was confirmed by a bull of Sixtus IV in 1474, with St. Francis as Superior General. The first monastery had been built in 1454 and was followed by several others. In 1482, he went to France by command of Sixtus IV, at the request of Louis XI, whose entire conversion he effected before the latter's death in 1483. St. Francis now established his Order in France, and Charles VIII and Louis XII became its special benefactors.

When his long life of penance was drawing to a close, St. Francis spent the last three months in his cell to prepare for death and eternity. He fell sick on Palm Sunday, 1508, and died shortly thereafter at ninety-one years of age. He was canonized in 1519 by Pope Leo X.

PRAYER God, the exultation of the humble, You raised St. Francis to the glory of Your Saints. Through his merits and example, grant that we may happily obtain the rewards promised to the humble. Amen.

ST. RICHARD, Bishop

April 3

BORN in 1197 at the manor of Wiche near Worcester, England, St. Richard, like so many other Saints, exhibited a great inclination to virtue from his childhood, spending his time in pious exercises or in study, while he showed himself averse to the ordinary amusements of his age. His greatest pleasure was to render service to others.

He went to Paris to continue his studies, and together with two chosen friends lived an austere life. On his return to England he took the degree of Master of Arts at Oxford and then went to Bologna, in Italy, to devote himself to the study of canon law. Finally, St. Edmund, Archbishop of Canterbury, summoned Richard to accompany him to France when he went there in exile. In France Richard was ordained to the priesthood.

Elevated to the Episcopal See of Chichester, he overcame many obstacles. As soon as he enjoyed sufficient liberty of action, he applied himself with all possible zeal to the government of his church. His firmness in maintaining ecclesiastical discipline and his charity to the poor commanded great admiration. He suffered much for two years at the hands of King Henry III.

The Pope commissioned Richard to preach a crusade against the Saracens. In fulfilling this mission he fell sick of a fever, which was the forerunner of his death in 1253. He was canonized in 1262 by Pope Urban IV.

PRAYER God, You made St. Richard an outstanding exemplar of Divine love and the Faith that conquers the world, and added him to the role of saintly pastors. Grant by his intercession that we may persevere in Faith and love and become sharers of his glory. Amen.

ST. ISIDORE OF SEVILLE

Bishop and Doctor of the Church

April 4

ST. ISIDORE was born at Cartagena in Spain, the son of Severinus and Theodora, illustrious for their virtue. St. Leander and St. Fulgentius, both Bishops, were his brothers, and his sister, Florentina, is also numbered among the Saints. From his youth he consecrated himself to the service of the Church and prepared himself for his sacred ministry by virtue and learning. He assisted his brother St. Leander, Archbishop of Seville, in the conversion of the Visigoths from the Arian heresy. On his brother's death, about the year 600, he succeeded him in the See of Seville.

Several Councils at which he assisted settled the discipline of the Spanish Church, and in that of Seville, in 619, he converted Gregory, a Eutychian Bishop from Syria. A few years before, in 610, the Archbishop of Toledo, in a Council held at Toledo, had been declared Primate of all Spain. Notwithstanding this, the personal merit of St. Isidore was so highly esteemed that he presided at the Fourth Council of Toledo, held in 633, although the Primate was present. This Council was the most famous of all the Spanish synods. At that time Toledo was the capital of Spain and the residence of the Visigothic kings.

St. Isidore was also a voluminous writer. He composed a work containing the whole circle of science, which shows his vast erudition. This is one of the earliest encyclopedias on record. The Saint was versed in the Latin, Greek, and Hebrew languages. He governed his church about thirty-seven years, continuing his assiduous labors up to a most advanced age. During the last six months of his life his charities became more profuse than ever. Perceiving his end approaching he went to church, received Holy Communion, remitted all the debts that were due to him, and caused his money to be distributed to the poor. He then returned home and calmly expired four days later, in 636.

PRAYER Lord, hear our prayers, which we offer on the commemoration of St. Isidore. May Your Church be instructed by his teaching. Amen.

ST. VINCENT FERRER,
Priest

April 5—*Patron of Builders*

AT VALENCIA in Spain, this illustrious son of St. Dominic came into the world on January 23, 1357. In the year 1374, he entered the Order of St. Dominic in a monastery near his native city. Soon after his profession he was commissioned to deliver lectures on philosophy. On being sent to Barcelona, he continued his scholastic duties and at the same time devoted himself to preaching.

At Lerida, the famous university city of Catalonia, he received his doctorate. After this he labored six years in Valencia, during which time he perfected himself in the Christian life. In 1390, he was obliged to accompany Cardinal Pedro de Luna to France, but he soon returned home. When, in 1394, de Luna himself had become Pope at Avignon he summoned St. Vincent and made him master of the sacred palace. In this capacity St. Vincent made unsuccessful efforts to put an end to the great schism. He refused all ecclesiastical dignities, even the cardinal's hat, and only craved to be appointed an apostolic missionary. Now began those labors that made him the famous missionary of the 14th century.

He evangelized nearly every province of Spain, and preached in France, Italy, Germany, Flanders, England, Scotland, and Ireland. Numerous conversions followed his preaching, which God Himself assisted by the gift of miracles. Though the Church was then divided by the great schism, the Saint was honorably received in the districts subject to the two claimants to the Papacy. He was even invited to Mohammedan Granada, where he preached the Gospel with much success. He lived to behold the end of the great schism and the election of Pope Martin V. Finally, crowned with labors, he died April 5, 1419 and was canonized in 1455.

PRAYER God, You raised up St. Vincent Your Priest for a ministry of evangelical preaching. Grant that we may see him reigning in heaven who while on earth proclaimed the future judgment. Amen.

ST. MARCELLINUS OF CARTHAGE, Martyr

April 6

ST. MARCELLINUS was the friend of St. Augustine (who dedicated his great work *The City of God* to him) and Secretary of State of the Roman Emperor Honorius. In 409, Honorius granted freedom of public worship to the Donatists, a rigid and repressive heretical group, who began to oppress the Catholics, culminating in the latter's appeal to the Emperor.

In 411, St. Marcellinus was sent to act as judge and assessor and bring about peace between the two groups. After weighing the evidence, he ruled that the Donatists had to relinquish their churches and return to the communion of their Catholic brothers. This judgment was carried out according to the severity of Roman law, despite the remonstrances of St. Augustine who had himself written against the Donatist heresy.

Two years later the Donatists got their revenge by accusing Marcellinus and his brother Apringus (who had also been active in their case) of involvement in the rebellion of Heraclion. General Maricus, who had been delegated to crush the rebellion and who was sympathetic to the Donatists, arrested the brothers and threw them into prison. Despite the intervention of St. Augustine on their behalf with the Judge Cecilian, St. Marcellinus and his brother were executed in 413.

PRAYER Almighty, ever-living God, You enabled St. Marcellinus to fight to the death for justice. Through his intercession enable us to bear all adversity and with all our strength to hasten to You Who alone are life. Amen.

ST. JOHN BAPTIST DE LA SALLE,
Religious

April 7

Patron of Teachers

FOUNDER of the Institute of the Brothers of the Christian Schools, St. John Baptist de La Salle is called the father of modern pedagogy. After completing his education he desired to enter the priesthood. He was ordained in 1678 and received his doctorate in theology in 1680.

Observing that the poor of his day were grossly neglected as far as their education was concerned,

St. John became the first to set up training colleges for teachers who would instruct the poor. Thus began the Institute of the Brothers of the Christian Schools, whose first novitiate was founded at Vangirard in 1691. St. John exhorted its members to have a father's love for their pupils, be ready to devote all their time and energies to them, and be as concerned to save them from wickedness as to dispel their ignorance.

In 1695, he drew up the Rule for his Brothers (which he later revised in 1705) and also wrote *The Conduct of Christian Schools,* which set forth his pedagogical system and has become a classic in the field of education. He died on April 7, 1719 and was canonized on May 24, 1900 by Pope Leo XIII.

PRAYER God our Father, You chose St. John Baptist de la Salle as an educator of Christian youth. Give Your Church good teachers today, who will dedicate themselves to instructing young people in human and Christian disciplines. Amen.

ST. JULIA BILLIART, Virgin

April 8

BORN in 1751 at Cuvilly, France, St. Julia gave evidence from her earliest years of exceptional traits of intelligence and devotion. By the age of fourteen, she had already taken a vow of chastity and was working to support her family which had become impoverished.

Suddenly, in 1773, her whole life was changed. She witnessed the attempted assassination of her father and the shock left her largely paralyzed. Undaunted, St. Julia continued her deeply spiritual life, and strenously fought against the Reign of Terror initiated by the Jacobins during the French Revolution. When calm was restored, this holy woman founded the Institute of the Sisters of Notre Dame in collaboration with Frances Blin, Viscountess of Gezaincourt, and Father Joseph Varin, of the "Fathers of the Faith" (a group standing in for the suppressed Society of Jesus). Her society had for its purpose the teaching and the salvation of the children of the poor.

In 1804, St. Julia was suddenly cured of her paralysis (which she had endured for twenty-two years) at the end of a mission given by Father Enfantin of the Fathers of the Faith. She was now able to consolidate and extend the new Institute as well as to give her personal assistance to the missions conducted by the Fathers of the Faith. After Father Varin's departure from Amiens, St. Julia had to struggle hard to preserve the distinctively modern character of her Institute. Her success can be seen in the modern cast of the Institute which has spread throughout the world. After having spent herself in the service of God, St. Julia died on April 8, 1816 and was canonized in 1970 by Pope Paul VI.

PRAYER Lord, our God, grant that Your faithful spouse, St. Julia, may kindle in us the flame of

Divine love which she enkindled in other virgins for the everlasting glory of Your Church. Amen.

ST. GAUCHERIUS, Abbot

April 9

ST. GAUCHERIUS was born at Meulan-sur-Seine, France, and received a good Christian education. At the age of eighteen he gave up the world and retired to Aureil to lead a solitary life. Gradually a community grew up around him and he gave them the Rule of St. Augustine. Many holy men were trained in this community: among them, St. Lambert, Faucherius, and St. Stephen of Grammont. St. Gaucherius died in 1140.

PRAYER Lord, amid the things of this world, let us be wholeheartedly committed to heavenly things in imitation of the example of evangelical perfection You have given us in St. Gaucherius the Abbot. Amen.

ST. FULBERT, Bishop

April 10

BORN in Italy, of humble parentage, St. Fulbert went to school in Rheims, France, and conducted himself so brilliantly that when his mathematics and philosophy teacher, Gerbert, became Pope Sylvester II, he received a post at Rome. Later, he returned to France and was appointed chancellor of Chartres, overseeing the cathedral schools of the diocese in this capacity.

St. Fulbert labored diligently and long and succeeded in making these schools the greatest educational center in France, frequented by students from Germany, Italy, and England. He was regarded as another Socrates and Plato, a bulwark against the rationalizing temper of his day.

Later, he became Bishop of Chartres, despite his protestations of unworthiness. His influence was vast in this position, since he became the recognized oracle of the spiritual and temporal leaders of France in addition to maintaining control of the cathedral schools. Yet he never allowed external affairs to interfere with the task of caring for his diocese. He preached regularly at the cathedral and strove to spread instruction throughout his diocese.

This great Saint had a deep devotion to Mary and composed several hymns in her honor. He is also responsible for the beautiful Easter hymn, *You Choirs of New Jerusalem.* After an episcopate of nearly twenty-two years, St. Fulbert died on April 10, 1029.

PRAYER God, Light and Shepherd of souls, You established St. Fulbert as Bishop in Your Church to feed Your flock by his word and form it by his example. Help us through his intercession to keep the Faith he taught by his word and follow the way he showed by his example. Amen.

ST. STANISLAUS, Bishop and Martyr

April 11—*Patron of Poland*

ST. STANISLAUS was born on July 26, 1030, at Sezepanow in the diocese of Cracow, Poland. In his childhood were laid the foundations of his future sanctity. After an early training in the schools of his native country and at the university of Gnesna, he was sent to Paris, where he spent seven years in the study of canon law and theology. Out of humility he refused the degree of doctor and returned home.

On the death of his parents he gave away his ample fortune to the poor, and received the order of priesthood from the Bishop of Cracow, who made him canon of the cathedral and, soon afterward, preacher and vicar-general. His sermons produced a wonderful reformation of manners. After the death of the Bishop he was unanimously chosen to succeed him in 1072.

Boleslaus II, then King of Poland, was leading an infamous life. The Saint reproached him in private with the irregularity of his conduct. The King at first seemed to repent, but he soon broke out again into enormous excesses. The Saint again remonstrated, and threatened excommunication. The King became enraged.

Finally, in 1079, after much patience, the Bishop pronounced upon him the sentence of excommunication. This cost him his life, for while he was in a small chapel outside of Cracow the

King and his guards entered. When the guards refused to obey the wicked order of the King to put the Bishop to death, the impious King murdered the holy Bishop with his own hands.

PRAYER God, for Your honor the holy Bishop Stanislaus fell before the swords of his persecutors. Grant that we may be strong in the Faith and persevere until death. Amen.

ST. GEMMA GALGANI, Virgin

***The Same Day*, April 11**
—Patron of Pharmacists

ST. GEMMA GALGANI was born at Camigliano near Lucca, Italy, on March 12, 1878. At twenty years of age, St. Gemma was attacked by tuberculosis of the spine. This disease was declared by the doctors to be hopelessly incurable. After countless novenas to St. Gabriel, she was completely cured on the first Friday of March, 1899.

At this time, apparently free from her recent illness, she sought to fulfill her lifelong wish of pursuing her religious vocation with the Passionist nuns, but her application, as previously, was rejected.

From 1899 on, this quiet and unexcitable girl who was endowed with a remarkably fervent religious disposition underwent many extraordinary religious experiences—all of which were carefully investigated by her confessor and spiritual director, Father Germano. The marks of Christ's crucifixion (*stigmata*) appeared intermittently for over eighteen months on her hands and feet, and she had ecstasies and visions.

In 1902, she was again stricken with an illness which was thought to be tuberculosis and she fell asleep in the Lord in 1903. The fame of her sanctity spread rapidly all over the world. She was beatified by Pius XI on March 14, 1933, and canonized by Pius XII on Ascension Day, 1940.

PRAYER God, You showered heavenly gifts on St. Gemma. Help us to imitate her virtues during our earthly life and enjoy eternal happiness with her in heaven. Amen.

ST. JULIUS, Pope

April 12

ST. JULIUS, a Roman, was elected Pope in 337, succeeding St. Mark, whose reign had been exceedingly brief. The Church was then in a troubled condition on account of the Arian agitators whose heresy had been condemned at Nicaea, but who were beginning to deceive Constantine the Emperor in regard to their real character. When the Emperor died, his three sons, Constantine, Constantius, and Constans, divided the Empire.

For a considerable time St. Athanasius, Bishop of Alexandria, had been an object of persecution to the Arians. Upon the accession of Pope Julius, their Bishop in the East sent three deputies to accuse St. Athanasius. At an impartial hearing the Bishop of Alexandria was acquitted of every accusation that had been brought against him. On the demand of the Arians, the Pope assembled a Council at Rome in 341, which confirmed St. Athanasius in his See in spite of the fact that the Arian Bishops refused to attend.

As the Arians still remained obstinate, Pope Julius convinced the Emperors Constans and Constantius to convoke a Council at Sardica in Illyricum. It began in May, 347, and confirmed the decrees of Nicaea, of which it is considered as an appendix or continuation. It declared St. Athanasius orthodox, and deposed certain Arian Bishops. In this Council it was decreed that any Bishop deposed by a synod in his province has a right to appeal to the Bishop of Rome.

In a letter to the Oriental Bishops of the Arian party, St. Julius appeals to the apostolic traditions in defense of the right of the Holy See to be consulted, a right which the Eastern Bishops admitted, but which they had slighted by their conduct. St. Julius occupied the Chair of St. Peter for fifteen years, two months, and six days. He died April 12, 352.

PRAYER God, Light and Shepherd of souls, You established St. Julius as Pope over Your Church to feed Your flock by his word and form it by his example. Help us through his intercession to keep the Faith he taught by his word and follow the way he showed by his example. Amen.

ST. MARTIN I, Pope and Martyr

April 13

A MEMBER of the Roman clergy, St. Martin was sent to Constantinople. Upon the death of Pope Theodore he was elected to succeed him, in the year 649. In the following October he held a Council in the Lateran Church, in which he condemned the leaders of the heresy of the Monothelites, a modification of that of the Eutychians. A document emanating from the Emperor Constans was also censured.

This incensed the Emperor, and he sent Olympius, his chamberlain, to Italy with orders to cause the Pope to be put to death, or to send him to the East as a prisoner. An attempt on the Saint's life in the Church of St. Mary Major was miraculously frustrated. Olympius now became reconciled to the Pope and went over to Sicily.

The Emperor then sent Calliopas and Pellurus to Rome, with orders to seize St. Martin. The

Pope, who lay sick, was seized, carried down the Tiber at midnight and conveyed to the East. After three months he arrived at the island of Naxos, where his guards kept him a whole year and subjected him to many indignities.

In 654, Martin reached Constantinople, and for three months he was confined in a dungeon. His sufferings were extreme, but like St. Stephen, he hoped that his persecutors would be brought to repentance. He was banished to Chersonesus in 655, while a terrible famine raged in that region. In his exile, Martin's sorrow was the greater because he regarded the Church as having abandoned him by electing a new Pope. Nonetheless, he prayed constantly for his sucessor, Eugene I. Martin died in 655, and is the last Pope to be venerated as a martyr.

PRAYER Almighty God, help us to bear worldly adversities with an unconquerable spirit. For You did not let St. Martin Your Pope and Martyr be terrified by threats or conquered by pains. Amen.

STS. TIBURTIUS, VALERIAN, AND MAXIMUS, Martyrs

April 14

THE Church has declared that these three Saints actually existed. However, because of the paucity of trustworthy historical material concerning their lives, she has seen fit to remove them from the liturgical calendar for the universal Church and relegated them to local calendars.

In actuality, these three Saints were Roman Martyrs of the 2nd and 3rd century, buried in the cemetery of Praetextatus. Their names were woven into the legend of St. Cecilia, Virgin and Martyr, which became very popular from the 6th century on. But there is no historical reason to believe that they had anything to do with her.

PRAYER Lord, we devoutly recall the sufferings of Sts. Tiburtius, Valerian, and Maximus. Give success to our joyful prayers and grant us also constancy in our Faith. Amen.

ST. PATERNUS, Bishop

April 15

ST. PATERNUS was born at Poitiers about the year 482. His father ended his days in solitude in Ireland. St. Paternus emulated his example and embraced monastic life in the diocese of Poitiers.

Later, he went to Wales, where he built a monastery called Llanpaternvaur. After visiting his father in Ireland, he returned to his monastery at Poitiers, or rather Ansion, in that diocese; but soon after, with a monk of that house, he embraced a hermit's life in the forest of Seicy. Here he converted a number of idolaters to the Faith and extended his apostolic labors as far as Bayeuse, with several priests as his fellow laborers.

At an advanced age he was consecrated Bishop of Avranches by Germanus of Rouen. He governed his diocese thirteen years and died about the year 550.

PRAYER God, You made St. Paternus an outstanding exemplar of Divine love and the Faith that conquers the world, and added him to the role of saintly pastors. Grant by his intercession that we may persevere in Faith and love and become sharers of his glory. Amen.

ST. BENEDICT JOSEPH LABRE, Mendicant

April 16

ST. BENEDICT Joseph Labre was born in France in 1748. He received a good education under the care of his pious parents and a priest of Amettes, the place of his birth.

From his childhood he performed various acts of penance for faults, even the most venial. In his twelfth year he began to learn Latin under the care of his uncle, a priest, and for four years he applied himself to this and other studies with pleasure. At sixteen, however, his thoughts turned so much to piety that a dislike of study seemed to gain upon him. Above all, he loved the Bible, and for the rest of his life always carried a copy.

At this period of his life he showed a desire to join the Trappists. Upon being refused, he next tried the Carthusians and remained six weeks among them; but such was not his vocation. Another trial of the monastic life, made among the

Cistercians, was equally a failure. He now took to the life of a pilgrim and sanctified himself by living on alms and practicing extreme poverty.

The last years of his life were spent in Rome, where he made pilgrimages to different sanctuaries. Gradually his health declined. In 1783, he seemed to be dying and yet he would spend hours in prayer. Finally, he was taken into a house out of charity, and died on April 16 of the same year.

St. Benedict represents a Western example of the Eastern ascetical vocation of the mendicant pilgrim or wandering holy man—"the fool of Christ."

PRAYER God, by Your grace St. Benedict Joseph persevered in imitating Christ in His poverty and humility. Through his intercession, grant that we may faithfully follow our vocation and reach that perfection which You held out to us in Your Son. Amen.

ST. STEPHEN HARDING, Abbot

April 17

ST. STEPHEN Harding was born at Dorset, England, early in the second half of the 11th century and was educated at the Sherborne Abbey. As a young man he traveled abroad and grew into a person of great charm and a first-rate scholar. Eventually, he became a monk at the Abbey of Molesme in Burgundy, where he came under the influence of the Abbot, St. Robert, and his zeal for reform.

In 1098, together with St. Robert, St. Alberic, and some twenty other monks of Molesme, St. Stephen founded a new monastery at Cîteaux. Here they lived a life that was simple and austere, in accord with the letter of the Rule of St. Benedict. Upon St. Alberic's death in 1108, St. Stephen became the third Abbot of Cîteaux and built up the community—undergoing many hardships because of his high ideals.

In 1112, St. Bernard arrived there with thirty of his followers, and the fortunes of the monastery took an upward turn. During the next eight years alone, a dozen more Cistercian houses had to be erected to hold those who flocked to the ideals of the new community, and many more followed. In 1119, St. Stephen drew up the "Charta of Charity," which defined the spirit of the Cistercian Abbeys and provided their unity, and has become a most important document in the history of Western monasticism.

The Cistercian life is an accurate barometer of St. Stephen's character; its high ideals, careful organization, austerity, and simplicity mirror the traits of this great Saint who ruled the community for twenty-five years. In 1133, he resigned his office because of near-blindness and advancing age, and on March 28, 1134, he passed on to his heavenly reward.

PRAYER Lord, amid the things of this world, let us be wholeheartedly committed to heavenly things in imitation of the example of evangelical perfection which You have given us in St. Stephen the Abbot. Amen.

ST. APOLLONIUS, Martyr

April 18

MARCUS AURELIUS was followed in 180 on the imperial throne by his son Commodus, a vicious prince. Yet toward the Christians he was not cruel, and the severity of the laws was relaxed. To the number of those influential persons who joined the ranks of Christians during the reign of Commodus, beginning in 180, belonged St. Apollonius, a man of importance and learning.

Severus, one of his slaves, accused him of being a Christian, and was put to death in virtue of an obscure law of Marcus Aurelius, who, though enforcing the punishment of convicted Christians, had decreed that their accusers should be put to death. After the execution of the slave, the judge sent an order to St. Apollonius to renounce his religion. St. Apollonius refused to submit, and was referred to the judgment of the Roman Senate.

He then composed an apology for the Christian religion, which he pronounced before that illustrious body. This eloquent discourse was filled with sacred and profane learning and concluded with the words: "We have hastened to honor Him because we have learned lofty commandments from Him. . . . Yet if it were a delusion (as you assert) which tells us that the soul is immortal, and that there is a judgment after death and a reward of virtue at the resurrection, and that God is the Judge, we would gladly be carried away by such a lie as that, which has taught us to lead good lives awaiting the hope of the future even while suffering adversities."

However, this magnificent discourse fell on deaf ears, and St. Apollonius was condemned by a decree of the Senate for refusing to abjure his Faith. He was beheaded in the sixth year of Commodus, about 186.

PRAYER God of power and mercy, through Your help St. Apollonius has overcome the tortures of his passion. Help us who celebrate his triumph to remain victorious over the wiles of our enemies. Amen.

ST. ELPHEGE, Bishop and Martyr

April 19

ST. ELPHEGE, born of noble and virtuous parents, abandoned the world at an early age and entered the monastery of Derherste in Gloucestershire. After some years he began to lead the life of a recluse in a cell in the neighborhood of the Abbey of Bath, of which he was appointed Abbot until 984, when, through the instrumentality of St. Dunsten, he was elected Bishop of Winchester. In 1006 he was appointed Archbishop of Canterbury.

This period in English history was greatly disturbed by the incursions of the Danes, who sacked and pillaged the country that was then governed by the weak King Ethelred. The Archbishop hurried to the scenes of blood and endeavored to turn the cruelty of the pagans from his people to himself.

Consequently, his cathedral was burned, he was made to endure great tortures, and for several months he was kept in prison. Refusing to use the goods of his church for his ransom, he was put to death while he prayed for his enemies. His martyrdom occurred April 19, 1012.

PRAYER God, You gave splendor to Your Church by granting St. Elphege the victory of martyrdom. Grant that, as he imitated the Lord's Passion, so we may follow in his footsteps and attain everlasting joys. Amen.

ST. MARCELLINUS, Bishop

April 20

ST. MARCELLINUS was born in Africa of noble parents. He journeyed to Gaul with Vincent and Domninus and preached the Gospel with great success in the vicinity of the Alps. Then he fixed his residence at Embrun, where he built an oratory, in which he spent his nights in prayer after consecrating the day to the works of the ministry.

His example and discourses converted a great number of the idolaters among whom he lived. When the whole city had been converted to Christianity, St. Eusebius of Verceil consecrated his oratory at his request.

St. Marcellinus himself received episcopal consecration, and worked with all his power for the spread of the Kingdom of God. He commissioned Vincent and Domninus to preach in several places that he could not visit in person. Heaven confirmed his apostolic labors with miracles. He died at Embrun in 374.

PRAYER God, Light and Shepherd of souls, You established St. Marcellinus as Bishop in Your Church to feed Your flock by his word and form it by his example. Help us through his intercession to keep the Faith he taught by his word and follow the way he showed by his example. Amen.

ST. ANSELM, Bishop and Doctor of the Church

April 21

ST. ANSELM was born of noble parentage in Piedmont about the year 1033. At the age of twenty-seven, St. Anselm adopted the monastic state in the monastery of Bec, studied under Lanfranc, and was made Prior in 1063 and Abbot in 1078.

Various voyages to England in the interest of his Abbey made him known in that country, and in 1093 he succeeded his old master, Lanfranc, as Archbishop of Canterbury. His resistance to the unjust measures of King William Rufus drew upon him the anger of that monarch. In 1097-98, he made a voyage to Rome, and spent some time in a monastery of Calabria, where he composed a work on the Incarnation. In the same year he assisted at the Council of Bari, and by his prayers prevented the Pope from excommunicating the King of England.

During his travels he composed several of his metaphysical works, and did not return to his See until after the death of King William Rufus in 1100. Differences with the new King caused him to undertake a second journey to Rome in 1103, and Pascal II upheld the authority of the Archbishop as his predecessor, Urban II, had done. He returned to England in 1106 and died in 1109.

St. Anselm was characterized by his spirit of recollection, which he preserved even in the most distracting occupations and by the metaphysical bent of his mind. His written works have deeply influenced Catholic philosophy and theology. In this field he is best known for his ontological argument for the existence of God.

He was also a strenuous defender of the rights of the Church against the usurpation of kings.

PRAYER Lord God, You endowed St. Anselm with heavenly doctrine. Through his help, may we faithfully keep that teaching and profess it in our conduct. Amen.

STS. EPIPODIUS AND ALEXANDER,
Martyrs

April 22—(St. Epipodius) *Patron of the Unmarried*

STS. EPIPODIUS and Alexander were two Christian young men of Lyons—both unmarried and of good position. During the fierce persecution of Marcus Aurelius in that city (178), they were arrested, imprisoned, and finally brought before the governor. Their ready acknowledgment of being Christians elicited the astonishment of the governor who was well aware of the fierce tortures and executions which had already been meted out to Christians.

However, the governor was not deterred in carrying out his task. He separated them and attempted to cajole Epipodius (the younger of the two) to abandon his Faith. But the loyal youth remained unmoved and continued to profess his Faith. Then he was stretched out on a rack and his sides were rent by iron claws. He was finally beheaded.

Two days later, it was St. Alexander's turn. Instead of being frightened by the reminder of his companion's fate, he thanked God for his example and expressed a firm desire to join him. He was scourged unmercifully but stood fast in the Faith. Finally, he was sentenced to be crucified, and the moment his battered body was fastened to the cross he passed on to his heavenly reward.

PRAYER May the prayer of Sts. Epipodius and Alexander make us pleasing to You, Lord, and strengthen us in professing Your truth. Amen.

ST. GEORGE, Martyr

April 23—*Patron of England*

THE devotion to this holy martyr can be traced at least to the 5th century, and if it can be proved that the oldest of the churches dedicated to his honor in Constantinople was built by Constantine the Great, then certainly to a much earlier date. Very little is known of him, as certain Acts forged by ancient heretics have cast no little obscurity over his life. It is supposed that he suffered martyrdom in the persecution under Diocletian at Nicomedia in the beginning of the 4th century.

Among the Greeks St. George is called "the Great Martyr," and his feast is kept as a holy day of obligation. His intercession was implored especially in battles, as he is said to have been a soldier. Under the first Norman kings he was chosen as Patron of England, and Edward III instituted an order of knighthood in his honor.

There are some who suppose that it was St. George who tore down the imperial edicts of persecution when they were first published at Nicomedia. He is generally represented as engaged in combat with a dragon. He died about the year 303.

PRAYER Lord, we acclaim Your might and humbly pray. Just as St. George imitated the Lord's Passion, so let him now come to the aid of our weakness. Amen.

ST. ADALBERT, Bishop and Martyr

***The Same Day*—April 23**

ADALBERT (whose Czech name is Vojtech) was born in Bohemia around the year 956 and completed his studies in Magdeburg. Returning home, he became a priest and eventually the second Bishop of Prague in 983.

After expanding his diocese to include Moravia, he labored to eradicate pagan customs in it. A feud between rival political factions hindered his work, so he went to Rome and became a Benedictine at the Abbey of Sts. Alexis and Boniface.

Returning to Prague at the people's request, Adalbert found the same situation and went back to Rome. Heeding the call of the Polish Duke Boleslaw the Great, the Saint undertook to evangelize the Prussians. He met with fierce resistance and was martyred on April 23, 997.

PRAYER God, You bestowed the crown of martyrdom on St. Adalbert, Your Bishop, who was animated by zeal for souls. By his intercession, grant that pastors may not be without their flocks' obedience nor flocks without their pastors' care. Amen.

ST. FIDELIS OF SIGMARINGEN, Martyr

April 24

ST. FIDELIS was born in 1577 at Sigmaringen, a town in the principality of Hohenzollern. In 1612 he received Holy Orders and soon afterward entered the Capuchin Order at Fribourg, changing his baptismal name, Mark, to Fidelis.

At the request of the Congregation of Propaganda he undertook, with eight Fathers of his Order, the mission among the Calvinists in the Canton of the Grisons in Switzerland, although his life was threatened. In spite of opposition he gained many converts. He spent much time at the foot of the altar or before his crucifix, preparing himself for the martyrdom of which he had a premonition.

On April 24, 1622, he made his confession, celebrated Mass, and preached at Gruch. At the end of his sermon he seemed in an ecstasy and foretold his death to several persons. From Gruch he went to Sewis where he was fired upon by a Calvinist, though without effect.

On his way back to Gruch, the Saint was attacked by an angry mob. He died praying for his attackers and with the Names of Jesus and Mary on his lips.

PRAYER God, You were pleased to adorn St. Fidelis, burning with love for You, with the palm of martyrdom in the propagation of the Faith. By his intercession grant that we may be grounded in love, and experience together with him the power of Christ's Resurrection. Amen.

ST. MARK,
Evangelist

April 25

Patron of Notaries

THE second Gospel was written by St. Mark, who, in the New Testament, is sometimes called John Mark. Both he and his mother, Mary, were highly esteemed in the early Church, and his mother's house in Jerusalem served as a meeting place for Christians there.

St. Mark was associated with St. Paul and St. Barnabas (who was Mark's cousin) on their missionary journey through the island of Cyprus. Later he accompanied St. Barnabas alone. We know also that he was in Rome with St. Peter and with St. Paul. Tradition ascribes to him the founding of the Church in Alexandria.

St. Mark wrote the second Gospel, probably in Rome sometime before the year 60 A.D.; he wrote it in Greek for the Gentile converts to Christianity. Tradition tells us that St. Mark was requested by the Romans to set down the teachings of St. Peter. This seems to be confirmed by the position which St. Peter has in this Gospel. In this way the second Gospel is a record of the life of Jesus as seen through the eyes of the Prince of the Apostles.

PRAYER God our Father, You helped St. Mark the Evangelist with Your grace so that he could preach the Good News of Christ. Help us to know You well so that we may faithfully live our lives as followers of Christ. Amen.

BL. ALDA OR ALDOBRANDESCA, Widow

April 26

BLESSED Alda was widowed after seven years of married life and left without children. She retired to a little cottage outside Siena, Italy, and devoted herself to almsgiving and mortification. She was favored with many visions of the earthly life of our Lord. Little by little she gave away all her possessions and ultimately began using a gourd for a drinking cup for lack of anything else to use.

At length, she decided to relinquish her solitude in order to devote herself to the care of the sick poor. She went to live in a hospital and her ecstatic states became the object of scorn on the part of some members of the staff, who to show her up as a fake went so far as to pierce her with sharp instruments and apply lighted candles to her hands. By her charity and humility, this great contemplative won them all over and effected many cures by her ministrations to the poor. She died in 1309.

PRAYER God, You inspired Blessed Alda to strive for perfect charity and so attain Your Kingdom at the end of her pilgrimage on earth. Strengthen us through her intercession that we may advance rejoicing in the way of love. Amen.

ST. ZITA, Virgin

April 27—*Patroness of Domestic Workers*

ST. ZITA was born into a poor but devout Christian family. Her elder sister became a Cistercian nun and her uncle Graziano was a hermit whom the local people regarded as a Saint. Zita herself showed a marked tendency to do God's will obediently whenever it was pointed out to her by her mother.

At the age of twelve Zita entered domestic service in the house of a well-to-do weaver in Lucca, Italy, eight miles from her native village of Monte Sagrati. As things turned out, she remained with that family for the last forty-eight years of her life. She found time every day to attend Mass and recite her plentiful prayers, as well as to carry out her household duties so punctiliously that she earned the resentment of the other servants. Indeed, her work was part of her religion! She used to say: "A servant is not pious if she is not industrious; work-shy piety in people of our position is sham piety."

At first, her employers were upset by her lavish gifts of food to the poor, but in time they were completely won over by her patience and goodness and she became practically a confidential family friend. St. Zita was given free reign over her working schedule and busied herself with visits to the sick and those in prison.

Word spread rapidly in Lucca of her good deeds and the supernatural manifestations that appeared to her. She was sought out by the prominent and at her death in 1278 the people acclaimed her as a Saint. She was canonized in 1696 by Pope Innocent III.

PRAYER Lord God, You showered heavenly gifts on St. Zita the Virgin. Help us to imitate her virtues during our earthly life and enjoy eternal happiness with her in heaven. Amen.

ST. PETER CHANEL, Priest and Martyr

April 28

THE protomarytr of the South Seas, St. Peter Chanel was born in Clet in the diocese of Belley, France, in 1803. He became a diocesan priest and in three years completely revitalized the first parish to which he was assigned.

Since his mind was set on missionary work, Peter joined the newly formed Society of Mary (Marists), which concentrated on missionary work at home and abroad. To his dismay, he was appointed to teach at the Seminary of Belley and remained there for the next five years, dilligently performing his duties.

In 1836, Peter was sent to the New Hebrides as the superior of a little band of missionaries. After a long and arduous ten-month journey, the band split up, with Peter and two others going to evangelize the island of Futuna.

Once there, they made headway in converting the island's populace, attracting even the son of the King. As a result, the King dispatched a group of warriors to set upon the saintly head of the missionaries.

On April 28, 1841, three years after his arrival, Peter was seized and clubbed to death by those he had come to save. And his death brought his work to completion—within five months the entire island was converted to the Faith. Peter was canonized in 1954 by Pope Pius XII.

PRAYER God, in order to spread Your Church You crowned St. Peter with martyrdom. Grant that in these paschal joys we may so frequent the mysteries of Christ's Death and Resurrection as to become witnesses of the new life. Amen.

ST. LOUIS DE MONTFORT, Priest

***The Same Day*—April 28**

LOUIS Mary Grignion was born to a poor family on January 21, 1673, at Montfort, France. He was educated at the Jesuit college in Rennes and was ordained there in 1700. He was assigned as chaplain to a hospital at Poitiers, and his much needed reorganization of the hospital staff caused great resentment, leading to his resignation. However, during his stay there he organized a group of women into the congregation of the Daughters of Divine Wisdom.

Eventually Louis went to Rome where Pope Clement XI appointed him missionary apostolic, and he began to preach in Britanny. His emotional style caused much reaction, but he was successful, especially in furthering devotion to the Blessed Virgin through the Rosary. He also wrote a popular book, *True Devotion to the Blessed Virgin.*

In 1715, Louis organized several priests and formed the Missionaries of the Company of Mary. He died in 1716 at Saint-Laurent-sur Sèvre, France, and was canonized in 1947 by Pope Pius XII.

PRAYER Gracious God, through Your servant St. Louis Your Word was spread. May we continue in our lives to live Your Word and spread devotion to the Mother of Jesus. Amen.

ST. CATHERINE OF SIENA,
Virgin and Doctor of the Church

April 29—
Patroness of Fire Prevention

THE year 1347 witnessed the birth of St. Catherine, the most remarkable woman of her age. In her childhood she consecrated her virginity to God. However her parents, wishing to see her married, began to thwart her pious inclinations. She finally became an object of persecution in her own house. She bore her trials with fortitude and joy, and persevered in her resolution of giving herself entirely to the Divine service. Eventually her parents relented, and she was left free to follow her pious inclinations.

In 1365, at eighteen years of age, she received the habit of the Third Order of St. Dominic. In 1374, during the great pestilence, she devoted herself heroically to the care of the infected. Meanwhile, she was considered to be a power for good, since thousands were converted by her exhortations.

Two years later she went to Avignon to intercede with the Pope for the Florentines, who had been interdicted for joining in a conspiracy against the temporal possessions of the Holy See in Italy. Through her influence Gregory XI returned to Rome, and she exhorted him to contribute, by all possible means, toward the peace of Italy.

Having lived to see the beginning of the great schism, she wrote to the cardinals who were the cause of it and to several princes, seeking to avert the terrible evil. The life of the Saint who had been glorified by God with wondrous gifts and miracles was brought to a close on April 29, 1380, at the age of thirty-three. She was canonized in 1461 by Pope Pius II.

St. Catherine has long been regarded as one of the finest theological minds in the Church—as is shown by her outstanding work, *Dialogue*—and in 1970 Pope St. Paul VI declared her a Doctor of the Church.

PRAYER God, You caused St. Catherine to shine with Divine love in the contemplation of the Lord's Passion and in the service of Your Church. By her help, grant that Your people, associated in the mystery of Christ, may ever exult in the revelation of His glory. Amen.

ST. PIUS V, Pope

April 30

MICHAEL GHISLIERI was born in Italy in 1504. His whole life was always guided by the most perfect maxims of Christian piety. At the age of fifteen he received the Dominican habit, and at once become a model of religious perfection. In 1528, he was ordained priest, and then taught philosophy and theology for sixteen years. He also filled other important positions in his Order.

Pope Paul IV in 1556 promoted him to the united Bishoprics of Nepi and Sutri in the Papal States, and in 1557 the same Pope created him Cardinal, but his humility and other virtues only became more conspicuous in this exalted position. Pius IV, who succeeded Paul IV in 1559, moved him to the diocese of Mondori in Piedmont. At the conclave which was held on the death of Pius IV, St. Charles Borromeo united the suffrages in favor of Cardinal Alexandrinus, as Ghislieri was called, and he became Pope under the title of Pius V in 1566.

His life as Sovereign Pontiff was as exemplary as it had been while he was a simple Dominican

Friar. It was during his pontificate that the celebrated victory of Lepanto was gained against the Turks under Don John of Austria. As a result of this victory he ordered the feast of the Holy Rosary to be observed on the first Sunday of October. He died in the year after this victory, on May 1, 1572, and was canonized in 1712 by Pope Clement XI.

PRAYER God, You providently raised up St. Pius in Your Church for the defense of the Faith and for more suitable Divine worship. Through his intercession, help us to participate in Your mysteries with a livelier Faith and a more fruitful love. Amen.

ST. JOSEPH THE WORKER,

Spouse of the Blessed Virgin Mary

May 1

IN an address to the Catholic Association of Italian Workers, May 1, 1955, Pope Pius XII proclaimed May 1 (May Day) the feast day of St. Joseph the Worker. He thus imparted special religious significance to an observance that had been strictly secular—the proper feast of labor throughout the world—and one that had been used by the enemies of the Church to further their evil designs.

Henceforth, May Day is to be "a day of rejoicing for the concrete and progressive triumph of the Christian ideals of the great family of labor. Acclaimed in this way by Christian workers and having received as it were a Christian baptism, the first of May, far from being a stimulus for discord, hate and violence, is and will be a recurring invitation to modern society to accomplish that which is still lacking for social peace."

Thus the humble carpenter of Nazareth, who was the support and guardian of the Divine Child and His Virgin Mother on earth, is now honored above all other men as the personification of the dignity of the manual laborer and the provident guardian of the worker's family.

PRAYER Lord God, You have created all things, and imposed on man the necessity of work. Grant that, following St. Joseph's example, and under his protection, we may accomplish the works You give us and obtain the rewards You promise. Amen.

ST. ATHANASIUS,

Bishop and Doctor of the Church

May 2

ST. ATHANASIUS, the great champion of the Faith, was born at Alexandria, about the year 296, of Christian parents. Educated under the eye of Alexander, later Bishop of his native city, he made great progress in learning and virtue. In 313, Alexander succeeded Achillas in the Patriarchal See, and two years later St. Athanasius went to the desert to spend some time in retreat with St. Anthony.

In 319, he became a deacon, and even in this capacity he was called upon to take an active part against the rising heresy of Arius, an ambitious priest of the Alexandrian Church who denied the Divinity of Christ. This was to be the life struggle of St. Athanasius.

In 325, he assisted his Bishop at the Council of Nicaea, where his influence began to be felt. Five months later Alexander died; on his deathbed he recommended St. Athanasius as his successor. In consequence of this Athanasius was unanimously elected Patriarch in 326.

His refusal to tolerate the Arian heresy was the cause of many trials and persecutions for St. Athanasius. He spent seventeen of the forty-six years of his episcopate in exile. After a life of virtue and suffering, this intrepid champion of the Catholic Faith, the greatest man of his time, died in peace on May 2, 373.

PRAYER Father, You gave us St. Athanasius, Your Bishop, to defend the Divinity of Your Son. Grant that we may enjoy his teaching and protection and grow continually in our knowledge and love of You. Amen.

STS. PHILIP AND JAMES, Apostles

May 3

(St. James) ***Patron of Hatmakers***

ST. PHILIP, a native of Bethsaida in Galilee, was called by our Lord the day after St. Peter and St. Andrew. We learn from tradition that he was then a married man, and that he had several daughters, three of whom reached eminent sanctity. Like the other Apostles, St. Philip left all things to follow Christ. His name is frequently mentioned in the Holy Gospels.

After the Ascension of his Divine Master, St. Philip preached the Gospel in that part of Asia

Minor called Phrygia, which was then a province of the Roman Empire. It is supposed that he was buried at Hierapolis in Phrygia.

ST. JAMES the Less, the author of the first Catholic Epistle, was the son of Alphaeus of Cleophas. His mother Mary was either a sister or a close relative of the Blessed Virgin, and for that reason, according to Jewish custom, he was sometimes called the brother of the Lord. The Apostle held a distinguished position in the early Christian community of Jerusalem. St. Paul tells us he was a witness of the Resurrection of Christ; he is also called a "pillar" of the Church, whom St. Paul consulted about the Gospel.

According to tradition, he was the first Bishop of Jerusalem, and was at the Council of Jerusalem about the year 50. The historians Eusebius and Hegesippus relate that St. James was martyred for the Faith by the Jews in the Spring of the year 62, although they greatly esteemed his person and had given him the surname of "James the Just."

Tradition has always recognized him as the author of the Epistle that bears his name. Internal evidence based on the language, style, and teaching of the Epistle reveals its author as a Jew familiar with the Old Testament, and a Christian thoroughly grounded in the teachings of the Gospel. External evidence from the early Fathers and Councils of the Church confirms its authenticity and canonicity.

The date of its writing cannot be determined exactly. According to some scholars it was written about the year 49 A.D. Others, however, claim it was written after St. Paul's Epistle to the Romans (composed during the winter of 57-58 A.D.). It was probably written between the years 60 and 62 A.D.

St. James addresses himself to the "twelve tribes that are in the Dispersion," that is, to Christians outside Palestine; but nothing in the Epistle indicates that he is thinking only of Jewish Christians. St. James realizes full well the temptations and difficulties they encounter in the midst of paganism, and as a spiritual father he endeavors to guide and direct them in the Faith. Therefore the burden of his discourse is an exhortation to practical Christian living.

PRAYER Lord God, we enjoy celebrating the annual feast of Your Apostles Sts. Philip and James. Through their prayers let us share in the Passion and the Resurrection of Your Son and help us merit Your eternal presence. Amen.

ST. GOTHARD (GODEHARD), Bishop

May 4

BORN in the Bavarian village of Reichersdorf about 960, Gothard was educated by the Canons of that area and showed so much promise that he attracted the attention of Archbishop Frederick of Salzburg. He became a priest and in 990 when the Benedictine Rule was restored to the Abbey of Neider-Altaich he received the monastic habit. He became Prior and eventually Abbot of the Abbey.

There was such good religious discipline under St. Gothard that the Emperor, St. Henry II, entrusted him with the reform of other monasteries. Over the course of twenty-five years he formed nine Abbots for various houses, and when St. Bernward died in 1022, St. Gothard was made Bishop of Hildesheim in his place, despite his pleas of age and lack of suitable qualifications.

In typical fashion, this dedicated servant of God set about reforming his diocese with all the vigor of a young man. He built and restored churches, fostered education, especially in the Cathedral school, established order throughout the diocese, and erected a hospice for the poor and sick at the edge of Hildesheim. He died in 1038. The pass and railroad tunnel from Switzerland into Italy takes its name from this Saint in whose honor the near-by hospice for travelers and its chapel were dedicated.

PRAYER God, You made St. Gothard an outstanding exemplar of Divine love and the Faith that conquers the world, and added him to the role of saintly pastors. Grant by his intercession that we may persevere in Faith and love and become sharers of his glory. Amen.

ST. JUTTA (JUDITH), Widow

May 5—*Patroness of Prussia*

A NATIVE of Thuringia, St. Jutta was born at Sangerhausen and emulated the life of another great Saint of that area, and contemporary of hers, St. Elizabeth of Hungary. She was married at the age of fifteen to a nobleman and became an admirable wife and mother, winning her husband over to her kind of spiritually-motivated life. The untimely death of her husband on a pilgrimage to the Holy Land left St. Jutta desolate and obliged to bring up her children by herself.

Influenced by their mother's splendid example, each of the children entered the religious life at maturity and left her free to follow the vocation to which she had long aspired. Divesting herself of her property, she spent the few remaining years of her life in religious retirement and care for the sick. She settled down in a dilapidated building about half a mile from Kulmsee in the territory of the military order of the Teutonic Knights, whose Grand Master was a relative of hers. Here she received and dispensed wonderful graces, gaining widespread renown as a Saint.

St. Jutta maintained that three things can bring one close to God—painful sickness, exile from home in some remote corner of a foreign country, and poverty voluntarily accepted for

God. After an entire life exemplifying this way of approach to God, St. Jutta died in 1260.

PRAYER God, You inspired St. Jutta to strive for perfect charity and so attain Your Kingdom at the end of her pilgrimage on earth. Strengthen us through her intercession that we may advance rejoicing in the way of love. Amen.

BLESSED EDWARD JONES AND ANTHONY MIDDLETON, Martyrs

May 6

EDWARD JONES from Wales and Anthony Middleton from Yorkshire were both educated at the Douai College in Rheims. They became priests and were sent to the English mission in the time of Elizabeth I. Middleton was the first to arrive in England, in 1586, and pursued the ministry for some time without being discovered, helped considerably by his youthful appearance and slight stature. Jones followed, in 1588, and quickly became known by the English Catholics as a devout and eloquent preacher.

The two men of God were hunted down and captured with the aid of spies posing as Catholics, and they were hanged before the very doors of the houses in Fleet Street and Clerkenwell where they were arrested. Their trial is regarded as full of irregularities; the reason for the summary justice dispensed to them was spelled out in large letters: "For treason and foreign invasion." After offering their death for the forgiveness of their sins, the spread of the true Faith, and the conversion of heretics, they died on May 6, 1590.

PRAYER Lord, we devoutly recall the sufferings of Blessed Edward and Anthony. Give success to our joyful prayers and grant us also constancy in our Faith. Amen.

BLESSED GISELE, Widow

May 7

BLESSED GISELE was given in marriage to St. Stephen of Hungary in 1008. She bore him a son, who went on to become St. Emeric, and fully supported him in his work of evangelization. After the death of her husband, Gisele retired to the Benedictine Abbey of Niederburg and spent her remaining time on earth in prayer and self-denial.

PRAYER God, You inspired Blessed Gisele to strive for perfect charity and so attain Your Kingdom at the end of her pilgrimage on earth. Strengthen us through her intercession that we may advance rejoicing in the way of love. Amen.

ST. DESIDERATUS, Bishop of Bourges

May 8

ST. DESIDERATUS was the son of Auginus and Agia, a worthy couple of Soissons, France. The wonderful Christian influence of his parents, who spent all their time and possessions in helping the poor, worked on Desideratus and his two brothers, Desiderius and Deodatus, to such an extent that all went on to become Saints.

Desideratus became Secretary of State for King Clotaire and had a telling effect on him for the good. Though surrounded by the worldly splendors of the royal court, the holy man of God lived a life of mortification and prayer. He also strove to eliminate heresy and simony. He often voiced a desire to retire to a monastery, but was always reminded by the King to put the people's welfare before his own.

In 541, Desideratus was appointed Bishop of Bourges and held the post for nine years; during that time his fame spread far and wide as a peacemaker and wonderworker. He took part in the Fifth Council of Orleans and the Second Council of Auvergne which dealt with the errors of Nestorius and Eutyches. He died on May 8, 550.

PRAYER God, You made St. Desideratus an outstanding exemplar of Divine love and the Faith that conquers the world, and added him to the role of saintly pastors. Grant by his intercession that we may persevere in Faith and love, and become sharers of his glory. Amen.

ST. PACHOMIUS, Abbot

May 9—*Founder of Christian Monasticism*

ST. PACHOMIUS was born about 292 in the Upper Thebaid in Egypt and was inducted into the Emperor's army as a twenty-year-old.

The great kindness of Christians at Thebes toward the soldiers became embedded in his mind and led to his conversion after his discharge. After being baptized, he became a disciple of an anchorite, Palemon, and took the habit. The two of them led a life of extreme austerity and total dedication to God; they combined manual labor with unceasing prayer both day and night.

Later, Pachomius felt called to build a monastery on the banks of the Nile at Tabennisi; so about 318 Palemon helped him build a cell there and even remained with him for a while. In a short time some one hundred monks joined him and Pachomius organized them on principles of community living. So prevalent did the desire to emulate the life of Pachomius and his monks become that the holy man was obliged to establish ten other monasteries for men and two nunneries for women. Before his death in 346, there were seven thousand monks in his houses, and his Order lasted in the East until the 11th century.

St. Pachomius was the first monk to organize hermits into groups and write down a Rule for them. Both St. Basil and St. Benedict drew from his Rule in setting forth their own more famous ones. Hence, though St. Anthony is usually regarded as the founder of Christian monasticism, it was really St. Pachomius who began monasticism as we know it today.

PRAYER Lord, amid the things of this world, let us be wholeheartedly committed to heavenly things in imitation of the example of evangelical perfection which You have given us in St. Pachomius. Amen.

ST. SOLANGE, Virgin and Martyr

May 10—*Invoked in Time of Drought*

ST. SOLANGE, the patroness of the province of Berry in France, was born at Villemont near Bourges in the 9th century. After the example of her poor but devout parents, the child was deeply religious and at the age of seven she is said to have taken a vow of chastity.

As she grew up, she was given the task of looking after the family sheep, and she obtained a great affinity for and power over animals. This saintly virgin also was endowed with the power of healing and effected many cures of the sick. Her fame spread throughout the country and everyone became aware of her beauty and holiness.

One day about the year 880, while she was tending her flock, one of the sons of the Count of Poitiers named Bernard approached and made advances toward her. Her resistance only served to inflame the attacker all the more, and he attempted to set her on the horse he was riding. Calling forth all her strength, the young girl twisted free and slid off the horse but was seriously injured by the fall. Driven by a demonic fury, the youth then thrust his sword into her, killing her on the spot.

In 1281, an altar was erected in her honor in the cemetery of the Church of St. Martin-du-Cros, as a result of the legend which said that St. Solange had arisen after being stabbed and carried her head in her hands up to that Church. Also, a field in which she used to pray was given the name: "The Field of St. Solange." She is invoked in time of drought.

PRAYER Lord God, you showered heavenly gifts on St. Solange. Help us to imitate her virtues during our earthly life and enjoy eternal happiness with her in heaven. Amen.

ST. FRANCIS DI GIROLAMO, Priest

May 11—*Apostle of Naples*

BORN at Taranto, Italy, in 1642, St. Francis entered the clerical state at the age of sixteen in his native town and then went to Naples to complete his education for the priesthood. After ordination, he taught in the Jesuit College of Nobles in Naples and was highly regarded by his students. He entered the Society of Jesus four years later and spent the last forty years of his life as a rural missionary working on the outskirts of Naples.

St. Francis was a powerful, spellbinding preacher and was characterized as "a lamb when he speaks but a lion when he preaches." He conducted at least 100 missions in the provinces but the people of Naples never allowed him to be away from them for too long. He was surrounded by people wherever he went; they hung on his every word and streamed to his confessional. He converted countless sinners—at least 400 hardened sinners are said to have come back to God every year through his work.

St. Francis sought out sinners everywhere—in hamlets, along back roads, and on street corners; he haunted the prisons, checked the brothels, and went down into the galleys in his ever-active quest. He even converted a number of Moorish and Turkish prisoners. However, his most spectacular conversion was that of Marie Alvira Cassier, a French woman who had killed her father and fled to the Spanish army in the guise of a man.

St. Francis also established a workingman's organization to help the Jesuits in their labors, founded a charitable pawnshop, and rescued countless children from conditions that spawn delinquency. He had an additional reputation as a wonderworker that led throngs of people to gather round his coffin at his death in 1716. He was canonized in 1839 by Pope Gregory XVI.

PRAYER Almighty, eternal God, You dedicated the joy of this day to the glorification of St. Francis. Mercifully grant that we may always strive to retain and complete by our works that Faith which he continually proclaimed with unwearying zeal. Amen.

STS. NEREUS, ACHILLEUS, AND PANCRAS, Martyrs

May 12

ACCORDING TO Pope St. Damasus, Nereus and Achilleus were Roman soldiers of the 1st century who became Christians and refused to remain in the service. They were martyred for the Faith and buried in the cemetery of Domitilla on the Via Ardeatina. The bas-relief of Achilleus being stricken is the oldest known representation of martyrdom.

The legendary Acts of these martyrs state on the other hand that they were servants of Flavia Domitilla, a niece of the Emperors Titus and Domitian, who became a Christian. They further relate that she was banished to the island of Pontia and was finally martyred at Terracina together with Nereus and Achilleus.

St. Pancras was a Phrygian of noble birth who was baptized at the age of fourteen and proceeded to give all his possessions to the poor. This drew the attention of the authorities to him and ultimately to the fact that he was a Christian. When he refused to renounce his Christianity, he was decapitated under Diocletian about 304.

PRAYER Almighty God, we have seen Your glorious Martyrs Nereus, Achilleus, and Pancras remain steadfast in their profession of Faith. May we also experience their piety in their intercession for us before You. Amen.

ST. ANDREW HUBERT FOURNET, Priest

May 13

BORN into a devout and wealthy family near Poitiers, France, in 1752, St. Andrew was bored by religion and life in general throughout his early years. Undisciplined and frivolous, he got into one scrape after another as a child. Later, he ran away from school and still later dallied with the idea of becoming a soldier while he was in the process of studying law! However, with the aid of a country uncle who happened to be a priest, Andrew threw off the yoke of his devilment and discovered that a vocation to the priesthood lay underneath.

After his ordination, he returned to his native village as the local curate but was still infected with a worldliness that was recognized and mocked by his parishioners in their form of address to him. Once again Divine Providence intervened through the casual criticism of a beggar to whom Andrew had refused an alms. Suddenly, he came to the realization that his way of life was not at all in accord with the spirit of the Gospel. He sold all his possessions, did away with all his petty pretensions, and lived an extremely simple life—even his manner of speech became simple.

During the French Revolution, he refused to swear allegiance to the revolutionary government and ministered to the people in secret. In

1792, he was prevailed upon by his Bishop to leave for Spain, but he returned five years later and tended in secret to the people's spiritual needs. With the coming of Napoleon to power, peace was restored and Andrew returned to his parish and strove to rekindle the people's faith through missions, preaching, and confessions.

In 1806, with the aid of St. Elisabeth Bichier he founded the Congregation of the Daughters of the Cross, whose rule he formulated. Aimed directly at the care of the sick and the education of the young, this Congregation played a large part in the renewal of religion in France after the Revolution. Though retiring from his parish in 1820, St. Andrew continued to direct the sisters till his death on May 13, 1834. More than once he miraculously multiplied food for the sisters and those in their care.

PRAYER God, You taught Your Church to observe all the heavenly commandments in the love of God. Help us to practice works of charity in imitation of Your Priest, St. Andrew, and merit to be numbered among the blessed in Your Kingdom. Amen.

ST. MATTHIAS, Apostle

May 14

FROM the Acts of the Apostles we learn that St. Matthias had been one of the companions of our Savior from the day of His baptism by St.

John; for when there was question of electing an Apostle to take the place of the apostate Judas, St. Peter spoke: "Of these men who have been in our company all the time that the Lord Jesus moved among us, from John's baptism until the day that He was taken up from us, one must become a witness with us of His Resurrection" (Acts 1:21).

Two men were proposed: Barsabbas and Matthias, and the latter was chosen by lot. About one hundred and twenty persons were present at this election. According to an ancient tradition handed down by Clement of Alexandria and confirmed by Eusebius and St. Jerome, St. Matthias was one of the seventy-two disciples of our Lord. It was after this occurrence that the Holy Spirit descended upon the Apostles, among whom St. Matthias was then numbered.

Clement of Alexandria writes that St. Matthias was remarkable for inculcating the necessity of mortifying the flesh with its irregular passions and desires. According to the Greeks, St. Matthias suffered martyrdom in Colchis, which is called Ethiopia. Colchis was a district of Asia Minor, situated on the shores of the Black Sea, south of the Caucasus Mountains.

PRAYER *Lord God, You chose St. Matthias to be an Apostle replacing Judas. Through his intervention may we enjoy the reward of Your love and be numbered among the elect. Amen.*

ST. ISIDORE, the Farmer

May 15—*Patron of Farmers*

ST. ISIDORE was born at Madrid, Spain, in the latter half of the 12th century. For the greater part of his life he was employed as a laborer on a farm outside the city. Many marvelous happenings accompanied his lifelong work in the fields and continued long after his holy death. He was favored with celestial visions and, it is said, the angels sometimes helped him in his work in the fields. St. Isidore was canonized in 1622.

In 1947, he was proclaimed the patron of the National Rural Life Conference in the United States.

PRAYER God, through the intercession of St. Isidore the holy Farmer grant that we may overcome all feelings of pride. May we always serve You with that humility which pleases You, through his merits and example. Amen.

ST. DYMPHNA,
Virgin and Martyr

The Same Day—May 15

Patroness of the Mentally Ill

ST. DYMPHNA was born in the 7th century. Her father, Damon, a chieftain of great wealth and power, was a pagan. Her mother was a very beautiful and devout Christian.

Dymphna was fourteen when her mother died. Damon is said to have been afflicted with a mental illness, brought on by his grief. He sent messengers throughout his own and other lands to find some woman of noble birth, resembling his wife, who would be willing to marry him. When none could be found, his evil advisers told him to marry his own daughter. Dymphna fled from her castle together with St. Gerebran, her confessor, and two other friends.

Damon found them in Belgium. He gave orders that the priest's head be cut off. Then Damon tried to persuade his daughter to return to Ireland with him. When she refused, he drew his sword and struck off her head. She was then only fifteen years of age.

Dymphna received the crown of martyrdom in defense of her purity about the year 620. She is the patron of those suffering from nervous and mental afflictions. Many miracles have taken place at her shrine, built on the spot where she was buried in Gheel, Belgium.

PRAYER Hear us, O God, our Savior, as we honor St. Dymphna, patron of those afflicted with mental and emotional illness. Help us to be inspired by her example and comforted by her merciful help. Amen.

ST. JOHN NEPOMUCENE,

Priest and Martyr

May 16

Patron of Confessors

IN his early childhood, John Nepomucene was cured of a disease through the prayers of his good parents. In thanksgiving, they consecrated him to the service of God.

After he was ordained, he was sent to a parish in the city of Prague. He became a great preacher, and thousands of those who listened to him changed their way of life.

Father John was invited to the court of Wenceslaus IV. He settled arguments and did many kind deeds for the needy people of the city. He also became the Queen's confessor. When the King was cruel to the Queen, Father John taught her to bear her cross patiently.

One day, about 1393, the King asked him to tell what the Queen had said in confession. When Father John refused, he was thrown into prison.

A second time, he was asked to reveal the Queen's confession. "If you do not tell me," said the King, "you shall die. But if you obey my command, riches and honors will be yours." Again Father John refused. He was tortured. The King ordered him to be thrown into the river. Where he drowned, a strange brightness appeared upon the water. Known as the "Martyr of the Confessional," he was canonized in 1729 by Pope Benedict XIII.

PRAYER God, we praise You for the grace You granted to St. John to offer his life in defense of the seal of confession. Grant that, through his prayers, we may use the Sacrament of Penance often and with great profit. Amen.

ST. PASCHAL BAYLON, Religious

May 17—*Patron of Eucharistic Congresses*

BORN at Torre Hermosa in the Kingdom of Aragon, in the year 1540, St. Paschal Baylon spent his early childhood as a shepherd. So great was his desire for instruction that while tending his sheep he carried a book with him and begged those he met to teach him the alphabet. Thus, in a short time he learned to read.

He led the solitary life of a shepherd until he was about twenty-four. By meditation, prayer, and the reading of pious works, he advanced rapidly in perfection, so that when he decided to embrace the religious state and petitioned the Franciscans to admit him into their Order, he had already reached an eminent degree of sanctity. When he decided to become a Religious, he purposely avoided rich monasteries, for he said, "I was born poor, and I am resolved to die in poverty and penance."

In 1564, he entered among the Reformed Franciscans in the Kingdom of Valentia and insisted upon becoming simply a lay brother. For twenty-eight years he lived a perfect life in the austere Order he had chosen, a life of extreme poverty and of constant prayer, which even his labors did not interrupt.

The Saint was characterized by intense devotion to our Lord in the Holy Eucharist. Toward the end of his life he frequently spent a great part of the night in prayer before the altar. God often favored him with ecstasies and raptures, but so great was his humility that he carefully avoided whatever might redound to his honor or praise. St. Paschal also had a great devotion to the Blessed Virgin. He died on May 17, 1592 and was canonized in 1690 by Pope Alexander VIII.

PRAYER God, You filled St. Paschal with a wondrous love for the sacred mysteries of Your Body and Blood. May we draw from this Divine Banquet the same spiritual riches he received. Amen.

ST. JOHN I, Pope and Martyr

May 18

A native of Tuscany in Italy, while he was still an archdeacon John was elected Pope upon the death of Pope Hormisdas in 523. At that time, the ruler of Italy was Theodoric the Goth who subscribed to the Arian brand of Christianity, but had tolerated and even favored his Catholic subjects during the early part of his reign. However, about the time of St. John's accession to the Papacy, Theodoric's policy underwent a drastic change as a result of two events: the treasonable (in the sovereign's view) correspondence between ranking members of the Roman Senate and Constantinople and the severe edict against heretics enacted by the Emperor Justin I, who was the first Catholic on the Byzantine throne in fifty years.

Spurred on by the appeals of Eastern Arians, Theodoric threatened to wage war against Justin but ultimately decided to negotiate with him through a delegation of five Bishops and four Senators. At its head he named Pope John—much against the latter's wishes. Little is known for certain about the nature of the message which the Pope bore and the manner in which he carried out his mission. What is known is that he succeeded in persuading the Emperor to mitigate his treatment of the Arians and thus avoid reprisals against the Catholics in Italy. The

Pope's visit also brought about the reconciliation of the Western and Eastern Churches which had been plagued by a schism since 482 when Zeno's *Henoticon* had been published.

However, Theodoric had been becoming more suspicious with each passing day. While waiting for the delegation to return, he ordered the execution of the philosopher Boethius and his father-in-law Symmachus on a charge of treason; and as he got word of the friendly relations between the Pope and the Emperor, he concluded that they were plotting against him. Hence, on the delegation's return to the capital city of Ravenna, Pope John was imprisoned by order of Theodoric and died a short time later as a result of the treatment he experienced there.

PRAYER God, the rewarder of those faithful to You, on this day You consecrated the martyrdom of Pope St. John. Hear the prayers of Your people and grant that we who venerate his merits may imitate the constancy of his Faith. Amen.

ST. YVES, Priest and Lawyer

May 19—*Patron of Lawyers*

BORN around 1253 at Kermartin in Brittany, St. Yves (Ivo) Helory was sent to Paris by his landowning father to receive a higher education, and at the end of ten years he had gained distinction in philosophy, theology, and canon law, as well as civil law. On his return to Brittany he was appointed a diocesan judge, first to the Bishop of Rennes and later to the Bishop of Treguier. In this capacity, he carried out his duties with equity, incorruptibility, and concern for the poor and the lowly.

His fame quickly spread and he became known as "the poor man's advocate." He pleaded for the poor in other courts, going so far as to pay their expenses and even visiting them in prison; his constant concern was to obtain justice for all. Accordingly, he constantly tried to reconcile quarrelling parties and have them arrive at an amicable agreement without incurring the costs of unnecessary lawsuits.

In 1284, Yves became a priest and from 1287 on devoted himself to parish work. But he made his legal knowledge ever available to any of his parishioners who needed it. He lived frugally and unassumingly, instructed the people in both spiritual and temporal matters, and preached the Word of God with power. On May 19, 1303, this "attorney who was a holy man" appeared before the Ultimate Judge to receive his reward. He was canonized in 1347 by Pope Clement VI.

PRAYER God, You taught Your Church to observe all the heavenly commandments in the love of God. Help us to practice works of charity in imitation of Your Priest, St. Yves, and merit to be numbered among the blessed in Your Kingdom. Amen.

ST. BERNARDINE OF SIENA, Priest

May 20—*Patron of Advertisers*

THE Republic of Siena was the country of St. Bernardine. He was born at Massa in that territory in 1380. Left an orphan at an early age, he was educated by his pious aunt, who loved him as if he had been her own son. Even his first years were brightened by his proficiency in study.

As a member of the Confraternity of Our Lady, he served the sick in the hospital; nor did he desist when the great pestilence broke out in 1400. He even persuaded other young men to share these arduous labors. Four years later he entered among the Fathers of the Strict Observance of the Order of St. Francis.

On becoming a priest he devoted himself to the office of preaching. For fourteen years his labors were confined to his own country, where devotion to the Holy Name of Jesus, which he extolled, became widespread. As his reputation spread, however, he gradually became the apostle of Italy in the 15th century. In 1427, he refused the Bishopric of Siena; in 1431, that of Ferrara; and again, in 1435, the diocese of Urbino. The wondrous results of his sermons became a byword.

Though he was followed by honors and applause, the most sincere humility appeared in his actions, and he always sought to conceal the talents with which God had endowed him. In 1435, he was appointed vicar-general of the Strict Observance, but after five years he obtained his release from this office and in his old age continued the work of preaching in Romania, Ferrara, and Lombardy. He died in 1444 and was canonized in 1450 by Pope Nicholas V.

PRAYER God, You gave St. Bernardine Your Priest an exceeding love for the Name of Jesus. Through his merits and prayers grant that we may ever be inflamed with love for You. Amen.

ST. GODRIC OF FINCHALE, Hermit

May 21

THIS long-lived Saint led a full life, pursuing a secular vocation until his middle years and a strictly religious one thereafter. Born about 1065 in Walpole, England, he started out as a peddler, and then took to the sea and became a prosperous trader. He made trips to Scotland, Flanders, and Scandinavia, and even steered the ship in times of danger. He still found time, however, to make pilgrimages to St. Andrew's in Scotland, Jerusalem, Compostela, and elsewhere.

In 1102, he assisted King Baldwin I of Jerusalem to escape after the Battle of Ramleh and earned the name of "pirate" from one of his contemporaries. After a brief stint as a steward to a Norfolk landowner he made two more pilgrimages, to St. Gilles in Provence and to Rome in the company of his mother, who walked barefoot all the way. Then in his middle years he tried his hand at book-learning, and lived for some time with an old recluse near Bishop Auckland.

In 1110, Godric retired to Finchale in a little hut and remained there in solitude for the rest of his life. Here he practiced fearsome penances and dispensed salutary spiritual advice to all who came to him. He gained a power over wild creatures that was looked upon as remarkable and was endowed with the ability of St. Thomas Becket whom he had never seen in the flesh.

It is also quite likely that this holy man was the first known lyrical poet in English as well as the author of the first known musical settings of English words. Four holy songs taken from his own lips have come down to us. Most remarkable of all is the fact that he was totally ignorant of music and attributed both words and melodies to the Blessed Virgin and his dead sister who appeared to him in a vision. He died in 1170.

PRAYER Lord God, You alone are holy and no one is good without You. Through the intercession of St. Godric help us to live in such a way that we may not be deprived of a share in Your glory. Amen.

ST. RITA OF CASCIA, Widow

May 22—*Patroness of Impossible Cases*

ST. RITA was born at Spoleto, Italy, in 1381. At an early age she begged her parents to allow her to enter a convent. Instead they arranged a marriage for her.

Rita became a good wife and mother, but her husband was a man of violent temper. In anger he often mistreated his wife. He taught their children his own evil ways. Rita tried to perform her duties faithfully and to pray and receive the Sacraments frequently.

After nearly twenty years of marriage, her husband was stabbed by an enemy but before he died he repented because Rita prayed for him.

Shortly afterward her two sons died, and Rita was alone in the world. Prayer, fasting, penances of many kinds, and good works filled her days. She was admitted to the convent of the Augustinian nuns at Cascia in Umbria, and began a life of perfect obedience and great charity.

Sister Rita had a great devotion to the Passion of Christ. "Please let me suffer like You, Divine Savior," she said one day, and suddenly one of the thorns from the crucifix struck her on the forehead. It left a deep wound which did not heal and which caused her much suffering for the rest of her life. She died on May 22, 1457, and was canonized in 1900 by Pope Leo XIII.

PRAYER God, through the prayers of St. Rita, may we learn to bear our crosses in life in the same spirit in which she bore hers. Amen.

ST. JOHN BAPTIST DEI ROSSI, Priest

May 23

BORN at Voltaggio, Italy, in 1698, St. John received an excellent education and was ordained in 1721. Shortly thereafter he was afflicted with epilepsy and devoted his ministry to the poor of the Campagna. For the next forty years he performed labors which would have taxed the strength of a robust man.

He ministered to the sick and poor in St. Gall, the night hospice for paupers founded by Celestine III, and in the hospital of the Trinity. Early in the morning and late every night he sought out the cattle-drivers and teamsters in the Roman market, gaining their confidence, instructing them, and preparing them for the Sacraments. Another class of people to whom his pity was extended comprised the homeless women and girls who wandered around begging or walked the streets by night. With the pittance he received in Mass stipends he rented a house behind St. Gall and housed them there.

As an assistant priest he spent many hours hearing confessions, especially of the poor and unlearned. On succeeding to the canonry of St. Mary in Cosmedin in 1735, he turned over all income to charitable causes and lived most frugally. He was given the unusual faculties of hearing confessions in any of the churches of Rome and was greatly in demand for parish missions. Often, he preached five and six times a day in churches, chapels, convents, hospitals, barracks and prisons.

Such extraordinary zeal and labor eventually took its toll and his health broke down. He retired to the hospital of the Trinity which he had so often frequented and died of a stroke on May 23, 1764. Since he died without a penny, this "Hunter of souls" was buried at the expense of the hospital. He was canonized in 1881 by Pope Leo XIII.

PRAYER Almighty, eternal God, You dedicated the joy of this day to the glorification of St. John. Mercifully grant that we may always strive to retain and complete by our works that Faith which he continually proclaimed with unwearying zeal. Amen.

STS. DONATIAN AND ROGATIAN, Martyrs

May 24

IN the 3rd century there lived at Nantes in Brittany two brothers named Donatian and Rogatian. The former had become a convert to Christianity and led such an edifying life that his example moved the heart of Rogatian to desire the Sacrament of Baptism. But the persecution of the Emperor Maximian was raging, and the Bishop was in concealment, so there remained no opportunity of receiving that Sacrament. The Emperor was in Gaul in 286, and it was probably about that time that the martyrdom of the two brothers occurred.

The prefect, who was probably the cruel Rictius Varus, accused St. Donatian of being a Christian and of having enticed others, particularly his brother, from the worship of the gods. Having confessed Christ, he was cast into prison. St. Rogatian was also apprehended and showed himself equally steadfast in the Faith.

Both spent the night in prayer. When brought before the prefect in the morning, they declared that they were ready to suffer anything for the Name of Jesus. Seeing them to be inflexible, the judge commanded them to be stretched on the rack and beheaded (St. Rogatian thus received a Baptism of blood). Their martyrdom occurred probably about the year 287.

PRAYER Lord, we devoutly recall the sufferings of Sts. Donatian and Rogatian. Give success to our joyful prayers and grant us also constancy in our Faith. Amen.

ST. BEDE THE VENERABLE, Priest and Doctor of the Church

May 25

ST. BEDE was born at Jarrow, England, in 673. He joined the Benedictines and was ordained priest in 702. He was considered far and wide as the most learned man of his day. His written works, most of which are extant, comprise all branches of knowledge: history, rhetoric, cosmography, orthography, astronomy, music, grammar, philosophy, poetry, exegesis and hagiography.

The best known and most authoritative of his historical works is the *Ecclesiastical History of the English People*, which is a complete history up to 731. He died in 735.

PRAYER God, You enlightened Your Church by the erudition of the Priest, St. Bede. Grant to

Your servants always to exemplify his wisdom and to be aided by his merits. Amen.

ST. GREGORY VII, Pope

***The Same Day*—May 25**

HILDEBRAND was born in Tuscany, Italy, and went to France where he embraced the monastic state in the renowned Abbey of Cluny. He was called back to Rome and soon gained a great reputation for learning and sanctity. He helped to carry out the reforms of Leo IX and succeeded him in 1073, taking the name of Gregory VII. Continuing the reforms of St. Leo, he worked especially to eradicate simony and the looseness of morals of the clergy, and to free the Church from the influence of temporal rulers.

Henry IV, the German Emperor, whom he had excommunicated for flagrantly denying the Church's authority to invest Bishops, came to him at Canossa and stood barefoot in the snow to beg for a pardon which the Pope granted. However, this famous act of repentance was a sham; when Henry seized Rome in 1084, he set up an antipope and forced Gregory into exile at Salerno, where the Saint died the following year—steadfast to the end. His last recorded words were: "I have loved justice and hated iniquity. . . ; therefore, I die in exile." He was canonized in 1606 by Pope Paul V.

PRAYER Grant to Your Church, O Lord, the spirit of fortitude and zeal for justice with which

You were pleased to let Pope St. Gregory shine forth. Renouncing iniquity, may she carry out with a willing love whatever things are right. Amen.

ST. MARY MAGDALEN DE PAZZI, Virgin

The *Same Day*—May 25

BORN of a noble Florentine family in 1566, Mary became a Carmelite nun in Florence at seventeen. God favored her with the most wonderful graces, and she lived in that mysterious sphere to which many Saints have been raised, called the Extraordinary Way. She was also endowed with the spirit of prophecy. She found her vocation in prayer and penance for the reform of all states of life in the Church and for the conversion of all men.

The last three years of her life were characterized by intense bodily and mental suffering, yet she prayed to suffer more, so great was her love for Jesus Christ Crucified. She died on May 25, 1607, shortly after Pope Leo XI, whose elevation to the papacy and subsequent death she had foretold. She was canonized in 1669 by Pope Clement IX.

PRAYER God, the lover of virginity, You conferred heavenly gifts on St. Mary the Virgin who was inflamed with love for You. Help us to imitate the example of purity and love given us by the one whom we honor this day. Amen.

ST. PHILIP NERI, Priest

May 26—*Patron of Rome*

ST. PHILIP was born in Florence in 1515, the very same year that St. Teresa was born at Avila in Spain. From his sixth year he was characterized by the most perfect obedience toward his parents. Having finished his classical studies at eighteen, he was sent to an uncle who lived near Monte Cassino. But St. Philip, desirous of serving God without worldly distractions, went to Rome in 1533 and became preceptor to the children of a Florentine nobleman.

Even at this period of his life he obtained a great reputation for sanctity. While teaching others he devoted himself to the study of philosophy and theology. His desire to save souls caused him to establish the Confraternity of the Blessed Trinity in 1548, with the object of serving pilgrims and the sick. In obedience to his confessor he became a priest in June 1551, at nearly thirty-six years of age.

He now began to dwell in a small community near the Church of St. Jerome, continuing his mortified life. In the same year he laid the foundation for the Congregation of the Oratory. In 1575, Gregory XIII approved it, and in 1583 gave to St. Philip the new Church of La Vallicella, which is still called La Chiesa Nuova—The New Church.

Here the Saint lived, edifying all Rome by his virtues and laboring zealously for souls in the ministry of the confessional. He enjoyed the favor of Popes Pius IV and V, Gregory XIII and XIV and Clement VIII, and the friendship of many great men, among whom was St. Charles Borromeo. After a life of penance and of eminent usefulness, St. Philip died in 1595 and he was canonized in 1622 by Pope Gregory XV.

PRAYER God, You never cease raising Your faithful servants to the glory of holiness. Grant that we may be inflamed by the fire of the Holy Spirit which so wonderfully burned in the heart of St. Philip. Amen.

ST. AUGUSTINE OF CANTERBURY, Bishop

May 27—*Apostle of England*

POPE St. Gregory the Great sent St. Augustine, a monk of the Benedictine monastery of St. Andrew in Rome, with 39 of his brethren, to England. Upon landing in England, St. Augustine was greeted by King Ethelbert of Kent, a pagan, who had married a Christian, Bertha. Shortly thereafter, in 597, St. Augustine baptized King Ethelbert together with many of his subjects. After being consecrated Bishop in Gaul by the Archbishop of Arles, St. Augustine became the Bishop of Canterbury.

By dint of hard and unremitting labor, this holy missionary in a few short years founded and directed the English hierarchy, thus sowing the seed which was to yield rich harvests of souls for Christ over the centuries. He died on May 27, 604 or 605.

PRAYER God, through the preaching of St. Augustine, Your Bishop, You led the English peoples to the Gospel. Grant that the fruits of his labor may perdure in Your Church with perennial fruitfulness. Amen.

ST. GERMANUS, Bishop of Paris

May 28

ONE of the glories of France in the 6th century, St. Germanus was born near Autun about 496. He was ordained by St. Agippinus, Bishop of the diocese, and subsequently chosen Abbot and administrator of St. Symphorianus in one of the suburbs of Autun. About the year 566, he was nominated to be Bishop of Paris by King Childebert I, but he continued to lead his former austere life. His example and his preaching brought about the conversion of many sinners and careless Christians. The King himself abandoned his total absorption in worldly affairs, and became a benefactor of the poor and the founder of many religious establishments.

Throughout his episcopate St. Germanus remained unwearying and fearless in his endeavors to halt civil strife, curb the licentiousness of the nobles, and check the viciousness of the Frankish Kings—but to no avail. He founded a monastery in Paris in whose church he was buried after his death on May 28, 576; it went on to become very famous under the name of Saint-Germain-des-Prés. At his death, he was mourned by the people and by King Chilperic, who composed the Bishop's epitaph, extolling his virtues, miracles, and zeal for the salvation of souls.

PRAYER God, Light and Shepherd of souls, You established St. Germanus as Bishop in Your Church to feed Your flock by his word and form it by his example. Help us through his intercession to keep the Faith he taught by his word and follow the way he showed by his example. Amen.

ST. MAXIMINUS OF TRIER, Bishop

May 29

A native of Poitiers, France, St. Maximinus left for Trier early in his life, drawn by the saintly reputation of its Bishop, St. Agritius. He received his education there and eventually succeeded to the episcopacy upon the death of St. Agritius in 325. This provided an ideal base for Maximinus to carry on his lifelong battle with Arianism, since Trier at that time was the usual residence of the Emperors of the West and the capital of the Western Empire.

Maximinus deemed it an honor to have St. Athanasius living under his protection during his first exile from 335-337; and he later provided equal protection for St. Paul, Patriarch of Constantinople, when he was banished by the same Emperor, Constantius, who for a while fell under the Arian influence. Afterward, St. Athanasius praised the nobility, vigilance, and fearless courage of his host who was also famous for his miracles.

St. Maximinus convened the Synod of Cologne which declared Euphratas a heretic and removed him from his See; he also participated in the Council of Sardica in 347. Perhaps his finest moment came when he was coupled with the great St. Athanasius and anathematized by the Arians at their Council of Philippopolis. This provided irrefutable evidence of his redoubtable opposition to Arianism and his marked success in that regard. Unfortunately, though he seems to have written much, we do not possess any of the works of this intrepid defender of the true Faith, who died about 349.

PRAYER *Father, You gave us St. Maximinus to defend the Divinity of Your Son. Grant that we may enjoy His teaching and protection and grow continually in our knowledge and love of You. Amen.*

ST. JOAN OF ARC,

Virgin

May 30

Patroness of France

ON January 6, 1412, Joan of Arc was born to pious parents of the French peasant class, at the obscure village of Domremy, near the province of Lorraine. At a very early age she heard voices: those of St. Michael, St. Catherine, and St. Margaret.

At first the messages were personal and general. Then at last came the crowning order. In May 1428, her voices told Joan to go to the King of France and help him reconquer his kingdom. For at that time the English King was after the throne of France, and the Duke of Burgundy (the chief rival of the French King) was siding with him and gobbling up ever more French territory.

After overcoming opposition from churchmen and courtiers, the seventeen-year-old girl was given a small army with which she raised the siege of Orleans on May 8, 1429. She then enjoyed a series of spectacular military successes, during which the King was able to enter Rheims and be crowned with her at his side.

In May 1430, as she was attempting to relieve Compiégne, she was captured by the Burgundians and sold to the English when Charles and the French did nothing to save her. After months of imprisonment, she was tried at Rouen by a tribunal presided over by the infamous Peter Cauchon, Bishop of Beauvais, who hoped that the English would help him to become Archbishop.

Through her unfamiliarity with the technicalities of theology, Joan was trapped into making a few damaging statements. When she refused to retract the assertion that it was the Saints of God who had commanded her to do what she had done, she was condemned to death as a heretic, sorceress, and adulteress, and burned at the stake on May 30, 1431. She was nineteen years old. Some thirty years later she was exonerated of all guilt and she was ultimately canonized in 1920 by Pope Benedict XV, making official what the people had known for centuries.

PRAYER Lord, You wondrously raised up St. Joan, Your Virgin, to defend the Faith and her country. Through her intercession grant that the Church may overcome the snares of her enemies and enjoy unbroken peace. Amen.

VISITATION OF THE BLESSED VIRGIN MARY

May 31

THIS feast commemorates the visit of the Blessed Virgin Mary to St. Elizabeth, in the mountains about six miles west of Jerusalem, upon being told by the Angel Gabriel that her aged cousin was with child. The feast was instituted in 1389 by Urban VI to obtain the end of the Western schism, and it was inserted in the Roman Calendar on July 2, the date on which it had already been celebrated by the Franciscans since 1263. It has now been assigned to the last day of May, between the Solemnity of the Annunciation of the Lord and the Birth of St. John the Baptist, to conform more closely to the Gospel account.

"Mary set out, proceeding in haste into the hill country to a town of Judah, where she entered Zechariah's house and greeted Elizabeth. When Elizabeth heard Mary's greeting, the baby stirred in her womb. Elizabeth was filled with the Holy Spirit and cried out in a loud voice: 'Blessed are you among women and blessed is the fruit of your womb. But who am I that the mother of my Lord should come to me? The moment your greeting sounded in my ears, the baby stirred in my womb for joy. Blessed is she who trusted that the Lord's words to her would be fulfilled.'

"Then Mary said: 'My being proclaims the greatness of the Lord, my spirit finds joy in God my savior' " (Luke 1:39-47).

PRAYER Father, under Your inspiration the Virgin Mary, pregnant with Your Son, visited St. Elizabeth. Grant that we may follow the guidance of the Spirit and praise You eternally with her in heaven. Amen.

ST. JUSTIN, Martyr

June 1—*Patron of Lecturers*

BORN at Nablus (ancient Shechem), Palestine, about 100, Justin came from a pagan family. At the age of thirty-three, after years of studying the various systems of philosophy, he became converted to Christianity by way of Platonism. Thereafter, his whole life was devoted to the propagation and defense of the Faith in Asia Minor and at Rome. Though he retained the garb of a philosopher, he is the most important Christian Apologist of the 2nd century and the first of whom we possess written works. These are the two *Apologies* (to the Emperor Antoninus and the Roman Senate) setting forth the moral values of Christianity, and the *Dialogue* demonstrating its truth to the Jew Trypho. They are invaluable for the information they contain about the Christian Faith and practice at that time.

In 165, while bearing witness to the Faith in Rome, he was denounced as a Christian, most likely at the instigation of a Cynic philosopher whom he had outshone in a public debate. Arrested and ordered to sacrifice to the gods, he replied: "No right-minded man forsakes truth for falsehood." The six others who were with him remained steadfast with him and they all attained the palm of martyrdom.

PRAYER God, in a wonderful manner You taught St. Justin the Martyr the lofty science of Jesus Christ manifested in the folly of the Cross.

Through his intercession grant that we may never fall into error but remain firm in the Faith. Amen.

STS. MARCELLINUS AND PETER, Martyrs

June 2

DURING the persecution of Diocletian, in 304, a Roman priest and an exorcist, named respectively Marcellinus and Peter, were apprehended and thrown into prison. While there, they zealously strengthened others of the faithful and made new converts, among whom was their jailer Arthemius together with his wife and daughter. They were all condemned to death; and Marcellinus and Peter were led to a wood called the Silva Nigra, where they were beheaded in secret so that their place of burial would remain unknown.

By an irony of Divine Providence, their names which were doomed to oblivion have been inserted in the Roman Canon (that is, Eucharistic Prayer I) at Mass where they have been perpetuated over the centuries. Pope Damasus composed an epitaph for the tomb of these two martyrs and stated that he learned about them from their executioner, who had subsequently become a Christian.

PRAYER God, You surround and protect us by the glorious confession of Your holy Martyrs, Sts. Marcellinus and Peter. Help us to profit from their example and be supported by their prayer. Amen.

STS. CHARLES LWANGA AND COMPANIONS, Martyrs

June 3—*Protomartyrs of Equatorial Africa*

KING MTESA of Uganda, in Equatorial Africa, had allowed the White Fathers to preach the Faith in his country with some good results. However, when his successor, King Mwanga, assumed power in 1885, he initiated a fierce persecution against "all those who pray," that is, all Catholics.

Among the victims of this persecution were the elite of the Ugandan youth—Charles Lwanga, the chief of the royal pages, and twenty-one of his companions. As their leader, Charles exhorted them by his words and left them an example by his death—since he was the first to be burned alive. Twelve others followed him on that same day, June 3, 1886; the rest were killed between May 26, 1886, and January 27, 1887.

These martyrs of Christ were beatified in 1920 and canonized in 1964 by St. Paul VI who declared: "These African martyrs inaugurate a new age. Africa is rising free and redeemed, bathed in their blood. Christianity has found a ready hearing in Africa, and we see this as a mysterious plan of God, a vocation proper to Africa, and a promise of historical significance. Africa is the new country of Christ. A clear witness of this fact is the direct simplicity and unshakable fidelity of these young African Christians."

PRAYER God, You made the blood of martyrs become the seed of Christians. May the field of Your Church, irrigated by the blood of St. Charles and his Companions, always produce rich harvests. Amen.

ST. FRANCIS CARACCIOLO, Religious

June 4

ST. FRANCIS, born in the Kingdom of Naples, was signally pious from his childhood. In his youth he determined to consecrate himself to God and he entered the priesthood at Naples, where he began to exercise his zeal, especially in assisting those condemned to die. By a providential disposition, he joined John Augustine Adorno and Fabricius Caracciolo in founding the Order of the Regular Clerics Minors.

Up to the time of his profession, he had borne the name of Ascanio, which he now changed for that of Francis, in honor of St. Francis of Assisi. Two years later, upon the death of Adorno, he became superior of the Order. To extend his Order he traveled three times to Spain, clad as a pilgrim and begging his bread along the road.

On these journeys he suffered great hardships, but he had the satisfaction of founding several houses in Spain, aided by the liberality of Philip II and his son, Philip III, who succeeded him in 1598. Such was the charity of the Saint that arriving in Rome he took up his abode in a hospice of the poor and associated with a leper. He breathed his last at Agnone, in the house of the Oratorian Fathers, June 4, 1608 and was canonized in 1807 by Pope Pius VII.

PRAYER God, You adorned St. Francis, the founder of a new Order, with a zeal for prayer and love for penance. Help Your servants to make such progress by imitating him that by praying unceasingly and bringing their bodies into subjection they may be worthy to attain heavenly glory. Amen.

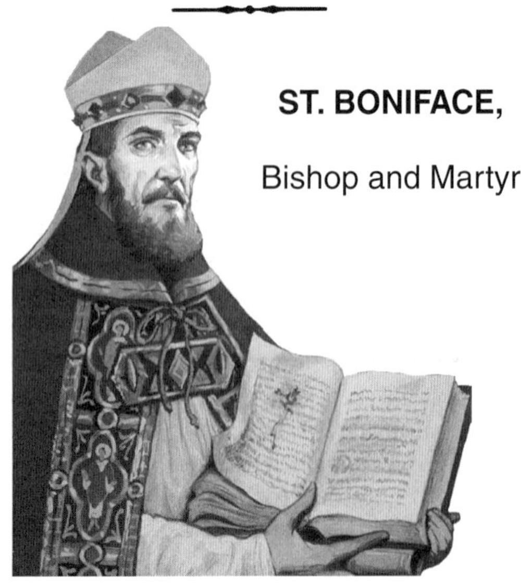

ST. BONIFACE,

Bishop and Martyr

June 5—*Apostle of Germany*

ST. BONIFACE, whose baptismal name was Winfrid, was born about the year 680 in Devonshire, England. From the age of thirteen he was educated in the Benedictine monastery of Exeter, where he later became a monk. He then passed on to that of Nursling in the diocese of Winchester, which enjoyed a great reputation for learning. After some time the Abbot appointed him to teach. At the age of thirty he was ordained to the priesthood.

With the permission of his Abbot, Boniface went to Friesland in 716, in order to preach to the idolaters. His first attempt was unsuccessful, and he was obliged to return to England, where he was chosen Abbot of his monastery, a dignity which he soon resigned.

In 719, he went to Rome and presented himself to Pope Gregory II, begging authority to preach to the idolaters. The Pope, having seen the letters of his Bishop, gave him ample power to preach the Faith to the heathens in Germany. In 745, the Saint chose Mainz as his Episcopal See, after he had established a number of dioceses in Germany. He ended his fruitful career by a glorious martyrdom in Friesland, where he had gone to preach the Faith. His death occurred on June 5, 755.

PRAYER Lord, let St. Boniface intercede for us, that we may firmly adhere to the Faith he taught, and for which he shed his blood, and fearlessly profess it in our works. Amen.

ST. NORBERT, Bishop

June 6

ST. NORBERT was born at Xanten in the Rhineland, about 1080. The early part of his life was devoted to the world and its pleasures. He even entered upon the ecclesiastical state in a worldly spirit. He was ordained subdeacon, but fear of greater restraint prevented him from receiving higher orders.

An accident became the occasion of a wonderful change of heart. A stroke of lightning frightened his horse, whereupon he was thrown to the ground and knocked senseless; on regaining consciousness, he became a sincere penitent. He left the court and withdrew to Xanten, where he began to lead a retired and penitential life.

A retreat he made in the monastery of St. Sigebert, near Cologne, completed his conversion, and he spent two years preparing himself for the priesthood, which he received at Cologne. Soon after, he resigned his ecclesiastical benefices, sold his property and gave the proceeds to the poor, and traveled to Languedoc, where Pope Gelasius II was at that time.

He went from place to place, preaching penance. Finally, he settled at Premontre, where he established the Order of Premonstratensians which became very numerous, even during the life of the holy founder. He was forced to accept the dignity of Archbishop of Magdeburg, about the year 1125, but in this exalted station he practiced the same austerity that had been familiar to him in the cloister.

His zeal effected a great reformation in his diocese, though, like other Saints, he had enemies in those to whom his life was a reproach. Together with St. Bernard he labored much to extinguish the disorders caused by the schism of the anti-Pope, Anacletus. Upon his return from a journey to Rome with Emperor Lothaire, he fell ill, and, after four months of sickness, died June 6, 1134. He was canonized in 1582 by Pope Gregory XIII.

PRAYER God, You made Your Bishop St. Norbert an outstanding minister of Your Church by his prayer and pastoral zeal. Through his prayers grant that Your faithful flock may always find pastors after Your heart and salutary pastures. Amen.

ST. ROBERT OF NEWMINSTER, Abbot

June 7

ST. ROBERT was born at Gargrave, England, at the beginning of the 12th century. He studied at the University of Paris, was ordained priest and served as a parish priest at Gargrave. Later he joined the Benedictines at Whitby and then the Cistercians at Fountains. In 1138, he founded the Abbey of Newminster at Morpeth, Northumberland, which became a place of pilgrimage.

As Abbot, he founded several new monasteries and also provided a fine example leading his monks to sanctity. He recited the entire Psalter of 150 psalms daily and he ate sparingly to maintain his self-denial. This holy man was also endowed with special power over evil spirits and he cured many possessed persons; he is sometimes pictured as holding the devil in chains and taming him with an upright crucifix.

Robert was a close friend of the simple hermit Godric and often visited him in his lonely hermitage at Finchale, where they would discourse about heavenly mysteries. At the moment of Robert's death, on June 7, 1159, his friend saw his soul ascending to heaven like a ball of fire.

PRAYER Lord, amid the things of this world, let us be wholeheartedly committed to heavenly things in imitation of the example of evangelical perfection You have given us in St. Robert the Abbot. Amen.

ST. MEDARD, Bishop

June 8

ST. MEDARD was born at Salency in Picardy, about the year 457. Under the care of his pious parents he made rapid strides in virtue, evincing particularly a great charity for the poor. At thirty-three years of age he was ordained to the priesthood and became a bright ornament of that holy state, preaching to the people by both word and example.

In 530, he became Bishop of Augusta Verumanduorum, being consecrated by St. Remigius, who had baptized King Clovis in 496. Though he was then seventy-two years old, he redoubled his labors, extending his zeal wherever the honor of God seemed to require it. He bore persecutions in silence and with patience. Though he had the affliction of beholding his diocese ravaged by the Huns and Vandals, it gave him a fresh opportunity to practice charity.

In 544, Radegondes, Queen of France, received the religious veil from his hands, and she was made a deaconess with the consent of her husband, King Clotaire, who, doing penance for the sins of his youth, allowed himself to be guided by the counsels of St. Medard. The Saint died either in 545 or 561 and the whole kingdom lamented his loss. A celebrated Benedictine Abbey afterward arose over his tomb at Soissons.

PRAYER God, Light and Shepherd of souls, You established St. Medard as Bishop in Your Church to feed Your flock by his word and form it by his example. Help us through his intercession to keep the Faith he taught by his word and follow the way he showed by his example. Amen.

ST. EPHREM, Deacon and Doctor of the Church

June 9

BORN at Nisibis, a city in Roman Mesopotamia, St. Ephrem was banished from his home by his pagan father for his Christian sympathies. He found refuge with St. James, Bishop of Nisibis, under whose guidance he received a thorough education. Baptized at eighteen years of age, he assumed a post as a teacher in the flourishing school of Nisibis. After the death of St. James he fled to Edessa, where, after entering the monastic life, he was ordained deacon.

He wrote many works in defense of the Catholic Church, on the various mysteries of Our Lord Jesus Christ and in honor of the Virgin Mary. Poet, exegete, and orator extraordinary, St Ephrem was called "The Prophet of the Syrians" and "The Lyre of the Holy Spirit." He died in 373, and was numbered among the Doctors of the Church in 1920 by Pope Benedict XV.

PRAYER Lord, graciously infuse the Holy Spirit into our hearts. By His inspiration, St. Ephrem the Deacon rejoiced in singing of Your mysteries and through His power he merited to be seated with You. Amen.

ST. LANDERICUS (LANDRY),
Bishop of Paris

June 10

ST. LANDERICUS (or Landry) was a sincere and dedicated servant of God who like his Lord Jesus Christ had great love for the poor and the lowly. As Bishop of Paris, from 650-661, he labored zealously to improve their lot. And when the proceeds from the sale of all his possessions did not suffice to relieve their hunger during a famine, he went so far as to sell some of the church vessels and furniture.

St. Landericus became increasingly aware that the sick poor of his diocese were not really cared for by the custom then in vogue of housing them in little hostels dependent on the casual alms of charitable persons. This led him to erect the city's first real hospital, dedicated to St. Christopher, which in time became the famous Hotel-Dieu.

Always on the alert to provide spiritual help for his people, this saintly Bishop welcomed the Benedictines into his diocese and encouraged them to set up the Abbey of St. Denis. In 653, in company with twenty-three other Bishops, he signed the foundation charter granted by King Clovis to the Abbey. He died about 661, after having commissioned the monk Marculfus to compile a collection of Ecclesiastical Formulas.

PRAYER God, You made St. Landericus an outstanding exemplar of Divine love and the Faith that conquers the world, and added him to the roll of saintly pastors. Grant by his intercession that we may persevere in Faith and love, and become sharers of his glory. Amen.

ST. BARNABAS, Apostle

June 11

THOUGH not one of the Twelve, St. Barnabas is considered an Apostle by the Church. He was a Jew of the tribe of Levi, but born in Cyprus, where the family settled. His success in preaching prompted the Apostles to change his name of Joseph to that of Barnabas—which means "son of exhortation" or "consolation." He also was noted for his generosity in the early Christian community of Jerusalem (Acts 4:36-37).

It was St. Barnabas who befriended the recently converted and former persecutor of the Church, Saul of Tarsus, and set him on the path to becoming the great Apostle Paul by introducing him to the Apostles (Acts 9:27). When St. Barnabas went to Antioch to consolidate the infant Church there, he asked St. Paul to share his labors. After laboring a year at Antioch, the two Apostles brought the offerings of the community to the famine-stricken poor of the Judean community (Acts 11:27-30).

Together with St. Paul, Barnabas preached the Faith in Cyprus and central Asia (Acts 13–14) and attended the First Council of Jerusalem (Acts 15:1-29). But on their return to Antioch they parted company when St. Barnabas wanted his nephew John Mark to accompany them on their second missionary journey while St. Paul did not (Acts 15:30-40); accordingly, St. Barnabas went back to Cyprus with John Mark (Acts 15:30-40). The subsequent events of the life of St. Barnabas are not known for certain, except that he was known to the Corinthians (1 Cor 9:6). A tradition relates that he died at Salamis in Cyprus, after being stoned.

PRAYER God, You commanded that St. Barnabas, who was full of Faith and the Holy Spirit, should be set apart to labor for the conversion of the Gentiles. May Christ's Gospel which he preached with great ardor continue to be preached faithfully by word and deed. Amen.

ST. GUY (VIGNOTELLI) OF CORTONA,
Priest
June 12

NOTHING is known about the birth and early life of St. Guy. We first meet him as a devout young Christian of Cortona, supplementing an inheritance by the work of his hands, and making available to the poor whatever he did not need for his own use. In 1211, he provided hospitality for St. Francis of Assisi on the latter's first visit to Cortona with one of his companions.

At the end of their common meal St. Guy asked to become a member of the followers of the Seraphic Saint. He was told that to do so he must abandon all things. Rising from the table, he immediately arranged for the sale of his possessions; then together with his guests he distributed the proceeds as alms. The next day he was invested with the Franciscan habit and a little convent was erected at Cortona although the new disciple received permission to occupy a small cell on a bridge over a stream.

Since St. Guy was evidently an educated man, he was ordained to the priesthood and gave ample evidence to his people of his great holiness, powerful eloquence, and extraordinary gifts. Among the miracles he performed were the raising of a girl who had drowned and the multiplication of a meal in time of famine. So when St. Francis spoke glowingly of him on a subsequent visit to Cortona, he was only telling the people what they were well aware of. St. Guy died at the age of sixty, about 1245, after receiving a vision of St. Francis coming once again to Cortona—this time to lead him to paradise!

PRAYER Lord God, You alone are holy and no one is good without You. Through the intercession of St. Guy help us to live in such a way that we may not be deprived of a share in Your glory. Amen.

ST. ANTHONY OF PADUA

June 13—*Patron of the Poor*

ST. ANTHONY, called "St. Anthony of Padua" on account of his long residence in that city, was a native of Lisbon in Portugal, where he was born in 1195, receiving the name of Ferdinand at his Baptism At an early age his parents placed him in the community of the Canons of the Cathedral of Lisbon, by whom he was educated. At fifteen he entered the Order of Regular Canons of St. Augustine near Lisbon. After two years he was sent to the convent of the Holy Cross of the same Order at Coimbra.

He had lived in this house eight years, intent on his studies, when the relics of five Franciscan martyrs were brought from Morocco to Portugal. This event inspired him to follow in the footsteps of these heroes of the Faith. When this became known his brethren offered extreme opposition, but he finally obtained the consent of the prior and passed over to the Franciscan Order.

After some time he obtained leave to go to Africa to preach to the Moors, but a severe illness obliged him to return to Spain. However, the vessel was driven to Sicily by contrary winds, and the desire to see St. Francis took him to Assisi, where a general chapter of the Order was in progress. At first he was entirely ignored in the Order, and he purposely kept himself in obscurity; but Providence soon revealed to the Franciscans what a treasure they had acquired, and St. Anthony was made professor of theology, which subject he later taught successively at Bologna, Toulouse, Montpellier, and Padua.

He gave up teaching to devote himself to preaching, for he was an accomplished orator, being at the same time filled with zeal for souls. In this work he traveled through France, Spain, and Italy. He was invested with several important dignities in his Order and labored hard to preserve monastic discipline, boldly opposing the famous General Elias, who sought to introduce relaxations. He died June 13, 1231, and was canonized the following year by Pope Gregory IX.

Though he was denied the grace of a martyr's death, St. Anthony was a martyr of the Word, a martyr of the road, a martyr of the crowds. So numerous were those who flocked to hear him that no church could house them and the Saint was often forced to preach in the open air.

Even during his lifetime, he was regarded as a legendary hero and striking miracles were related about him: his sermon to the fish at Rimini, the mule that knelt before the Blessed Sacrament, the Psalter that was stolen and returned (on account of which he has become the patron of those who have lost something), and the story of how his host saw him holding the Child Jesus in his arms when he looked through his window.

PRAYER Almighty, ever-living God, You gave Your people the extraordinary preacher St. Anthony and made him an intercessor in difficulties. By his aid grant that we may live a truly Christian life and experience Your help in all adversities. Amen.

ST. METHODIUS,

Patriarch of Constantinople

June 14

THE son of a rich and distinguished Sicilian, St. Methodius received an excellent education in his native Syracuse. He went to Constantinople to obtain a position at court, but instead decided to enter the religious life. He constructed a monastery on the island of Chios and was then summoned to Constantinople by its Patriarch St. Nicephorus.

When the second Iconoclastic persecution erupted, under Leo the Armenian, he fearlessly defended the cult of sacred images. After the deposition and exile of St. Nicephorus, however, St. Methodius was commanded to bring Pope Paschal I an account of the state of things in the Near East. So he made his way to Rome and remained there until Leo's death. In 821, he returned under the new Emperor Michael the Stammerer, but was flogged, deported, and confined on the island of Antigoni in the Propontus for seven years.

Upon the death of the Emperor in 842, his widow Theodora became Regent for her infant son Michael III, and she appointed St. Methodius Patriarch of Constantinople. The holy man—rendered a scarecrow of his former self by his sufferings and privations—immediately convoked a Council which reaffirmed the lawfulness of venerating sacred images. To stress this fact, an annual Feast of Orthodoxy was instituted, and it continues to be observed on the First Sunday of Lent in all Byzantine Churches.

This heroic Patriarch, who went to his heavenly reward on June 14, 847, was a prolific writer but we possess only fragments of his many poetical, theological, and controversial works, and a complete *Life of St. Theophanes*.

PRAYER God, Light and Shepherd of souls, You established St. Methodius as Bishop in Your Church to feed Your flock by his word and form it by his example. Help us through his intercession to keep the Faith he taught by his word and follow the way he showed by his example. Amen.

ST. GERMAINE COUSIN, Virgin

June 15

FROM her birth in 1579 until her death in 1601, the short life of this remarkable servant of God was filled with sickness and suffering. Her right hand was withered and paralyzed at birth, and she later suffered from scrofula. She lost her mother when she was still only a child, never knew affection from her father, was subjected to constant mistreatment by her stepmother, and was denied a real place of her own in the family home. She was relegated to tending sheep around the surrounding area of Toulouse, France, and practically forbidden to come into contact with her stepbrothers and stepsisters.

However, her inner life was the exact opposite. St. Germaine's pure soul was in constant touch with her Maker, Who had led her to the heights of perfection. Her only book was the Rosary which she rejoiced in reciting every day. Nor could anything deter her from attending daily Mass; it was even reported that she once had walked over flood waters to reach the church in time.

St. Germaine's burning love for God spilled over into love for her neighbors. She often gathered the local children about her and taught them the rudiments of the Faith, and she fed the poor with crusts of dry bread that were doled out to her. Once her stepmother angrily accused the Saint of stealing bread and hiding it in her apron; but when the apron was opened it exposed a bunch of beautiful summer flowers. About half a century after her death (at the age of twenty-two), her body was found to be incorrupt, and when exposed for a year it became the object of veneration and the source of miracles. She was canonized in 1867 by Pope Pius IX.

PRAYER Lord God, You showered heavenly gifts on St. Germaine the Virgin. Help us to imitate her virtues during our earthly life and enjoy eternal happiness with her in heaven. Amen.

ST. JOHN FRANCIS REGIS, Priest

June 16—*Patron of Medical Social Workers*

THIS Saint was a descendant of the nobility of Languedoc, France, where he was born in 1597. He was educated at the Jesuit College of Beziers, and in his nineteenth year he entered the Jesuit novitiate at Toulouse, taking his vows two years later. After finishing his course in philosophy in 1621, he was sent to teach the classics in several colleges. He began his study of theology at Toulouse in 1628; in 1630, he was ordained priest, and the following year, having finished his studies, he made his Third Probation. He was now fully prepared for his lifework and entered upon his apostolic career in the summer of 1631.

Two years later he went to the diocese of Viviers at the invitation of the Bishop, giving missions over the whole diocese. He labored diligently, for both priests and people, and numerous conversions resulted. Crosses which followed the Saint, as the shadow follows the body, were not wanting, but he turned them to his spiritual advantage.

St. Francis longed to devote himself to the conversion of the Indians in Canada, but Divine Providence kept him in France until his death. Incredible were the hardships he endured on his apostolic journeys over rugged mountains in the depth of winter, but nothing could arrest his zeal. He died in 1640 and was canonized in 1737 by Pope Clement XII.

PRAYER Almighty, eternal God, You dedicated the joy of this day to the glorification of St. John. Mercifully grant that we may strive to retain and complete by our works that Faith which he continually proclaimed with insatiable zeal. Amen.

ST. HARVEY (HERVE), Abbot

June 17—*Invoked against Eye-Sores*

ST. HARVEY is one of the most popular saints of Brittany, and makes up a considerable part of the folklore of that area. However, reliable details about his life are few and far between.

A biography dating from the late Middle Ages makes him the son of a British bard; born in Brittany during the 6th century, St. Harvey was blind from birth. His father died while the Saint was still an infant, and his mother entrusted him at the age of seven to a holy man called Arzian, and herself retired to a monastery.

After learning everything Arzian could teach him, St. Harvey joined his uncle Urzel who had founded a monastic school at Plouvien, helping him out with the students and the farm. In time, he himself became Abbot of the community and it flourished under his leadership. He ultimately resettled it at Lanhorneau in Finistere, and made it famous throughout the country.

St. Harvey is portrayed as a wandering monk and minstrel, and many popular tales are told about his person. He never was ordained, but he performed some of his most outstanding miracles as the result of his order of Exorcist. He also took part in the condemnation of the tyrant Conover in 550. He is invoked for eye-troubles of all types.

PRAYER Lord, amid the things of this world, let us be wholeheartedly committed to heavenly things in imitation of the example of evangelical perfection You have given us in St. Harvey the Abbot. Amen.

ST. GREGORY BARBARIGO, Bishop

June 18

ST. GREGORY was born in 1625, of a distinguished Venetian family. A brilliant student, he embraced a diplomatic career and accompanied the Venetian Ambassador, Contarini, to the Congress of Münster in 1648. Then he became a priest and was soon thereafter consecrated as the first Bishop of Bergamo by Pope Alexander VII.

Later on he was elevated to the rank of Cardinal and also given authority over the diocese of Padua. He guided his flock with pastoral wisdom and deep understanding.

St. Gregory Barbarigo worked unceasingly in carrying out the reforms set forth by the Council of Trent. Through his efforts the seminaries of both Bergamo and Padua were substantially enlarged. At Padua he also added a library and a printing press. He died in 1697 and was canonized in 1960 by Pope St. John XXIII.

PRAYER God, You willed that St. Gregory, Your Bishop, should shine forth with pastoral solicitude and compassion for the poor. Help us who celebrate his merits to imitate the example of his charity. Amen.

ST. ROMUALD, Abbot

June 19

ST. ROMUALD was born at Ravenna about the year 956. In spite of an innate desire for virtue and sanctity, his early life was wasted in the service of the world and its pleasures. Then one day, obliged by his father, Sergius, to be present at a duel fought by him, he beheld him slay his adversary. The crime made such an impression upon him that he determined to expiate it for forty days, as though it were entirely his own. For this purpose he retired to a Benedictine monastery of St. Apollinare, near Ravenna, where he became Abbot (996-999). After founding several monasteries he laid the foundations of the austere Order of Camaldoli in Tuscany.

Like all the Saints, he fought a lifelong battle against the assaults of devils and men. In the beginning of his spiritual life he was strongly assailed by numerous temptations, which he conquered by vigilance and prayer. More than one attempt was made on his life, but Divine Providence enabled him to escape from the danger. Like many servants of God, he also became the victim of calumny, which he bore in patience and silence. In his old age he increased his austerities instead of diminishing them.

Romulad died in the monastery of Castro, which he founded in Marquisate of Ancona. on June 19, about the year 1027. He was canonized in 1582 by Pope Gregory XIII.

PRAYER Lord, amid the things of this world, let us be wholeheartedly committed to heavenly things in imitation of the example of evangelical perfection You have given us in St. Romuald the Abbot. Amen.

ST. SILVERIUS, Pope and Martyr

June 20

ST. SILVERIUS was subdeacon when, on the death of St. Agapetus, he was chosen Pope in 536. Shortly after his election, the victorious Belisarius, general of the Emperor Justinian, waging war against the Goths, appeared before the gates of Rome. At the persuasion of Pope Silverius, the senate and people admitted him into the city.

The Empress Theodora, who favored the sect of the Acephali or Ultra-Eutychians, endeavored to draw the Pope into connivance with her party, but the Sovereign Pontiff could not be deceived, though he foresaw that his resistance would cost him his life. The Empress now entered into an intrigue with Vigilius, Archdeacon of the Roman Church, promising him the papacy if he would condemn the Council of Chalcedon. To this he basely agreed.

Hereupon, the Archdeacon was sent to Rome with a letter for Belisarius, commanding him to drive out St. Silverius and to contrive the election of Vigilius After some hesitation, and, like Pilate, shifting the responsibility, the general decided to obey. Being lured into the hands of his enemies, St. Silverius was conducted to Patara in Lycia and Vigilius became Pope.

When Justinian, the Emperor, learned the true state of affairs, he gave orders that St. Silverius should be sent back to Rome. His enemies intercepted him on the road and Vigilius had him taken to the island of Palmaria. He died there a short time afterward, in 537. Ironically, the death of St. Silverius was of no benefit whatever to the heretics, for once Vigilius had actually become Pope he gave up all dalliance with them.

PRAYER Almighty God, help us to bear worldly adversities with an unconquerable spirit. For You did not let St. Silverias Your Pope and Martyr be terrified by threats or conquered by pains. Amen.

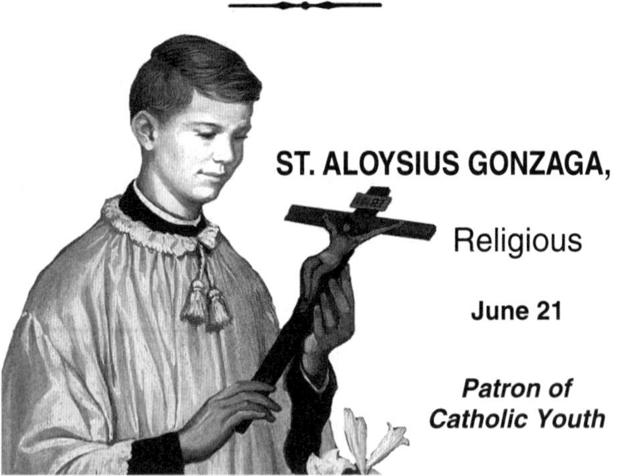

ST. ALOYSIUS GONZAGA,

Religious

June 21

Patron of Catholic Youth

THIS youthful scion of the illustrious house of Gonzaga, son of Ferdinand, Marquis of Castiglione, was born at Castiglione in the diocese of Brescia, March 9, 1568. From his tenderest years St. Aloysius devoted himself heart and soul to the service of his Creator. His memory has come to us with the sweet fragrance of the most unsullied purity. He united an innocence perfectly angelic with a penance truly heroic.

At fourteen years of age he accompanied his father to Spain, where the latter went to attend the Empress, Maria of Austria, wife of Maximilian II. Philip II made him page to Prince James, elder brother of Philip II. His innocence remained uncontaminated amid the vanities of the court, nor could the world draw his heart from God.

On his return to Italy in 1584, he manifested his desire to enter the Society of Jesus. In spite of opposition, he finally succeeded in carrying out his intentions and became a novice at Rome in 1585, during the pontificate of Pope Pius V. He made his profession November 20, 1587, and soon after received minor orders.

From the beginning of his religious life St. Aloysius was a model of perfection. During an epidemic in Rome in 1591, he distinguished himself by his charity toward the sick in the hospital. These labors brought on him the illness that ended in his death. His last days were the faithful echo of his briefly consummated life. He exchanged time for eternity on June 21, 1591, at twenty-four years of age. St. Aloysius was canonized in 1726 by Pope Benedict XIII.

PRAYER God, Author of all heavenly gifts, You gave St. Aloysius both a wonderful innocence of life and a deep spirit of penance. Through his merits grant that we may imitate his penitence. Amen.

ST. PAULINUS OF NOLA, Bishop

June 22

BORN in 353 at Bordeaux, Gaul, of a senatorial family, St. Paulinus was educated under the poet Ausonius, and became governor of the province of Campania. He married a Spanish Christian lady named Therasia and for fifteen years displayed his talents in honorable employments in Gaul, Italy, and Spain. His conversations with St. Ambrose at Milan, St. Martin whom he met at Vienne, and St. Delphinus, Bishop of Bordeaux, resulted in his being baptized by the latter in 390.

After the death of his only child he and his wife took a vow of chastity, gave away their considerable wealth, and retired to Spain to embrace the religious life. In 394, he was ordained in Barcelona at the insistence of the people, and together with his wife settled at Nola, Italy, near the tomb of St. Felix, where they founded a home for monks and the poor and lived a very austere life. Because of his widespread reputation for holiness, he was made Bishop of Nola in 409.

His sanctity brought St. Paulinus in contact with the most eminent Saints of his time, such as Augustine and the ones already mentioned above. He had an intense devotion to the saints and respect for their relics. His poetic works, many of them in honor of St. Felix, place him beside Prudentius as the foremost Christian Latin poet of the patristic age. He died in 431.

PRAYER God, You willed that St. Paulinus, Your Bishop, should shine forth with pastoral solicitude and compassion for the poor. Help us who celebrate his merits to imitate the example of his charity. Amen.

STS. JOHN FISHER, Bishop, AND THOMAS MORE, Martyrs

The Same Day—June 22
(St. Thomas) Patron of Lawyers

ST. JOHN FISHER was born in Beverley, Yorkshire, in 1459, and educated at Cambridge, from which he received his Master of Arts degree in 1491. He occupied the vicarage of Northallerton, 1491-1494; then he became proctor of Cambridge University. In 1497, he was appointed confessor to Lady Margaret Beaufort, mother of Henry VII, and became closely associated in her endowments to Cambridge; he created scholarships, introduced Greek and Hebrew into the curriculum, and brought in the world-famous Erasmus as Professor of Divinity and Greek.

In 1504, he became Bishop of Rochester and Chancellor of Cambridge, in which capacity he also tutored Prince Henry who was to become Henry VIII. St. John was dedicated to the welfare of his diocese and his university. From 1527, this humble servant of God actively opposed the King's divorce proceedings against Catherine, his wife in the sight of God, and steadfastly resisted the encroachment of Henry on the Church. Unlike the other Bishops of the realm, St. John refused to take the oath of succession which acknowledged the issue of Henry and Anne as the legitimate heir to the throne, and he was imprisoned in the Tower in April 1534. The next year he was made a Cardinal by Paul III, and Henry retaliated by having him beheaded within a month.

A half-hour before his execution, this dedicated scholar and churchman opened his New Testament for the last time and his eyes fell on the following words from St. John's Gospel: "Eternal life is this: to know You, the only true God, and him whom You have sent, Jesus Christ. I have given You glory on earth by finishing the work You gave me to do. Do You now, Father, give me glory at Your side" (17:3-5). Closing the book, he observed: "There is enough learning in that to last me the rest of my life." He was canonized in 1935 by Pope Pius XI.

ST. THOMAS MORE was born at London in 1478. After a thorough grounding in religion and the classics, he entered Oxford to study law. Upon leaving the university he embarked on a legal career which took him to Parliament. In 1505, he married his beloved Jane Colt who bore him four children, and when she died at a young age he married a widow, Alice Middleton, to be a mother for his young children. A wit and a reformer, this learned man numbered Bishops and scholars among his friends, and by 1516 wrote his world-famous book *Utopia*.

Henry VIII appointed him to a succession of high posts, and finally made him Lord Chancellor in 1529. However, he resigned in 1532, at the height of his career and reputation, when Henry persisted in holding his own opinions regarding marriage and the supremacy of the Pope.

The rest of his life was spent in writing mostly in defense of the Church. In 1534, with his close friend, St. John Fisher, he refused to render allegiance to the King as the Head of the Church of England and was confined to the Tower. Fifteen months later, and nine days after St. John Fisher's execution, he was tried and convicted of treason. He told the court that he could not go against his conscience and wished his judges that "we may yet hereafter in heaven merrily all meet together to everlasting salvation." And on the scaffold he told the crowd of spectators that he was dying as "the King's good servant—but God's first." He was beheaded on July 6, 1535, and canonized in 1935 by Pope Pius XI.

PRAYER God, You consummated the form of the true Faith in martyrdom. Through the intercession of Sts. John and Thomas, grant that we may confirm by the testimony of our lives that Faith which we profess with our tongues. Amen.

ST. ETHELREDA (AUDRY), Virgin

June 23

THIS holy virgin was the third daughter of Annas, the saintly King of East Anglia. Three of her sisters, Sexburga, Ethelborga, and Withburga, are numbered among the Saints. She came into this world at Exning, a village in Suffolk. To comply with the desire of her parents she married Prince Tonbert, but she remained a virgin, for they lived in perpetual continence. Three years after her marriage her husband died and she retired to the island of Ely, where she lived a secluded life of contemplation for five years.

Her fame reached the ears of Egfrid, the powerful King of Northumberland, who extorted her consent to marry him; and thus for the second time she became engaged in the state of matrimony. With her second husband she lived, as she had done with the first, more as his sister than as his wife, devoting her time to the exercises of devotion and charity. Finally, after twelve years of wedded life, upon the advice of St. Wilfrid and more or less with her husband's consent, she embraced the religious life. She retired to the monastery of Coldinghan near Berwick, where she lived in obedience to the Abbess, St. Ebba.

In the year 672, she returned to the isle of Ely and founded a monastery. Her life henceforward was one of great austerity and perfection. She became a model of virtue to all her Sisters. Sufferings were her delight. She thanked God when, in her last sickness, she had much to suffer. After a lingering illness she expired in peace on June 23, 679.

PRAYER *Lord God, You showered heavenly gifts on St. Ethelreda. Help us to imitate her virtues during our earthly life and enjoy eternal happiness with her in heaven. Amen.*

BIRTH OF ST. JOHN THE BAPTIST

June 24

THE feast of the Nativity, or birthday, of St. John the Baptist, the precursor of the Messiah and born six months before Him, is observed on June 24, and is one of the oldest feasts in the liturgy of the Church. He was the son of Zechariah and Elizabeth, a cousin of the Blessed Virgin Mary. Tradition places the home and birthplace of the Baptist near the village of Ain-Karim, six miles west of Jerusalem, where a Franciscan church marks the site. The church is called "St. John in the Mountains."

What we know of this Saint, than whom a greater prophet had not arisen, from his sanctification before his birth to his martyrdom under King Herod, is set down in Holy Scripture. He has always had a chief place in the veneration given by Holy Church to the heroic servants of God. While the feast of other Saints is celebrated on the day of their death, when their final victory is won, the birthday of St. John the Baptist is his feast day, as he was *born* free from original sin. We have also the feast of the Birth of Mary Immaculate.

Thirty years after the birth of Jesus, John began his mission on the banks of the Jordan. He was the last of the prophets of the Old Covenant. His work was to prepare the way and announce the coming of the long-expected Messiah, the Redeemer, in Whom all flesh would see "the salvation of God."

Before St. John was born, an angel announced that "many would rejoice in his birth," and so June 24 is ranked among the joyous feasts of the year. In former times, and in other lands, it was observed with greater holiday rejoicing and greater outward display than in our age. On the eve of St. John's day "St. John's fires" were lighted on the hills and mountains in many countries, as they are still lighted in some places. "Scarce had the last rays of the setting sun died away, when all the world over, immense columns of flame arose from every mountain top, and in an instant every town and village and hamlet was lighted up." (Dom. P. L. P. Guéranger)

PRAYER God, You raised up St. John the Baptist to prepare a perfect people for Christ. Fill Your people with the joy of possessing Your grace and direct the minds of all the faithful in the way of peace and salvation. Amen.

ST. PROSPER OF REGGIO, Bishop

June 25

THIS 5th century Saint is shrouded in obscurity; beginning with the 9th century he was venerated in the Italian province of Emilia, although he may have been a native of Spain originally. A questionable tradition asserts that St. Prosper distributed all his goods to the poor in order to fulfill our Lord's precept to the rich young man. He became a Bishop and his beneficent episcopate lasted twenty-two years.

On June 25, 466, he passed on to his heavenly reward, surrounded by his priests and deacons, and he was buried in the church of St. Apollinaris, which he had built and consecrated, outside the walls of Reggio. In 703, his relics were transferred to a great new church erected in his honor by Bishop Thomas of Reggio. And fittingly enough he is the principal patron of that city.

PRAYER God, You made St. Prosper an outstanding exemplar of Divine love and the Faith that conquers the world, and added him to the roll of saintly pastors. Grant by his intercession that we may persevere in Faith and love, and become sharers of his glory. Amen.

ST. ANTHELM, Bishop of Belley

June 26

ST. ANTHELM, rightfully regarded as the greatest ecclesiastic of his age, was born about 1107 in Savoy of a noble family, who educated him for the Church. After ordination he was made provost and secretary of the province of Geneva and increased the earnings of his diocese by astute management. Up to that time, he was a high-minded young priest, hospitable and generous, but, as his background might suggest, primarily interested in the things of the world.

However, his outlook changed drastically as a result of a chance visit to the Carthusian monastery at Portes. So at the age of thirty he resigned his ecclesisatical benefice, left the world, and donned the habit of St. Bruno. Two years later (1139), he became Prior of the motherhouse of his Order, the Grande Chartreuse, which soon began to flourish under his direction. He increased the number and the fervor of those in the community, repaired its buildings, and brought the other monasteries into relation with it; in the process he also became the first Master General of the Order.

In 1152, he retired to Portes, looking forward to a life of solitude. But God had other plans for him. He was appointed Prior of Portes and succeeded in reforming that monastery as well. Two years later he returned to the Grande Chartreuse but still was denied solitude. In 1159, a schism occurred in the Church between the supporters of the canonically elected Pope, Alexander III, and a rival put forward by the powerful Emperor Frederick Barbarossa. St. Anthelm supported the true Pope by a strong and vociferous campaign that resulted in the Pope's triumph and in the appointment of Anthelm as Bishop of Belley.

Prevailed upon to accept the episcopacy, St. Anthelm applied himself to it in characteristic fashion, showing himself to be a brilliant administrator, dedicated reformer, and fearless battler for truth. He did not even hesitate to reprove the Pope when in 1175 the latter lifted the excommunication which the Saint had imposed on Count Hubert of Marienne for glaring misdeeds. Shortly afterward, the Pope commissioned St. Anthelm to go to England and try to reconcile King Henry II and St. Thomas Becket; but he was prevented from going by his death which took place on June 26, 1178.

PRAYER God, You made Your Bishop St. Anthelm an outstanding minister of Your Church by his prayer and pastoral zeal. Through his prayers grant that Your faithful flock may always find pastors after Your heart and salutary pastures. Amen.

ST. CYRIL OF ALEXANDRIA,

Bishop and Doctor of the Church

June 27

ST. CYRIL was born in Alexandria, Egypt, about 374. He strenuously defended the Divine maternity of the Blessed Virgin against Nestorius, Bishop of Constantinople, who maintained that Jesus Christ, as man only, was born of Mary, and that His Divinity was acquired after His human birth because of His great merits.

He presided over the General Council of Ephesus, at which Nestorius and his doctrines were condemned. However, St. Cyril paid dearly for this victory in the form of many sufferings at the hands of Nestorius and his followers. He left many exegetical treatises and an apologetical work against Julian the Apostate. He died in 444.

PRAYER God, You made St. Cyril, Your Bishop, the invincible champion of the Divine Maternity of the Blessed Virgin Mary. Grant that we who believe her to be truly the Mother of God may be saved through the Incarnation of Christ Your Son. Amen.

ST. IRENAEUS, Bishop and Martyr

June 28

WE know very little about the life of St. Irenaeus, who is one of the most important theologians of the 2nd century. He was born about 130 in Asia Minor and placed in the care of St. Polycarp. the disciple of St. John the Apostle, and Bishop of Smyrna. He studied in Rome and later became a priest of Lyons in Gaul. In 178, he succeeded St. Pothinus as Bishop of Lyons.

Through his preaching he converted many to the Faith and his writings did much to combat the heresies that were rampant, especially those of the Gnostics and Valentinians. His principal works are: *Against Heresies* and *The Proof of the Apostolic Preaching*. Accordingly, he is regarded as a link between the East and West. He died a martyr in 202 during the persecution of Septimus Severus.

PRAYER God, You enabled St. Irenaeus, Your Bishop, to strengthen the truth of Faith and the peace of the Church. Through his intercession may we be renewed in Faith and love and always strive to foster unity and concord. Amen.

STS. PETER AND PAUL, Apostles

June 29

St. Peter

Patron of Fishermen and Watchmakers

ST. PETER was a fisherman of Galilee, named Simon, and the son of John. His brother Andrew introduced him to Christ about whom they had probably heard from John the Baptizer, and he became His disciple, ultimately giving up his family and possessions to follow Him. Christ changed his name to Peter (Rock) and made him the Rock on which His Church was to be built. After His Resurrection, Jesus conferred the primacy on Peter and he became the Vicar of Christ and the head of the Apostles, the first Pope.

The Gospels speak about Peter more than any other Apostle. He was honored on many occasions; several miracles were performed for his benefit; Christ stayed at his home, preached from his boat, sent him the first message of the Resurrection, and appeared to him personally. Often Peter acted as spokesman for the other Apostles. Finally, mention is made of his defects: his anger, imperfect faith, impetuosity, and his triple denial of Christ.

After the Ascension Peter began his work as head of the Church. He directed the election of Matthias, delivered the first public Apostolic sermon, cured a man lame from birth, and received a Divine commission to receive Gentiles into the Church. After the execution of James, the brother of John, by Herod Agrippa, Peter was miraculously rescued from prison. He presided at the Apostolic Council of Jerusalem in the year 50, when it was officially declared that the Gentile converts to the Faith were not subject to the Jewish law of circumcision. Afterward, he went to Antioch, where it was decided that not even the Jews were bound to observe the Mosaic Law.

St. Peter dwelt in Rome intermittently for 25 years as founder and first Bishop of the Church there. Finally, in the last year of Nero's reign, 67, he was crucified with his head downward, at his own request, not deeming himself worthy to die as did his Divine Master. Two Epistles of the New Testament are attributed to him and the Gospel of St. Mark, who was his disciple, has been called "The Gospel of Peter."

St. Paul

Patron of Public Relations

ST. PAUL, the indefatigable Apostle of the Gentiles, was converted from Judaism on the road to Damascus (see p. 46).

He remained some days in Damascus after his Baptism, and then went to Arabia, possibly for a year or two, to prepare himself for his future missionary activity. Having returned to Damascus, he stayed there for a time, preaching in the synagogues that Jesus is the Christ, the Son of God. For this he incurred the hatred of the Jews and had to flee from the city. He then went to Jerusalem to see Peter and pay his homage to the head of the Church.

Later he went back to his native Tarsus (Acts 9:30) and began to evangelize his own province until called by Barnabas to Antioch. After one year, on the occasion of a famine, both Barnabas and Paul were sent with alms to the poor Christian community at Jerusalem. Having fulfilled their mission, they returned to Antioch.

Soon after this Paul and Barnabas made the first missionary journey (44/45–49/50), visiting the island of Cyprus, then Pamphylia, Pisidia, and Lycaonia, all in Asia Minor, and establishing churches at Pisidian Antioch, Iconium, Lystra, and Derbe.

After the Apostolic Council of Jerusalem Paul, accompanied by Silas and later also by Timothy and Luke, made his second missionary journey (50–52/53), first revisiting the churches previously established by him in Asia Minor and then passing through Galatia. At Troas a vision of a Macedonian was had by Paul, which impressed him as a call from God to evangelize Macedonia. He accordingly sailed for Europe, and preached the Gospel in Philippi, Thessalonica, Beroea, Athens, and Corinth. Then he returned to Antioch by way of Ephesus and Jerusalem.

On his third missionary journey (53/54–58) Paul visited nearly the same regions as on the second, but made Ephesus, where he remained nearly three years, the center of his missionary activity. He laid plans also for another missionary journey, intending to leave Jerusalem for Rome and Spain. But persecutions by the Jews hindered him from accomplishing his purpose. After two years of imprisonment at Caesarea he finally reached Rome, where he was kept another two years in chains.

The Acts of the Apostles gives us no further information on the life of this Apostle. We gather, however, from the Pastoral Epistles and from tradition that at the end of the two years St. Paul was released from his Roman imprisonment, and then traveled to Spain, later to the East again, and then back to Rome, where he was imprisoned a second time, and in the year 67 was beheaded.

St. Paul's untiring interest in and paternal affection for the churches established by him have given us fourteen canonical Epistles. It is, however, quite certain that he wrote other letters which are no longer extant. In his Epistles, St. Paul shows himself to be a profound religious thinker, and he has had an enduring formative influence in the development of Christianity. The centuries only make more apparent his greatness of mind and spirit.

PRAYER God, You give us a holy joy as we celebrate the solemnity of the Apostles Sts. Peter and Paul. Grant that Your Church may follow their teaching and example in all things, for it is through them that Christianity began its development. Amen.

FIRST MARTYRS OF THE CHURCH OF ROME

June 30

FOR varying and valid reasons, the new reformed liturgical Calendar of the Church has suppressed many names of ancient martyrs. In exchange this feast has been inserted into the Calendar on the day following that of Sts. Peter and Paul in honor of the first martyrs of the Church of Rome who were put to death at the Vatican Circus at the time of the persecution under Nero (in the year 64).

Whatever was the real cause of the conflagration which erupted within the confines of the Palatine and the Celius and ravaged the city for six days and seven nights, the wicked Emperor elected to hold Christians responsible for it—most of them slaves, enfranchised, and foreign. The cruelty and injustice of the ensuing repression, which had the victims torn to pieces by wild beasts or burned like living torches, eventually evoked the indignation of pagans such as Tacitus. The feast of these Christian martyrs had been celebrated on June 27 in Rome from 1923 on.

PRAYER God, You consecrated the copious firstfruits of the Roman Church with the blood of Martyrs. Grant that we may be strengthened in virtue by the agony of such a struggle and always rejoice in their victory. Amen.

ST. JUNIPERO SERRA, Priest

July 1

MIGUEL José Serra was born on the island of Majorca on November 24, 1713, and took the name of Junipero when in 1730 he entered the Franciscan Order. Ordained in 1737, he taught philosophy and theology at the University of Padua until 1749.

At the age of 37, he landed in Mexico City on January 1, 1750, and spent the rest of his life working for the conversion of the peoples of the New World.

In 1768, Father Serra took over the missions of the Jesuits (who had been wrongly expelled by the government) in the Mexican province of Lower California and Upper California (modern California). An indefatigable worker, Serra was in large part responsible for the foundation and spread of the Church on the West Coast of the United States when it was still mission territory.

He founded 21 missions and converted thousands of Indians. The converts were taught sound methods of agriculture, cattle raising, and arts and crafts.

Junipero was a dedicated religious and missionary. He was imbued with a penitential spirit and practiced austerity in sleep, eating, and other activities. On August 28, 1784, worn out by his apostolic labors, Father Serra was called to his eternal rest. He was canonized by Pope John Francis on September 23, 2015. His statue, representing the State of California, is in National Statuary Hall.

PRAYER Almighty, eternal God, You dedicated the joy of this day to the glorification of St.Junipero. Mercifully grant that we may strive to retain and complete by our works that Faith which he continually proclaimed with insatiable zeal. Amen.

ST. BERNARDINO REALINO, Priest

July 2

ST. BERNARDINO REALINO was born into a noble family of Capri, Italy in 1530. After receiving a thorough and devout Christian education at the hands of his mother, he went on to study medicine at the University of Bologna, but after three years he switched to law and received his doctorate in 1563. Word of his learning, dedication, and legal brilliance spread rapidly, and in 1564 he was summoned to Naples to assume the position of auditor and lieutenant general.

Shortly afterward, this exemplary young man came to the realization that he had a religious vocation and, aided by our Lady's appearance to him, joined the Society of Jesus, being ordained in 1567. For three years he labored unstintingly at Naples, devoting himself wholeheartedly to the service of the poor and the youth, and then he was sent to Lecce where he remained for the last forty-two years of his life.

St. Bernardino won widespread recognition as a result of his ceaseless apostolic labors. He was a model confessor, a powerful preacher, a diligent teacher of the Faith to the young, and a dedicated shepherd of souls, as well as Rector of the Jesuit College in Lecce and Superior of the community there. His charity to the poor and the sick knew no bounds and his kindness brought about the end of vendettas and public scandals that cropped up from time to time.

So greatly was this Saint loved and appreciated by his people that in 1616 as he lay on his deathbed the city's magistrates formally requested that he should take the city under his protection. Unable to speak, St. Bernardino bowed his head. He died with the names of Jesus and Mary on his lips and was canonized in 1947 by Pope Pius XII.

PRAYER God, You taught Your Church to observe all the heavenly commandments in the love of God and neighbor. Help us to practice works of charity in imitation of Your Priest, St. Bernardino, and merit to be numbered among the blessed in Your Kingdom. Amen.

ST. THOMAS, Apostle

July 3

Patron of Architects

ST. THOMAS was a Jew, called to be one of the twelve Apostles. He was a dedicated but impetuous follower of Christ. When Jesus said that He was returning to Judea to visit His sick friend Lazarus, Thomas immediately exhorted the other Apostles to accompany Him on the trip which involved certain danger and possible death because of the mounting hostility of the authorities. At the Last Supper, when Christ told His Apostles that He was going to prepare a place for them to which they also might come because they knew both the place and the way, Thomas pleaded that they did not understand and received the beautiful assurance that Christ is the Way, the Truth, and the Life.

But St. Thomas is best known for his role in verifying the Resurrection of His Master. Thomas' unwillingness to believe that the other Apostles had seen their Risen Lord on the first Easter Sunday merited for him the title of "doubting Thomas." Eight days later, on Christ's second apparition, Thomas was gently rebuked for his skepticism and furnished with the evidence he had demanded—seeing in Christ's hands the point of the nails and putting his fingers in the place of the nails and his hand into His side. At this, St. Thomas became convinced of the truth of the Resurrection and exclaimed: "My Lord and my God," thus making a public Profession of Faith in the Divinity of Jesus.

St. Thomas is also mentioned as being present at another Resurrection appearance of Jesus— at Lake Tiberias when a miraculous catch of fish occurred. This is all that we know about St. Thomas from the New Testament.

Tradition says that at the dispersal of the Apostles after Pentecost this Saint was sent to evangelize the Parthians, Medes, and Persians; he ultimately reached India, carrying the Faith to the Malabar coast, which still boasts a large native population calling themselves "Christians of St. Thomas." He capped his life by shedding his blood for His Master, speared to death at a place called Calamine.

PRAYER Almighty God, let us proudly rejoice as we celebrate the feast of St. Thomas the Apostle. May we be helped by his patronage and, believing, have life in the Name of Jesus Christ Your Son Whom he confessed to be the Lord. Amen.

ST. ELIZABETH OF PORTUGAL

July 4—*Patroness of Third Order of St. Francis*

THE father of St. Elizabeth was Peter III, King of Aragon. She came into the world at the royal palace in Saragossa in 1271, and received the name of Elizabeth after her aunt, St. Elizabeth of Hungary, who several years before had been canonized by Pope Gregory IX.

Her grandfather, James I, who then occupied the throne of Aragon, took upon himself the care of her education, but he died before she was six years of age. Her early years were spent in the most extraordinary piety and at the age of twelve she was given in marriage to Dionysius, King of Portugal. However, her husband left her free to practice her devotions, and she lived on the throne with the virtue and regularity of a Religious. Eventually, her patience and gentleness succeeded in converting the King, who had been leading a licentious life. Charity to the poor was one of her characteristic virtues, and her works for the good of her fellowmen knew no bounds.

Her virtue also had to pass through the crucible of suffering. One of the keenest pangs she endured came from the revolt of her son, Alfonso, against his own father, and the unjust treatment of the latter, who suspected her of favoring his son. The King, however, soon acknowledged his error and made amends, and the saintly woman succeeded in effecting a reconciliation between father and son.

After the death of her husband she took the habit of the Third Order of St. Francis and retired to a convent of Poor Clares, near which she dwelt in a house she had erected. Hearing that her son, Alphonsus IV, King of Portugal, had gone to war with her grandson, Alfonso XI, King of Castile, she set out on a journey to reconcile them and succeeded. This was her last act of mercy, for having arrived at Estremoz, on the frontiers of Castile where her son was, she fell ill. After receiving the Last Sacraments, she died on July 4, 1336, and was canonized in 1625 by Pope Urban VIII.

PRAYER God, Author and Lover of charity, You endowed St. Elizabeth with the wondrous grace of bringing dissidents together. Through her intercession enable us to practice works of peace so that we may be called children of God. Amen.

ST. ANTHONY ZACCARIA, Priest

July 5

BORN at Cremona, Italy, in 1502, of noble parents, St. Anthony lost his father when he was young. But his mother succeeded in compensating for his loss, and saw to it that he received a solid training, inculcating in him compassion for the poor and afflicted. He studied medicine at the University of Padua and returned home at the age of twenty-two as a full-fledged physician. But he quickly realized that his vocation consisted in healing souls as well as bodies.

Accordingly, the devoted young man studied theology but continued to practice medicine. At the same time, he assisted the dying spiritually, taught catechism to the young, and placed himself completely at the service of everyone. After his ordination in 1528, he was encouraged to go to Milan where there were greater opportunities for serving his fellowman. He joined the Confraternity of Eternal Wisdom whose purpose was to carry out various works of mercy; then with the help of Luigia Torelli, Countess of Guastella, he founded a community called the Angelicals, with the aim of rescuing fallen women and girls and those in danger of falling into sin.

In 1530, St. Anthony and two other zealous priests founded a congregation of priests to help regenerate and revive the love of Divine worship and a proper Christian way of life by frequent preaching and faithful administration of the Sacraments. This was the Order of Clerks Regular of St. Paul, and its early members banded with St. Anthony to minister night and day to the people of Milan, who were stricken by wars, plague, and neglect of the clergy. He died in 1539, at thirty-seven, worn out by his many labors. He was canonized in 1897 by Pope Leo XIII.

PRAYER Lord, grant us, in the spirit of St. Paul the Apostle, to learn the knowledge of Jesus Christ which surpasses all understanding. Taught by this knowledge, St. Anthony continually preached the word of salvation in Your Church. Amen.

ST. ATHANASIUS THE ATHONITE, Abbot

***The Same Day*—July 5**

IN THE words of Athanasius' biographer, "Trebizonde witnessed his birth (about 920), Byzantium enabled him to grow spiritually, and Kyminas and Athos rendered him pleasing to God." In 963, he founded the celebrated monasteries on Mount Athos which still house monastic communities— but only after he had overcome the opposition of the hermits who were there first. He died in 1003 when the cupola of his church fell in.

PRAYER Lord, amid the things of this world, let us be wholeheartedly committed to heavenly things in imitation of the example of evangelical perfection You have given us in St. Athanasius. Amen.

ST. MARIA GORETTI

Virgin and Martyr

July 6

Patroness of Youth

ST. MARIA GORETTI, called by Pope Pius XII "the St. Agnes of the 20th century," was born on a small farm near Ancona, Italy, in 1890. The third of seven children, she was, in the words of her mother, "happy, good, openhearted, without whim, but with a sense and seriousness beyond her years, and never disobedient." Her father died when she was nine, and Maria helped out with the younger children and the housework while her mother ran the farm. She received First Communion at eleven and strove with all her strength to do better each day.

Six months later, this heroic maiden was severely tried for her Faith. The Goretti family shared a home with the partner of their father and his son, Alexander, a wicked-minded youth who began making sinful advances toward Maria. She repelled them immediately but said nothing about them for he threatened to kill her and her mother if she did. Finally, lust drove the tragic Alexander to attack outright, but again the Saint resisted him with all her strength, crying out repeatedly: "No, it's a sin! God does not want it!" Thereupon, the attacker, overwhelmed by fear and anger, began to strike at her blindly with a long dagger, and several blows passed clear through her body.

St. Maria was rushed to the hospital at Nettuno and surgeons worked feverishly to save her life, but it soon became evident that nothing could be done. The next morning she was given Communion but first queried about her attitude toward Alexander. She replied clearly that she forgave him, that she would pray for his repentance, and that she wished to see him in heaven. On July 6, 1902, this saintly maiden died and went to meet her heavenly Spouse for Whose love she had been willing to give her life.

On July 25, 1950, she was raised to sainthood by Pope Pius XII, with her mother, brothers, and sisters present, a unique event in the history of the Church. By that time her prayers for her murderer had long since been heard and answered. After eight years of unrepentant imprisonment, Alexander had a complete change of heart; released for good behavior after twenty-seven years, he hastened to beg forgiveness of the Saint's mother and then became a Capuchin laybrother, who gave evidence at the canonical inquiry about Blessed Maria and lived to see her canonized.

PRAYER God, Author of innocence and Lover of chastity, You conferred on St. Maria Your handmaid the grace of martyrdom at a youthful age. Through her intercession grant us constancy in Your commandments, You Who gave the crown to a virgin who fought for You. Amen.

BLESSED RALPH MILNER AND ROGER DICKENSON, Martyrs

July 7

BLESSED Ralph Milner and Roger Dickenson lived at a time in the history of England when Catholics of that country risked imprisonment and death to practice and spread their Faith. Ralph Milner was an elderly and illiterate farmer from the district of Flacsted in Hampshire brought up as a Protestant. Influenced by the good lives led by his Catholic neighbors, he took instructions in the Faith and was received into the Church.

On the very day of his First Communion, this devout convert was seized and imprisoned. Though he remained in prison for a number of years, he was often granted parole; at such times he would obtain alms and spiritual succor for his fellow prisoners, and by utilizing his overall knowledge of the country he would help missionary priests move about and work more easily. It was in this way that he met and aided a secular priest named Roger Dickenson.

Roger Dickenson was a native of Lincoln and a priest of the College of Rheims who was sent on mission in 1583. He had already been arrested once but been able to escape when his guards got drunk. The second time he was arrested with Ralph Milner and both were put on trial for the Faith. The judge took especial pity on Milner who was getting old and had eight children; seeking any pretext to set him free, he urged the saintly farmer to make a visit to the nearby parish church as a matter of form and he would be freed since this would be tantamount to reconciliation with the Church of England.

However, the blessed martyr, aided by God's grace, stood firm and refused to make the least deceitful gesture, preferring to share the fate of his friend Father Dickenson. Accordingly, both of these servants of God were executed at Winchester on July 7, 1591. They were beatified in 1929 by Pope Pius XI.

PRAYER God, You surround and protect us by the glorious confession of Your holy Martyrs, Blessed Ralph and Roger. Help us to profit from their example and be supported by their prayer. Amen.

ST. GRIMBALD, Abbot of Newminster

July 8

ST. GRIMBALD was born in Flanders in the 9th century and became a monk of St. Bertin. King Alfred became acquainted with him when passing through the neighborhood on his way to Rome while still a youth. Once established on his throne, the King called the Saint, as well as other learned foreigners, to England to promote learning among his people.

Grimbald was especially noted for his knowledge of the Scriptures and his skill in music, and on his arrival in 885 was sent to Oxford to direct the school recently set up there. However, he was soon obliged to leave Oxford because of the jealousy and opposition of the masters who were already there. He retired to Winchester, where he continued to enjoy the esteem and reverence of the King.

On the advice of Grimbald, King Alfred planned the foundation of the New Minster in that city, a project which was completed by his son Edward. St. Grimbald was placed at the head of the new religious establishment, with the title of Abbot, though by his own request the church was served by secular canons.

When he had spent eighteen years in England and was well advanced in years, the holy Abbot fell seriously ill. After devoutly receiving Viaticum, he spent three days in close communion with his Lord. On the fourth day, July 8, 903, the community gathered around him in prayer and St. Grimbald breathed forth his last.

PRAYER Lord, amid the things of this world, let us be wholeheartedly committed to heavenly things in imitation of the example of evangelical perfection You have given us in St. Grimbald the Abbot. Amen.

ST. VERONICA GIULIANI, Virgin

July 9

ST. VERONICA was born at Mercatello in Urbino, Italy, in 1660, of a well-to-do family. Though she was a very religious person by nature, her father insisted that she marry when she came of age and paraded suitors before her. This so worried the girl that she became ill; only then did her father realize the genuine character of her vocation and allow her to enter the Capuchin convent of Poor Clares at Citta di Castello in Umbria, at the age of seventeen. She was to remain there for the rest of her life.

After her profession, she had a vision of Jesus bearing His Cross, and she began to feel acute pain over her heart. In 1693, she had another vision, in which she was offered the chalice of Christ's sufferings; when she accepted it, after a fierce struggle, her body and soul ever afterward carried the marks of our Lord's sufferings. The next year, the imprint of the crown of thorns appeared on her head, and on Good Friday, 1697, the impress of the five sacred wounds.

As a result of these mystical experiences, she became the object of close vigilance on the part of her superiors and the competent religious authorities. Thus, though this caused her much distress and suffering, it also ensured that her mystical experiences were well attested, making her an outstanding case in the history of mystical phenomena. Her humble obedience convinced all of the truth of these mystical experiences.

St. Veronica also possessed a large dosage of common sense and an admirable degree of efficiency. She was novice-mistress of her convent for thirty-four years and diligently laid the foundation for the Sisters under her charge to progress in humility, obedience, and charity. She became Abbess eleven years before her death and labored for the improvement of the convent even in its physical entity. She died on July 9, 1727, leaving behind a catalogue of her religious experiences entitled *Diary of the Passion*, written at the request of her confessor. She was canonized in 1839 by Pope Gregory XVI.

PRAYER Lord Jesus, You wondrously impressed the marks of Your Passion upon St. Veronica the Virgin. May we crucify our flesh and thus come to the eternal joys of heaven. Amen.

ST. ULRIC, Bishop of Augsburg

July 10

THE son of Count Hucbald of Suabia, St. Ulric was born at Augsburg in 890 and was educated in the Abbey of St. Gall from the age of seven on. At sixteen, he was given into the care of Bishop Adalbero of Augsburg who made him his chamberlain and later ordained him. The young man was wise in the ways of God and carried out his duties with utmost reverence and great prudence. He was zealous at prayer, diligent in study, and magnanimous toward the poor. Aware of the fragile character of chastity, he shunned every hint of danger, saying: "Take away the fuel, and you take away the fire."

In 923, King Henry the Fowler made St. Ulric Bishop of Augsburg. Since the Magyars had recently pillaged Germany, plundered the city, and destroyed the cathedral, the saintly man's first task was to raise the people's spirit. He built a small temporary church and provided for the instruction, relief, and comfort of his flock—working long hours and praying unceasingly. He made a visitation of his diocese annually and held synods of the clergy semi-annually.

In 955, the Magyars once again attacked Augsburg. This time, however, they were stopped and hurled back; and the people attributed this triumph to the prayers of their holy Bishop who had continued in prayer for his flock, like Moses on the mountain. In his later years, St. Ulric retired to St. Gall and died there in 973. Miracles recorded at his tomb influenced Pope John XV to canonize him in 993—the first solemn canonization by a Pope on record.

PRAYER God, You willed that St. Ulric, Your Bishop, should shine forth with pastoral solicitude and compassion for the poor. Help us who celebrate his merits to imitate his charity. Amen.

ST. BENEDICT,
Abbot

July 11

Patron of Poison Sufferers

THE Patriarch of Western monasticism was born at Nursia, in central Italy, about 480. In his youth, seeing the corruption of the world, he left home to live a hermit's life of penance and prayer in a cave in the mountain of Subiaco, near Rome, where he was instructed in Christian asceticism by St. Romanus, a Solitary of the vicinity.

His reputation for sanctity gathered a large number of disciples around him, for whom he erected monasteries in which they lived a community life under a prescribed rule. In the year 529, he left Subiaco for Monte Cassino, and there founded the great Abbey which became the center of religious life in Europe.

The principles of the Rule written by St. Benedict became the basis of religious life for all Western religious orders and congregations after his time. It shows the way to religious perfection by the practice of self-conquest, mortification, humility, obedience, prayer, silence, retirement, and detachment from the world and its cares.

St. Scholastica, the sister of St. Benedict, was the first Benedictine nun. She presided over a monastery of nuns near Monte Cassino. St. Benedict died March 21, 543, as he stood before the altar of Monte Cassino immediately after receiving Holy Communion.

PRAYER God, You established St. Benedict the Abbot as an admirable teacher in the school of Divine servitude. Teach us never to prefer anything to Your love and always to run the way of Your Commandments with most generous dispositions. Amen.

ST. JOHN GUALBERT, Abbot

July 12

THE city of Florence gave to the world St. John Gualbert. Although he enjoyed the benefits of an early Christian education, his youthful heart was soon attracted to the vanities of the world. A painful incident was the means God made use of to open his eyes. Hugo, his only brother, had been murdered and St. John had resolved to avenge his death. On a certain Good Friday he met his enemy in a place where there was no escape for the latter. St. John drew his sword and would have killed his adversary on the spot, but the latter threw himself on his knees begging him by the Passion of Jesus Christ to spare his life. St. John was touched at the words, embraced his enemy, entered a church and prayed with many tears for the pardon of his sins.

He now entered the Order of St. Benedict, in which he made such great progress in virtue that after the death of the Abbot the monks wished to impose this dignity upon him, but the Saint absolutely refused to accept it. Sometime later he left the monastery with one companion in quest of greater solitude.

Having visited the hermitage of Camaldoli, he finally settled at Valle Ombrosa in Tuscany. Together with two hermits whom he found there, he and his companions built a small monastery, observing the primitive rule of St. Benedict. Thus was laid the foundation of the Order of Vallombrosa. The humility of the Saint was such that he would never allow himself to be promoted, even to Minor Orders. His charity for the poor caused him to make a rule that no indigent person should be sent away without an alms. He founded several monasteries, reformed others, and succeeded in eradicating the vice of simony from the part of the country where he lived. He died on July 12, 1073, at about eighty years of age, and was canonized in 1193 by Pope Celestine III.

PRAYER Lord, amid the things of this world, let us be wholeheartedly committed to heavenly things in imitation of the example of evangelical perfection You have given us in St. John the Abbot. Amen.

ST. HENRY II, Emperor

July 13—*Patron of the Disadvantaged*

ST. HENRY, son of Henry, Duke of Bavaria, and of Gisella, daughter of Conrad, King of Burgundy, was born in 972. He was educated under the care of St. Wolfgang, Bishop of Ratisbon. In 995, St. Henry succeeded his father as Duke of Bavaria, and in 1002 upon the death of his cousin, Otho III, he was elected Emperor.

Firmly anchored upon the great eternal truths, which the practice of meditation kept alive in his heart, he was not elated by this dignity and sought in all things the greater glory of God. He was watchful over the welfare of the Church and zealous for the maintenance of ecclesiastical discipline through the instrumentality of the Bishops. He gained several victories over his enemies, both at home and abroad, but he used these with great moderation and clemency.

In 1014, he went to Rome and received the imperial crown at the hands of Pope Benedict VIII. On that occasion he confirmed the donation, made by his predecessors to the Pope, of the sovereignty of Rome and the exarchate of Ravenna. Circumstances several times drove the holy Emperor into war, from which he always came forth victorious. He led an army to the south of Italy against the Saracens and their allies, the Greeks, and drove them from the country.

The humility and spirit of justice of the Saint were equal to his zeal for religion. He cast himself at the feet of Herebert, Bishop of Cologne, and begged his pardon for having treated him with coldness, on account of a misunderstanding. He wished to abdicate and retire into a monastery, but yielded to the advice of the Abbot of Verdun, and retained his dignity.

Both he and his wife, St Cunegundes, lived in perpetual chastity, to which they had bound themselves by vow. The Saint made numerous pious foundations, gave liberally to pious institutions and built the cathedral of Bamberg. His holy death occurred at the castle of Grone, near Halberstad, in 1024. He was canonized in 1146 by Pope Eugene III.

PRAYER God, You filled St. Henry with the abundance of Your grace to govern his earthly empire worthily, and called him to share Your glory in heaven. Through his intercession help us to shun the allurements of the world and come to You with pure minds. Amen.

ST. CAMILLUS DE LELLIS, Priest

July 14—*Patron of Hospitals and the Sick*

ST. CAMILLUS was born in 1550, in a small town of the Kingdom of Naples. In his youth he became a soldier and for some time led a wayward life. He lost so much in gaming that he was forced to work as a laborer on a building belonging to the Capuchins. An exhortation made to him by the guardian of the convent touched him and he resolved to change his conduct.

He now begged to be admitted into the Order, but Divine Providence willed otherwise. Twice he received the Capuchin habit, but he was obliged each time to leave the novitiate, as he could not be admitted to profession on account of an ulcer on one of his legs. He later went to Rome and entered the Hospital of Incurables, and after some time was appointed its administrator. Regarding himself as the servant of the sick, he rendered them the most humiliating services.

At the age of thirty-two he undertook to study, beginning the first elements of grammar with the children. Having been ordained priest, he laid the foundation of the Congregation of Regular Clerics to administer to the sick. He had obstacles to encounter, but he triumphed over them all and succeeded in obtaining from the Apostolic See the approbation of his Institute.

Henceforth his life was entirely devoted to the sick and the dying, and after his death this work was continued by the Order he had founded. The Saint had as confessor another Saint, namely, Philip Neri, the founder of the Oratory, who preceded him to the tomb. St. Camillus was endowed by God with the spirit of prophecy and other supernatural gifts. He died on July 14, 1614, and was canonized in 1746 by Pope Benedict XIV.

PRAYER God, You adorned St. Camillus, Your Priest, with the singular grace of charity toward the sick. By his merits, pour forth the spirit of Your love into us, so that by serving You in our brothers here on earth we may safely come to You at the hour of death. Amen.

ST. KATERI TEKAKWITHA, Virgin

***The Same Day*—July 14**

KATERI was born near the town of Auriesville, New York, in the year 1656, the daughter of a Mohawk warrior. She was four years old when her mother died of smallpox. The disease also attacked Kateri and transfigured her face. She was adopted by her two aunts and an uncle.

Kateri became converted as a teenager. She was baptized at the age of twenty and incurred the great hostility of her tribe. Although she had to suffer greatly for her Faith, she remained firm in it. Kateri went to the new Christian colony of Indians in Canada. Here she lived a life dedicated to prayer, penitential practices, and care for the sick and aged. Every morning, even in bitterest winter, she stood before the chapel door until it opened at four and remained there until after the last Mass. She was devoted to the Eucharist and to Jesus Crucified. She died on April 7, 1680, at the age of twenty-four, and was canonized in 2012 by Pope Benedict XVI. She is known as the "Lily of the Mohawks."

PRAYER Lord, You called the Virgin, St. Kateri, to shine forth among the Indian people as an example of purity of life. Grant, through her intercession, that all peoples of every tribe, tongue, and nation, may be gathered into Your Church and proclaim Your greatness in one song of praise. Amen.

ST. BONAVENTURE

July 15

Bishop and Doctor of the Church

ST. BONAVENTURE, widely known as "The Seraphic Doctor," was born at Bagnorea in Tuscany, in 1221. He was originally called John but received the name of Bonaventure in consequence of an exclamation of St. Francis of Assisi, when, in response to the pleading of the child's mother, the Saint prayed for John's recovery from a dangerous illness, and, foreseeing the future greatness of the little John, cried out, "O buona ventura"—O good fortune!

At the age of twenty-two St. Bonaventure entered the Franciscan Order. Having made his vows, he was sent to Paris to complete his studies under the celebrated doctor Alexander of Hales, an Englishman and a Franciscan. After the latter's death he continued his course under his successor, John of Rochelle. In Paris he became the intimate friend of the great St. Thomas Aquinas. He received the degree of Doctor, together with St. Thomas Aquinas, ceding to his friend, against the latter's inclination, the honor of having it first conferred upon him. Like St. Thomas, he enjoyed the friendship of the holy King, St. Louis.

At the age of thirty-five he was chosen General of his Order and restored a perfect calm where peace had been disturbed by internal dissensions. He did much for his Order and composed the life of St. Francis. He also assisted at the translation of the relics of St. Anthony of Padua. He was nominated Archbishop of York by Pope Clement IV, but he begged not to be forced to accept that dignity. Gregory X obliged him to take upon himself a greater one, that of Cardinal and Bishop of Albano, one of the six suffragan Sees of Rome. Before his death he abdicated his office of General of the Franciscan Order. He died while he was assisting at the Second Council of Lyons, on July 15, 1274, and was canonized in 1482 by Pope Sixtus IV.

PRAYER Almighty God, today we celebrate the heavenly birthday of St. Bonaventure, Your Bishop. Let us benefit by his wonderful teaching and always be inspired by his burning charity. Amen.

OUR LADY OF MOUNT CARMEL

July 16

THIS is the patronal feast of the Carmelites. The Order of Carmelites takes its name from Mount Carmel, which was the first place dedicated to the Blessed Virgin and where a chapel was erected in her honor before her Assumption into heaven.

July 16 is also the feast of the "Scapular of Mount Carmel." On that day in 1251, pious tradition says, the Blessed Virgin appeared to St. Simon Stock, General of the Carmelites at Cambridge, England, showed him the scapular and promised supernatural favors and her special protection to his Order and to all persons who would wear her scapular.

To obtain the indulgences and other benefits promised to those who wear the Carmelite scapular, a person must be invested by a priest who has the requisite faculties and must lead a consistent Christian life.

PRAYER Lord, let the motherly prayer of the glorious Virgin Mary come to our help. Through her support help us to reach the true mount which is Christ. Amen.

THE BLESSED MARTYRS OF COMPIÈGNE

July 17

IN October, 1789, in the first fervor of the French Revolution, the National Assembly suspended all monastic vows, and in February, 1790, it decreed that these vows were not recognized by the law. Two months later, it instructed local assemblies to inventory all monastic goods. The official in charge of this at Compiègne was a former monk of Cluny, and in August he took inventory of the Carmel located there.

The Carmel was made up of fifteen choir sisters and three lay sisters. Two were golden jubilarians and one was ready for profession when the ban had been levied. The Prioress was Mother Theresa of St. Augustine, and all the nuns were committed to the royal family of France. The holy women immediately saw through the protestations of liberation mouthed by the public officials and rejected the opportunity set before them to go out into the new world of enlightenment.

At first, they were allowed to receive state pensions equal to their monastic property, but in September, 1792, they were cast out of their convent and obliged to live as private citizens. Yet the nuns remained undaunted in their desire to retain their religious way of life. Dividing themselves into four groups, they continued to follow their Rule. This continuation of their monastic life, coupled with their previous renunciation of the oath of allegiance to the new constitution, brought about the arrest and imprisonment of the nuns, on June 22, 1794.

On July 17, after having suffered brutalities and indignities in being transferred to Paris, the sixteen nuns were led before the revolutionary tribunal. They conducted themselves with the utmost courage and wisdom, clearly bringing out the point that they were being condemned for the Catholic Faith.

As they went forth to the place of execution, these holy women sang the *Salve Regina* and *Veni Creator*, and their saintly demeanor reduced the astonished crowd to silence. On reaching the scaffold, they renewed the vows of their Baptism and religious profession. Then as they individually went forth to give their lives for their Divine Bridegroom they kept singing "Praise the Lord, all you nations" in steadily diminishing chorus. They thus bore a unique collective witness to Christ, with a joy that no man could take from them! They were beatified in 1906 by Pope St. Pius X.

PRAYER God, You surround and protect us by the glorious confession of Your holy Martyrs. Help us to profit from their example and be supported by their prayers. Amen.

ST. FREDERICK, Bishop and Martyr

July 18

ST. FREDERICK, a member of an illustrious family among the Frisians, was educated by the clergy of the church of Utrecht. Filled with piety and learned in spiritual things, he was ordained by Bishop Ricfried and given the task of instructing catechumens. In 820, Frederick succeeded the same prelate as Bishop of Utrecht.

He was consecrated in the presence of the Emperor, Louis the Debonair, who advised him to stamp out the remaining vestiges of idolatry in Friesland. Frederick took the advice and sent zealous laborers into the north to extirpate the paganism still lurking there. He reserved for himself the most troublesome territory, Walcheren, an island belonging to The Netherlands which was rampant with incestuous marriages contracted within the forbidden degrees.

The Saint worked unceasingly to eradicate this evil from the people, by means of assiduous exhortations, tears, watchings, prayer, and fasting. He called an assembly of the principal people of the land and set forth the ways and means by which such an abomination could be eliminated for good. In this way, he put an end to many such marriages and brought back to God numberless persons who were truly contrite.

At the same time, hearing of some of the numerous immoralities attributed to the Emperor's second wife, the saintly Bishop went to the court to which he had free access and boldly admonished her. Though he did so with apostolic freedom and true charity, thinking only of her welfare, St. Frederick incurred the wrath and resentment of her husband.

Thus it was not very surprising on July 18, 838, as St. Frederick stepped down from the altar after saying Mass and was on his way to the side chapel to make his thanksgiving, that he was set upon by two assassins and stabbed to death. He died with the words of Psalm 116 on his lips: "I will praise the Lord in the land of the living." And the reputation of his sanctity spread quickly far and wide.

PRAYER You gave splendor to Your Church by granting St. Frederick the victory of martyrdom. Grant that, as he imitated the Lord's Passion, so we may follow in his footsteps and attain everlasting joys. Amen.

ST. ARSENIUS, Monk

July 19

IT IS probable that St. Arsenius was born in Rome about 354, became a deacon, and later was tutor to the sons of Emperor Theodosius I of Constantinople. He lived in splendor—wearing lavish clothes, residing in sumptuous quarters, and commanding a host of servants. However, after ten years of this kind of life he was surfeited and left Constantinople for Alexandria.

It is certain that (about 400) he joined the desert monks in the Wadi Natrun (Scetis) and then at Canopus and Troe. As lavishly as he had lived before so lowly did he live now—wearing the meanest of clothes, practicing the severest penances, and devoting himself to unceasing prayer. He shunned the company of his fellow men but was filled with compassion for them.

Forty-four maxims and moral anecdotes have been left us by him—each clearly demonstrating the desert fathers' shrewdness about human nature. One example is the following: "I have often been sorry for having spoken, but never for having held my tongue." He also had the gift of tears to a surprising degree. He died about the age of ninety-five in 449.

PRAYER God, You called St. Arsenius to seek Your Kingdom in this world through the pursuit of perfect charity. Grant that we may be strengthened by his intercession and advance in the way of love with joyful hearts. Amen.

ST. ANSEGISUS, Abbot

July 20

ST. ANSEGISUS was born about 770 in Lyonnais, France, and when he was eighteen entered the Abbey of Fontanelle where one of his relatives, St. Gerwold, was Abbot. There he exhibited such holiness and outstanding knowledge that Charlemagne appointed him to administer and reform the Abbeys of St. Sixtus at Rheims and St. Menge near Chalens. After successfully completing this task, he was appointed Abbot of St. Germer in Flay which was literally falling apart.

He became an adviser of the Emperor and carried out several political missions for him. When Louis the Debonair became Emperor, Ansegisus was transferred to the Abbey of Luxeuil. For five years he labored night and day to undo the effects of the destruction wrought there by the Vandals, and to restore discipline and prosperity to it. Once again, after he had succeeded, this holy man was handed another difficult task. In 823, he was sent back to the Abbey of Fontanelle.

Under his rule the Abbey flourished; its library and its *scriptorium* (the room where its scribes and copyists worked) gained widespread fame. In addition, the Abbey became recognized for the work of St. Ansegisus himself, who put together a collection of capitularies (laws or ordinances promulgated by the Frankish kings) which remained an official lawbook in the Empire.

St. Ansegisus was a virtuous and dedicated monk, a diligent scholar, and an outstanding reformer and administrator. He infused new life into five houses of God which were dying of waste and negligence. At the same time, he remained humble and ever aware that he had no lasting home on earth, and on July 20, 833, he exchanged it for his everlasting home in heaven.

PRAYER Lord, amid the things of this world, let us be wholeheartedly committed to heavenly things in imitation of the example of evangelical perfection You have given us in St. Ansegisus the Abbot. Amen.

ST. LAWRENCE OF BRINDISI,
Priest and Doctor of the Church
July 21

ST. LAWRENCE was born at Brindisi, Italy, and at the age of sixteen entered the Capuchin Franciscan community at Verona. At the University of Padua he made rapid progress in his studies of philosophy and theology and showed a remarkable facility for languages. He mastered Greek, Latin, Hebrew, French, Spanish, German, and Bohemian and acquired a wide knowledge of the Scriptures. After his ordination he labored as a domestic missionary and was called to Rome by Clement VIII to work for the conversion of the Jews.

In 1598, he was sent with eleven other Capuchins to establish Capuchin communities throughout Germany and Austria which were threatened by Lutheranism at that time. While in the imperial realm, the fame of his holiness, wisdom, and administrative ability led the Emperor, Rudolf III, to appoint him to organize the Catholic princes against the invading Turks. At the Battle of Stuhlweissenburg, though the Christians were outnumbered four to one, St. Lawrence roused the low spirits of the soldiers with a powerful oration, mounted a horse and rode before the army with a crucifix held high. The Turks were repulsed and Europe was saved.

At the successful conclusion of his other German projects, the Saint returned to seek seclusion in Italy, only to find that he had been elected the Minister General of the Order. He died in 1619 at Lisbon, Portugal, while on a mission to present the grievances of the people of Naples to their sovereign, King Philip III of Spain. Though he was a very active person, St. Lawrence was also a man of prayer as well as of deep learning. He was canonized in 1881 by Pope Leo XIII, and in 1960 he was made a Doctor of the Church.

PRAYER God, for the glory of Your name and the salvation of souls, You favored St. Lawrence, Your Priest with the spirit of wisdom and fortitude. Grant that in the same spirit we may recognize our obligations and with his help carry them out. Amen.

ST. MARY MAGDALENE

July 22

ST. MARY, whom Jesus converted, and who witnessed His last moments with Mary, His

Mother, and St. John, was called Magdalene from the town of Magdala in Galilee. Clement of Alexandria and others identify her with the woman who washed Jesus' feet with her tears. Others regard her as Mary, the sister of Martha and Lazarus. She followed Jesus with other devout women during His Public Life. After His Resurrection, Jesus appeared first to Mary Magdalene and then to His Apostles.

It is an ancient tradition in Provence, France, that St. Mary Magdalene or Mary the sister of Lazarus, together with Lazarus, Martha, and some other disciples of our Lord, being expelled by the Jews, put to sea and landed at Marseilles; and that St. Lazarus became the first Bishop of that See.

The feast of St. Mary Magdalene is celebrated by the Greeks as well as the Latins on this date. However, in the instructions given with the latest edition of the Roman Calendar, the Latin Church has stipulated that the feast is solely that of the woman to whom Christ appeared and not that of the sister of Lazarus or the penitent woman.

PRAYER God, it was to St. Mary Magdalene before all others that Your Son committed the message of Easter joy. Through her intercession may we one day contemplate Him reigning in glory. Amen.

ST. BRIDGET, Religious

July 23

Patroness of Sweden

ST. BRIDGET was the daughter of a royal Prince of Sweden, named Birger, and of Ingeburdis, a descendant of the Gothic Kings. From these pious parents she inherited a great love for the Passion of our Lord. Her father consecrated all Fridays to special acts of penance, and from her childhood St. Bridget loved to meditate upon the Passion of Christ. In obedience to her father, at the age of sixteen she married Ulfo, Prince of Nericia in Sweden, by whom she had eight children, the last of whom, Catherine, is now honored among the saints.

Later the holy couple bound themselves by a vow of chastity and made a pilgrimage to Compostela in Galicia. On their return to Sweden, Ulfo, with his wife's consent, entered a Cistercian monastery, where he died soon after in the odor of sanctity. After his death St. Bridget renounced her rank of princess and changed her habit.

In 1344, she built the great monastery of Wastein, which became the motherhouse of a new Order, that of the Brigittines. She next undertook a pilgrimage to Rome and to Palestine. Having satisfied her devotion at the holy places sanctified by the life and Passion of our Redeemer, she returned to Rome, where she lived a year longer. During this time she was sorely afflicted by sickness, but endured it with heroic patience and resignation. Her son, Birger, and her daughter, Catherine, were with her in her last moments. Having given them her final instructions, she received the Last Sacraments and died in 1373.

PRAYER Lord God, You revealed heavenly secrets to St. Bridget as she meditated on the Passion of Your Son. Grant that we Your servants may attain the joyful contemplation of Your glory. Amen.

ST. JOHN BOSTE, AND BL. GEORGE SWALLOWELL AND JOHN INGRAM, Martyrs

July 24

THESE three dedicated servants of God all died for the Faith near Durham, England, in 1594 and are known as the Durham Martyrs. John Boste was born about 1544 and educated at Queen's College, Oxford; though he became a fellow of that College with excellent prospects before him, he gave everything up and joined the Church at the age of twenty-two. In 1580, he was ordained at Rheims and returned to labor in England the next year. He labored for a few years with such zeal and success that the Earl of Huntington, then Lord President of the North, wanted to capture him more than any other priest in his jurisdiction.

At length he was treacherously betrayed and captured at his hiding place near Durham. He was sent to London, where he was committed to the Tower and cruelly tortured on the rack to induce him to betray his friends. As a result, he was obliged to walk for the rest of his life with his body bent and leaning on a staff. When he gave no information, the holy priest was sent back to Durham for trial.

Arraigned with him was a converted Protestant minister named George Swallowell, who had been wavering in his resolution. Father Boste's resolute, bold, joyful, and pleasant bearing had a calming effect on the convert who was moved to profess his Faith openly at court and receive public absolution from the priest. A few days later he was martyred at Darlington. For his part, Father Boste was also condemned and executed at Dryburn, outside Durham, on July 24, 1594, while praying for his executioner.

John Ingram was another priest who was condemned at the same time at Durham. Educated at New College, Oxford, he was converted and educated at Rheims and Rome where he received the priesthood in 1589. In 1592, he was sent to the Scottish mission. At the end of 1593, he was arrested and transported to London. Though undergoing excruciating tortures he steadfastly refused to betray his friends, even writing letters of encouragement to his fellow prisoners. Finally, two days after the death of John Boste, he was hung, drawn, and quartered at Gateshead for his priesthood.

All three Martyrs were beatified in 1929 by Pope Pius IX, and John Boste was canonized in 1970 by Pope St. Paul VI.

PRAYER God, You surround and protect us by the glorious confession of Your holy Martyrs, John Boste, George Swallowell, and John Ingram. Help us to profit from their example and be supported by their prayer. Amen.

ST. JAMES, Apostle

July 25—*Patron of Laborers*

THIS Saint is usually called "the Greater" in order to distinguish him from the other Apostle James, the "brother" of the Lord, who is called "the Less." He was the brother of St. John the Evangelist (sons of Zebedee and Salome) and came from Bethsaida in Galilee, where his father owned a fishing boat.

The two youths were fishing with their father when Jesus came by and invited them to follow him. They became such dedicated and zealous followers that our Lord styled them *Boanerges*, or sons of thunder. They were present at the cure of St. Peter's mother-in-law, the raising of Jairus' daughter, and the Transfiguration, and were near Christ in His Agony in the garden.

One day their mother asked Jesus to assure a place of honor for her sons in His future Kingdom. When He asked if they were able to bear the cup of His sufferings, their answer was typical of them: indeed they could! And indeed they did!

After the dispersion of the Apostles, St. James preached the Gospel in Spain and then returned to Jerusalem, where he was the first of the Apostles to drink the cup of Christ's sufferings. By order of Herod Agrippa he was beheaded at Jerusalem around the feast of Easter, in the year 44.

PRAYER Almighty, ever-living God, through the blood of St. James You consecrated the first fruits of the ministry of Your Apostles. Grant that Your Church may be strengthened by his confession and always enjoy his patronage. Amen.

ST. CHRISTOPHER, Martyr

The Same Day,* July 25—*Patron of Motorists

ST. CHRISTOPHER is one of the most popular Saints of the East and West. There are many legends concerning this Saint, often confused and contradictory. One of the most popular legends holds that St. Christopher was a giant who helped people across a raging stream. It is believed that he carried the Christ Child across this same stream. Hence, his name Christopher, Christbearer. He is the patron of motorists, and is invoked against storms, plagues, etc. He died a martyr during the reign of Decius in the 3rd century.

PRAYER Almighty and ever-living God, graciously pour out Your Spirit upon us. Let our hearts be filled with that true love which enabled Your holy Martyr Christopher to overcome all bodily torments. Amen.

STS. JOACHIM AND ANN,

Parents of Mary

July 26—(St. Ann) ***Patroness of Christian Mothers***

STS. JOACHIM and ANN, both of the tribe of Judah of the royal house of David, are venerated by the Church as the parents of the Blessed Virgin Mary who was probably their only child. The other Mary mentioned in the Gospels as the sister of the Mother of God was, it is believed, her cousin; for this was a customary way of designating relatives in the East.

St. Ann has been honored from early Christian times. Churches were dedicated to her honor, and the Fathers, especially of the Eastern Churches, loved to speak of her sanctity and privileges. She is often represented as teaching her little daughter to read the Scriptures.

ST. JOACHIM has been honored from time immemorial in the Churches of the East, and since the 6th century public devotion to him has been observed in all countries. However, as in the case of St. Ann, the Gospel tells us nothing about his life.

Tradition, grounded on very old testimonies, informs us that Sts. Joachim and Ann in their old age came from Galilee to settle in Jerusalem, and there the Blessed Mother of God was born and reared; there also they died and were buried. A church was built during the 4th century, possibly by St. Helena, on the site of the home of Sts. Joachim and Ann in Jerusalem.

PRAYER Lord, God of our fathers, through Sts. Joachim and Ann You gave us the Mother of Your Incarnate Son. May their prayers help us to attain the salvation You promised to Your people. Amen.

STS. NATHALIA, AURELIUS, LILIOSA, FELIX, AND GEORGE, Martyrs

July 27

DURING the 8th century, the Mohammedans ruled Cordova, Spain, and initiated a persecution of the Christians. Nathalia and Aurelius were converted Moslems who decided to practice the Faith openly. After setting aside enough money to take care of their daughter's future, they gave the rest of their possessions to the poor and practiced penance and devotion.

Their example proved to be an inspiration for a relative of Aurelius named Felix and his wife Liliosa, who had been practicing her Faith in secret. They joined Liliosa and Aurelius in visiting and ministering to the Christians in prison.

They were quickly arrested and cast into prison along with a beggar named George, who belonged to the monastary of St. Sabas in Jerusalem and had toured Egypt and Europe in search of alms for his house. They were all condemned to death—the first four for giving up the Moslem religion and George for insulting Mohammed. On July 27, 852, these saintly followers of Christ achieved the martyrdom they so avidly sought.

PRAYER Almighty, ever-living God, You conferred on Sts. Nathalia, Aurelius, Liliosa, Felix, and George the grace to suffer for Christ. Extend Your Divine help also to our weakness, so that just as they never shrank from dying for You we may remain steadfast in our confession of You. Amen.

ST. SAMSON, Bishop of Dol

July 28

ONE of the greatest of the Welsh saints, Samson was born about 490 and brought up in the Abbey of Llanwit, then ruled by St. Illtud. He was ordained and decided to increase his austerities, fervor, and prayer life. Retiring to another community in the neighborhood, he eventually became its Abbot.

However, he was so struck by the superior learning of some Irish monks who paid him a visit that he accompanied them to Ireland and remained a considerable time, laboring for the Faith. As time went on, the gift of miracles, which he already enjoyed, attracted so much attention that his humility could not tolerate it. Returning to his own country, he lived for a while as a hermit on the banks of the Severn.

The holy monk was consecrated Bishop by St. Dubricius and as the result of a vision crossed the sea to Brittany in company with other monks. With the aid of land given him, the saintly Bishop established a monastery at a place later called Dol, which became an important Episcopal See. His influence can be gauged by the fact that he visited King Childebert I to intercede on behalf of the dispossessed Breton ruler Judual.

St. Samson was a tireless traveler, great ascetic, and fearless monk who rendered innumerable benefits to his adopted country as well as a dedicated pastor who zealously looked after his flock. He died in 565 and was immediately honored in England, Normandy, and Brittany; later his cult spread to Italy.

PRAYER God, by Your ineffable mercy, St. Samson proclaimed the unsearchable riches of Christ. Through his intercession help us to grow in the knowledge of You and faithfully walk before You according to the truth of the Gospel, filled with every good work. Amen.

ST. MARTHA, Virgin

July 29—*Patroness of Cooks*

ST. MARTHA was the sister of Mary and Lazarus with whom she lived at Bethany, a village two miles from Jerusalem, a little beyond Mount Olivet, now bearing the name of El' Azaryth or Lazarich. The family, it appears, was of some importance in the country and, as is known from the Gospels, intensely devoted to Our Blessed Lord, Who was frequently their guest.

Martha is the prototype of the busy housewife because of the incident narrated in the Gospel when she asked Christ to rebuke her sister who was sitting at His feet leaving all the work to her. Instead, she heard the sublime answer that Mary had chosen the good part. Again, it was Martha who at the death of her brother had the Faith to declare that God would accomplish anything that Jesus willed, and she heard the words, "I am the Resurrection and the Life," to which she replied with a magnificent act of Faith: "I believe You are the Messiah, the Son of God." Finally, Martha was serving at table when Mary anointed Christ's feet with precious nard.

There is an untrustworthy Provençal legend that after our Lord's Ascension St. Martha traveled to France with her brother and sister, and Lazarus became Bishop of Marseilles. In 1187, her alleged relics were discovered at Tarascon, France, and placed in a magnificent crypt in the collegiate church there.

PRAYER Almighty, ever-living God, Your Son was a frequent Guest in St. Martha's home. Through her intercession grant that we may faithfully minister to our brethren and merit to be received in Your heavenly home. Amen.

ST. PETER CHRYSOLOGUS,

Bishop and Doctor of the Church

July 30

BORN at Imola, Italy, in 406, St. Peter was baptized, educated, and ordained a deacon by Cornelius, Bishop of Imola. St. Peter merited being called "Chrysologus" (golden-worded) because of his exceptional oratorical eloquence.

In 433, Pope Sixtus III consecrated him Archbishop of Ravenna. He practiced many corporal and spiritual works of mercy, and ruled his flock with utmost diligence and care. He extirpated the last vestiges of paganism and other abuses that had sprouted among his people, cautioning them especially against indecent dancing. "Anyone who wishes to frolic with the devil," he remarked, "cannot rejoice with Christ."

He also counseled the heretic Eutyches (who had asked for his support) to avoid causing division but to learn from the other heretics who were crushed when they hurled themselves against the Rock of Peter. He died at Imola, Italy, in 450, and in 1729 was made a Doctor of the Church, largely as a result of his simple, practical, and clear Sermons which have come down to us, nearly all dealing with Gospel subjects.

PRAYER God, You made St. Peter Chrysologus an outstanding preacher of Your Incarnate Word. Through his intercession, grant that we may contemplate the Mystery of Your salvation in our heart and faithfully bear witness to it by our deeds. Amen.

ST. IGNATIUS OF LOYOLA, Priest

July 31—*Patron of Retreats*

ST. IGNATIUS was born of a noble family in 1491, in the Castle of Loyola in Guipuscoa, Spain. Reared in the Court of Ferdinand V of Aragon, the husband of Isabella of Castile, he entered the army and distinguished himself by his valor. He was wounded at the siege of Pam-

plona, in a war between Charles V and Francis I, King of France. During his convalescence he read the "Lives of the Saints" which effected his conversion from worldliness to piety. Henceforth, his life belonged entirely to God.

After a general confession in the monastery of Monserrat, he spent ten months in the solitude of Manresa, where he composed his *Spiritual Exercises*, and then made a pilgrimage to Rome and the Holy Land. On his return to Spain he began his studies, and in 1528 he went to Paris to continue them. Here his virtue and wisdom gained him a few companions, and these became the nucleus of the Society of Jesus. At Montmarte they vowed to go to Palestine, or to offer themselves to the Pope to be employed in the service of God in some other manner. Receiving ordination at Venice together with his companions, St. Ignatius went to Rome where he was graciously received by Pope Paul III.

In 1540, Pope Paul III approved the Society and it soon made rapid progress, spreading to India in the East and to Brazil in the West. St. Ignatius continued to reside in Rome, employed in consolidating and governing his Society. There he became the friend of St. Philip Neri. He was General of the Society more than fifteen years. He died peacefully on July 31, 1556, and was canonized in 1622 by Pope Gregory XV.

PRAYER God, You raised up St. Ignatius in Your Church to inspire men to work for Your greater glory. Grant that we may labor on earth with his help and after his example and merit to be crowned with him in heaven. Amen.

ST. ALPHONSUS LIGUORI, Bishop and Doctor of the Church

August 1—*Patron of Confessors and Theologians*

ST. ALPHONSUS was born in the village of Marianella near Naples, Italy, September 27, 1696. At a tender age his pious mother inspired him with the deepest sentiments of piety. The education he received under the auspices of his father, aided by his own intellect, produced in him such results that at the early age of sixteen he graduated in law. Shortly after, he was admitted to the Neapolitan bar. In 1723, he lost a case, and God made use of his disappointment to

wean his heart from the world. In spite of all opposition he now entered the ecclesiastical state. In 1726, he was ordained priest. He exercised the ministry at various places with great fruit, zealously laboring for his own sanctification.

In 1732, God called him to found the Congregation of the Most Holy Redeemer, with the object of laboring for the salvation of the most abandoned souls. Amid untold difficulties and innumerable trials, St. Alphonsus succeeded in establishing his Congregation, which became his glory and crown, but also his cross. The holy founder labored incessantly at the work of the missions until, about 1756, he was appointed Bishop of St. Agatha, a diocese he governed until 1775, when, broken by age and infirmity, he resigned this office to retire to his monastery where he died.

Few Saints have labored as much, either by word or writing, as St. Alphonsus. He was a prolific and popular author, the utility of whose works will never cease. His last years were characterized by intense suffering, which he bore with resignation. His happy death occurred at Nocera de Pagani, August 1, 1787. He was canonized in 1839 by Pope Gregory XVI and declared Doctor of the Church in 1871 by Pope Pius IX.

PRAYER God, You constantly introduce new examples of virtue in Your Church. Walking in the footsteps of St. Alphonsus Your Bishop, may we be consumed with zeal for souls and attain the rewards he has won in heaven. Amen.

ST. EUSEBIUS OF VERCELLI, Bishop

August 2

BORN of a noble Sardinian family, St. Eusebius was taken to Rome by his mother while still an infant. There he received a Christian education and was ordained a lector by Pope St. Sylvester. Later, he went to Vercelli in Piedmont where he joined the clergy of that Church and was made Bishop about 340. Eusebius was the first Bishop in the Western Church to unite the clerical with the monastic life, for he lived in community with his clergy, anticipating the practice of the regular canons; at the same time, he also succeeded in forming a renowned clergy.

St. Eusebius was a strenuous upholder of the Orthodox Faith against the inroads of Arianism.

At the heavily pro-Arian Council of Milan in 355 he positively refused to subscribe to the condemnation of St. Athanasius, the greatest champion of the Faith of the time. As a consequence, the Emperor banished him to Scythopolis in Palestine, where he had to undergo great suffering for the Faith at the hands of the Arians; he was next removed to Cappadocia and some time later to Upper Thebes in Egypt.

After his release upon the death of the Emperor Constantius in 361, this Saint stopped at Alexandria where he met St. Athanasius. He also traveled through other parts of the East and strengthened many in the Faith. On returning to Vercelli, he encountered St. Hilary of Poitiers who like himself had been one of the exiled Bishops; and both of them exerted their zeal against Auxentius, the Arian Bishop of Milan. St. Eusebius died in peace at Vercelli in 370.

PRAYER Lord, God, help us to imitate the constancy of St. Eusebius, Your Bishop, in professing the Divinity of Your Son. In this way by remaining firm in the Faith he taught, we may be enabled to share in the life of Your Son. Amen.

ST. PETER JULIAN EYMARD, Founder

***The Same Day*—August 2**

PETER Julian Eymard was born at La Mure d'Isère in the Diocese of Grenoble, France, on February 4, 1811. In 1831 he entered the Grenoble Seminary, and was ordained a priest in 1835. After five years of pastoral ministry, he joined the Marist Fathers and served as spiritual director of their junior seminary at Belley, and later as provincial at Lyons.

In 1856 Peter was dispensed from his vows as a Marist, and he thereupon organized a religious institute dedicated to the Blessed Sacrament. Archbishop Sibour of Paris approved Peter's group, which was engaged in perpetual adoration of and devotion to the Blessed Sacrament. Eventually Pope Pius IX approved the institute as a congregation of priests.

Peter also founded a congregation of nuns and a priests' Eucharistic league, along with the Confraternity of the Blessed Sacrament, while writing several books on the Most Blessed Sacrament. He died on August 1, 1888, and was canonized in 1962 by Pope St. John XXIII.

PRAYER God, You endowed St. Peter Julian with wondrous love for the sacred mysteries of the Body and Blood of Your Son. May we deserve to obtain the same fruit that he received from the Divine Banquet. Amen.

ST. LYDIA

August 3—*Patroness of Dyers*

ST. LYDIA was a woman of Thyatira in the district of Lydia, the west-central portion of the Roman province of Asia, a district famed for its purple dyes. She was living as a dealer in purple goods at Philippi when St. Paul first came to the city about the year 55. Till then she had been a "worshiper of God," the technical name for a partial convert to Judaism. Under the influence of St. Paul's powerful preaching she received Christian Baptism—together with her entire household. This conversion represents the first one mentioned in Europe.

Since Lydia was apparently a wealthy woman, she then insisted on providing hospitality for St. Paul and his companions Luke and Silas during their stay at Philippi. St. Luke later wrote a record of this event in his history of the early Church, known as the Acts of the Apostles (chapter 16, verses 11 to 15).

PRAYER Pour forth on us, Lord, that spirit of knowledge and love of You with which You filled Your handmaid, Lydia. Help us to serve You sincerely by closely imitating her and so please You by our Faith and works. Amen.

ST. JOHN VIANNEY, Priest

August 4—*Patron of Priests*

UNIVERSALLY known as the "Curé of Ars," St. John Mary Vianney was ordained a priest in 1815. Three years later he was made parish priest of Ars, a remote French hamlet, where his reputation as a confessor and director of souls made him known throughout the Christian world. His life was one of extreme mortification.

Accustomed to the most severe austerities, beleaguered by swarms of penitents, and besieged by the devil, this great mystic manifested imperturbable patience. He was a wonder-worker loved by the crowds, but he retained a childlike simplicity, and he remains to this day the living image of the priest after the Heart of Christ.

He heard confessions of people from all over the world for sixteen hours each day. His life was filled with works of charity and love. It is reported that the staunchest of sinners were converted at his mere word. He died on August 4, 1859, and was canonized on May 31, 1925 by Pope Pius XI.

PRAYER Almighty and merciful God, in St. John Vianney You have given us a Priest who was outstanding in pastoral zeal. Through his intercession help us to win men for Christ and together with them attain eternal glory. Amen.

DEDICATION OF ST. MARY OF THE SNOWS

August 5

THERE is an ancient and popular tradition in Rome, according to which, during the reign of Pope Liberius in the 4th century, the Blessed Virgin appeared to a patrician named John, declaring that she wished a church to be dedicated to her honor on a spot which she indicated by a miraculous fall of snow in summer. John founded and endowed the church in 352, during the reign of the same Pope Liberius (352-366). Hence, it came to be called the Liberian Basilica.

Sixtus III enlarged and consecrated it under the title of the Virgin Mary about the year 435. The principal facade was added in 1741 by Benedict XIV. It bears the title of St. Mary Major, or the Greater, because it is in dignity, if not in antiquity, the first church in Rome among those dedicated to the Blessed Virgin. From the fact that the holy crib of Bethlehem is preserved in this church, it also bears the title of *Sancta Maria ad Praesepe* (at the Crib). St. Mary Major is one of the three patriarchal churches in which the Pope officiates on certain occasions, and in which there is an altar reserved only for him, St. Peter's and St. John Lateran being the others.

PRAYER Lord, forgive the sins of Your people. May we who cannot please You by our unaided efforts attain salvation through the intercession of the Mother of Your Son. Amen.

THE TRANSFIGURATION

August 6

WHILE Jesus was in Galilee, about one year before His Passion, He manifested His glory to three of His most beloved disciples—the same who were afterward witnesses of His Agony in the Garden: Peter and the two sons of Zebedee, James and John. He led them to the summit of Mount Tabor, as it is generally believed—this mountain, situated in Galilee, best answering the description of the evangelists.

The face of the Divine Savior became resplendent as the sun and His garments white as snow. Moses and Elijah appeared at His side and conversed with Him on the death He was to suffer at Jerusalem. Peter, in admiration, exclaimed: "Lord, it is good for us to be here!" He then proposed to erect three tents: one for the Savior, another for Moses, and a third for Elijah.

While he was still speaking, a luminous cloud enveloped them and a voice was heard proceeding from it: "This is My beloved Son in Whom I am well pleased; hear Him." The three Apostles fell prostrate; but Jesus touched them and commanded them to arise. When they arose, the vision had vanished and our Lord stood beside them in His ordinary guise.

It was fitting that those who so soon should behold Jesus in the depths of the humiliation to which His sacred humanity was to be subject in Gethsemane should catch a glimpse of that glorified humanity and of His Divinity, that they might be strengthened against temptation.

PRAYER God, in the glorious Transfiguration of Your only Son You confirmed the mysteries of Faith by the witness of the fathers and wonderfully foreshadowed the adoption of sons. Help us Your servants to listen to Your beloved Son and become coheirs with Him. Amen.

STS. SIXTUS II, Pope and Martyr, **AND COMPANIONS,** Martyrs

August 7

ST. SIXTUS (Xystus), elected to the Roman See in 257, was a good and peace-loving Pontiff. After reigning for twelve months, he was arrested on August 6, 258, at the cemetery of the Praetextatus in virtue of the recent edict of Valerian prescribing death for the leaders of the Christians. Accordingly, he was slain on the spot (although there is a possibility that he was first taken away and examined and then brought back for execution). With him there were also martyred Sts. Felicissimus, Agapitus, and four other deacons. St. Lawrence, archdeacon of Sixtus, was also martyred there three days later.

PRAYER Almighty God, You gave Sixtus and his companions the grace to lay down their lives for Your word and as a witness to Christ. By the power of the Holy Spirit, help us to be quick to believe and unwavering in the profession of our Faith. Amen.

ST. CAJETAN, Priest

The Same Day—August 7

ST. CAJETAN came into the world in 1480. Under the care of his pious mother he grew up in the tenderest sentiments of virtue. Entering the ecclesiastical state, he went to Rome, hoping there to lead an obscure life, but Pope Julius II forced upon him the office of protonotary apostolic. Upon the death of this Pope, however, he resigned the office and returned to Vicenza, his native city.

Both in Rome and Vicenza, the Saint devoted himself as a member of pious confraternities to promoting the glory of God and the salvation of souls. After some time he went to Venice and took up his abode in the hospital of that city. Having returned to Rome, he formed the idea of founding a society in which the members would endeavor to live like the apostles of old. His companions in this enterprise were John Peter Caraffa, afterward Pope Paul IV, Paul Consiglieri, and Boniface de Colle. Thus began the Order of Regular Clerics, now known as Theatines. It was approved by Clement VII in 1524.

During the sack of Rome by the Constable de Bourbon, St. Cajetan was most cruelly treated. In 1530, he succeeded Caraffa as General of the Order and filled the office three years. In spite of his numerous occupations the Saint spent many hours of the day in prayer and was often favored with extraordinary ecstasies. Worn out by labors, he died at Naples, on August 7, 1547, and was canonized in 1671 by Pope Clement X.

PRAYER God, You enabled St. Cajetan, Your Priest, to lead an apostolic life. Through his example and intercession, help us always to trust in You and seek Your Kingdom unceasingly. Amen.

ST. DOMINIC,
Priest

August 8

Patron of Astronomers

ST. DOMINIC, a native of Calaroga in Old Castile, Spain, was of the illustrious house of the Guzmans. At the age of fourteen he was sent to the schools of Valencia, which were soon after transferred to Salamanca. Having finished his education, he received the habit of the Regular Canons of St. Augustine in the diocese of Osma.

Devoting himself with ardor to the work of his own sanctification, he also labored for the salvation of others by preaching the Word of God.

He accompanied his Bishop on a mission imposed by Alphonsus IX, King of Castile. In France they became acquainted with the ravages of the Albigensian heresy. Both the Bishop and his companion proceeded to Rome, where they obtained permission from Innocent III to preach the Gospel among the heretics. They now began to labor with great zeal. To provide for the education of children, St. Dominic established a convent of nuns at Prouille, which became the nucleus of the Order of Dominican nuns. St. Dominic succeeded the Bishop of Osma as superior of the missions in Languedoc. Together with several companions of his labors, he laid the foundations of his Order, the Rules of which were approved by Pope Honorius III in 1216.

Some time later, the Pope created the office of Master of the Sacred Palace, or the Pope's domestic theologian, and St. Dominic was the first to fill it. The active life of the Saint was spent in traveling for the interests of God and His Church, preaching the Gospel, lecturing on theology and establishing houses of his Order which, even during his lifetime, made great progress and of which Honorius III, in 1220, made him General. His saintly life was happily terminated at Bologna, Italy, August 6, 1221, and he was canonized in 1234 by Pope Gregory IX.

The Saint is frequently pictured with a dog holding a torch in its mouth, which symbolized the fire of his zeal for souls.

PRAYER God, let St. Dominic help Your Church by his merits and teaching. May he who was an outstanding preacher of truth become a most generous intercessor for us. Amen.

ST. ROMANUS, Martyr

August 9

THIS Saint is an unknown Roman martyr whose cult was non-existent in the Church until the 12th century. His legendary acts tells us that St. Romanus was a soldier in Rome at the time when St. Lawrence had been imprisoned for his refusal to surrender the treasury of the Roman Church to the Empire. As he beheld the endurance and fortitude of St. Lawrence during his persecution and marveled at his virtuous courage and heroic patience, St. Romanus was so inspired that he approached the holy martyr and asked to be received into the Faith.

St. Lawrence first gave the necessary instructions to St. Romanus and then he baptized him in the prison. This brave Roman soldier then publicly proclaimed his conversion to Christianity to his fellow-soldiers, and he was immediately arrested and convicted. St. Romanus thereupon achieved the crown of martyrdom by being beheaded on August 9, 258, the day before the execution of St. Lawrence.

PRAYER Almighty and ever-living God, graciously pour out Your Spirit upon us. Let our hearts be filled with that true love which enabled Your holy Martyr Romanus to overcome all bodily torments. Amen.

ST. LAWRENCE, Martyr

August 10—*Patron of the Poor and of Cooks*

IN 257, when St. Sixtus became Pope, he ordained St. Lawrence deacon, and though he was still young appointed him the first of the seven deacons who served in the Church of Rome. To this office was annexed the care of the treasury of the Church and the distribution of its revenues among the poor. In that same year, the Emperor Valerian published his edict of persecution and commanded all Bishops, priests, and deacons to be put to death immediately. St. Sixtus was arrested twelve months later. As the holy man was led to execution, St. Lawrence followed him in tears. Sixtus at the same time ordered him to distribute the treasures of the Church among the poor. St. Lawrence did as he was commanded, selling even the sacred vessels to increase the sum.

At that time the Church of Rome, besides providing for its ministers, maintained fifteen hundred poor people and even sent alms to distant countries. The Prefect of Rome commanded St. Lawrence to surrender the treasures of the Church, and he promised to show them to him.

On the third day, instead of gold and silver he exhibited the poor whom he had gathered together.

The enraged Prefect commanded that he should be slowly roasted on a gridiron. The order was mercilessly executed but the martyr, strengthened by Divine grace, endured his suffering with heroic fortitude and even found strength to jest at the expense of his torments and his persecutor. To his last breath the holy deacon prayed for the conversion of the city of Rome, that the Faith of Christ might thence spread throughout the world. Several senators, who had witnessed his execution, were converted to Christianity and gave decent burial to his body. His martyrdom occurred in the year 258.

PRAYER God, by his ardent love for You St. Lawrence exhibited faithful service and attained a glorious martyrdom. Help us to love what he loved and to practice what he taught. Amen.

ST. CLARE, Virgin

August 11—*Patroness of Television*

ASSISI, the birthplace of St. Francis, had also the honor of giving birth to St. Clare, his spiritual daughter. She was born in 1193. From her childhood she desired to consecrate herself to Jesus Christ. Having heard of St. Francis and his sanctity, she contrived to be taken to him by a pious matron. The conversation of St. Francis

made her resolve to abandon the world. On March 18, 1212, together with another young woman, she went to the Portiuncula, where St. Francis prayed, and received the penitential habit.

At first St. Francis placed her in a Benedictine convent of nuns. She persevered in her resolution, in spite of the opposition of her friends and relatives. Later her sister Agnes joined her. St. Francis then placed them in a separate house. Soon after, her mother and several other ladies, some of high nobility, united themselves to her. The foundation of Poor Clares, or the Second Order of St. Francis, was thus laid. Within a few years St. Clare founded a number of other monasteries and her Order spread to Germany and Bohemia.

The austerities these religious women practiced had scarcely ever been known among their sex. Together with other mortifications, their fast was perpetual. Such was the spirit of poverty of St. Clare that when, after her profession, she fell heiress to the large fortune of her father, she gave all of it to the poor. She would accept no revenues for her monastery. When the army of Frederick II was devastating the valley of Spoleto some of the soldiers placed a ladder against the convent wall. St. Clare caused herself to be carried to a window, and, holding the monstrance with the Blessed Sacrament in sight of the enemies, she prostrated herself before the Eucharistic God. Her prayer was heard, and the enemies, struck with a sudden panic, fled in terror. St. Clare's life came to an end, on August 11, 1253. She was canonized in 1255 by Pope Alexander IV.

PRAYER God, in Your mercy You led St. Clare to embrace poverty. Through her intercession help us to follow Christ in the spirit of poverty and to contemplate You in the heavenly Kingdom. Amen.

ST. EUPLIUS, Martyr

August 12

ON August 12, 304, during the persecution of Diocletian at Catania, Sicily, a deacon named Euplius was brought to the governor's hall and staunchly professed his Faith. With the

Book of Gospels in his hand, he was called before the governor Calvisian and commanded to read from it. The Saint read the passage: "Blest are they who suffer persecution for justice' sake, for theirs is the Kingdom of heaven."

Euplius then read the passage: "If anyone will come after Me, let him deny himself and take up his cross and follow Me." Questioned by the governor as to what this meant, the youth replied: "It is the law of my Lord, which has been delivered to me." Calvisian asked: "By whom?" Euplius replied: "By Jesus Christ, the Son of the living God." With that, the governor ordered that he be led away to be tortured.

At the height of his torment, Eupilius was asked if he still persisted in his Christianity. He answered: "What I said before, I say again: I am a Christian and I read the Sacred Scriptures." He added that he would never give up the Scriptures and preferred death to life on earth, for he would thereby obtain eternal life. The governor realized that Euplius was firm in his refusal to adore the pagan gods, so he ordered him to be put to death. With the Book of Gospels hung around his neck, St. Euplius was led to the place of execution and beheaded—praising God all the while.

PRAYER God of power and mercy, through Your help St. Euplius has overcome the tortures of his passion. Help us who celebrate his triumph to remain victorious over the wiles of our enemies. Amen.

ST. PONTIAN, Pope and Martyr, AND ST. HIPPOLYTUS, Priest and Martyr

August 13

ST. PONTIAN succeeded St. Urban in the Pontifical See in 230. After the assassination of Alexander Severus in 235, he was exiled by the Emperor Maximus to the mines of Sardinia. He bore his sufferings and persecution patiently for Christ and attained the crown of martyrdom in that same year.

Exiled together with St. Pontian was a priest named Hippolytus, one of the most important 3rd century theologians of the Roman Church. Born about 170, he was already a priest and a personage of note when Origen heard him preach at Rome in 202. During the first part of his life he produced the Scriptural writings which constitute the best part of his works (he wrote the earliest known commentary on Scripture, that of the Book of Daniel), and defended the Faith.

About 215, he wrote the *Apostolical Tradition* (for which he is probably best known) which contains the earliest known ritual of ordinations and is the equivalent of a *Roman Ritual.* After becoming involved in unfortunate controversies and even regarded as a kind of antipope, Hippolytus returned to the fold and continued to defend the Church against all her enemies. Finally, he gave his life for the Faith together with Christ's Vicar on earth.

PRAYER Lord, may the outstanding constancy of Your Martyrs increase our love for You and fill our hearts with ever greater firmness of Faith. Amen.

ST. MAXIMILIAN MARY KOLBE,
Priest and Martyr
August 14

MAXIMILIAN was born in 1894 in Poland and became a Franciscan. He contracted tuberculosis and, though he recovered, he remained frail all his life. Before his ordination as a priest, Maximilian founded the Immaculata Movement devoted to Our Lady. After receiving a doctorate in theology, he spread the Movement through a magazine entitled "The Knight of the Immaculata" and helped form a community of 800 men, the largest in the world.

Maximilian went to Japan where he built a comparable monastery and then on to India where he furthered the Movement. In 1936 he returned home because of ill health. After the Nazi invasion in 1939, he was imprisoned and released for a time. But in 1941 he was arrested again and sent to the concentration camp at Auschwitz.

On July 31, 1941, in reprisal for one prisoner's escape, ten men were chosen to die. Father Kolbe offered himself in place of a young husband and father. And he was the last to die, enduring two weeks of starvation, thirst, and neglect. He was canonized in 1981 by Pope St. John Paul II.

PRAYER Lord, You inflamed St. Maximilian with love for the Immaculate Virgin and filled him with zeal for souls and love for neighbor. Through his prayers, grant that we may work strenuously for Your glory in the service of others and so be made conformable to Your Son until death. Amen.

BLESSED EBERHARD, Abbot

***The Same Day*—August 14**

BORN into the ducal family of Suabia, Eberhard became provost of the cathedral chapter of Strasbourg. In 934, seeking greater closeness to God, he withdrew to the hermitage of Einsiedeln in Switzerland which was under the wing of his old friend Blessed Benno, former Bishop of Metz. However, Eberhard's privacy was short-lived; his reputation for spiritual wisdom and sanctity drew large numbers, necessitating the construction of a monastery to house them and a church in which they could worship God.

After Benno's death, Eberhard became first Abbot of Our Lady of the Hermits and succeeded in obtaining certain concessions from the Emperor, Otto I. The monastery received the right of free election of Abbots, and won exemption from civil and episcopal jurisdiction.

When a bitter famine broke out in Alsace, Burgundy, and Upper Germany in 942, Blessed Eberhard and his followers relieved the people's hunger by supplying large quantities of corn. A legend says that when the consecration of the

Abbey church of Einsiedeln took place in 948, it was graced with the presence of our Lord Himself, assisted by the four Evangelists and Sts. Peter and Gregory the Great. At his death in 958, this holy man was buried near Blessed Benno in the church he had built.

PRAYER Lord, amid the things of this world, let us be wholeheartedly committed to heavenly things in imitation of the example of evangelical perfection You have given us in Bl. Eberhard the Abbot. Amen.

ASSUMPTION OF THE BLESSED VIRGIN

August 15

ON November 1, 1950, Pope Pius XII defined as a truth revealed by God that the Immaculate Mother of God, Mary ever Virgin, when the course of her life on earth was finished, was taken up body and soul into heaven. Such is the dogma of the Assumption of the Blessed Virgin.

"It was surely fitting, it was becoming, that she should be taken up into heaven and not lie in the grave till Christ's second coming, [one] who had passed a life of sanctity and of miracles such as hers. . . . Who can conceive that God should so repay the debt, which He considered to owe to His Mother for the elements of His human Body, as to allow the flesh and blood from which it was taken to molder in the grave? Or who can conceive that that virginal frame which never sinned was to undergo the death of a sinner? . . .

"She died, then, because even our Lord and Savior died. But though she died as well as others, she died not as others die; for, through the merits of her Son, by whom she was what she was, by the grace of Christ which in her had anticipated sin, which had filled her with light, which had purified her flesh from all defilement, she had been saved from disease and malady, and all that weakens and decays the bodily frame" (Cardinal Newman).

Jesus and Mary both passed through the gate of death into heaven. In her own way, Mary was crucified with Jesus. She patiently stayed on earth, after His Ascension, so long as God willed.

From her place in heaven she still abides invisibly with us, ever our refuge, our comfort, our hope. Through the Communion of Saints, of which she is the Queen, we share in the joy and glory of her Assumption, to which the Entrance Song of the Mass of August 15 gives us the key.

PRAYER Almighty, ever-living God, You raised to eternal glory the body and soul of the immaculate Virgin Mary, Mother of Your Son. Grant that our minds may always be directed heavenward and that we may deserve to share in her glory. Amen.

ST. STEPHEN, King

August 16—*Patron of Hungary*

THE son of Geysa, the fourth Duke of the Hungarians, and of Sarboth, his wife, who had both been recently converted to Christianity, St. Stephen was born in 977 at Gran, then the capital of Hungary. After a Christian education under the care of St. Adalbert, Bishop of Prague, and of Theodatus, a virtuous Italian Count, he succeeded his father upon the latter's death in 997.

He established a solid peace with all neighboring nations and then turned his attention to rooting idolatry out of his country. His methods were those of persuasion and exhortation, but many of his subjects, on account of their attachment to the religion of their ancestors, rebelled and besieged their King in Vesprin. St. Stephen prepared himself for battle by fasting, almsgiving, and prayer, and though his forces were inferior in number to those of the rebels he nevertheless completely routed them.

The work of propagating the Faith now went on with renewed vigor. Churches, monasteries, and Bishoprics were founded, and the King sent an embassy to Rome to obtain from Pope Sylvester II the confirmation of his foundations; and, in order to gratify the wish of his subjects, he also besought for himself the title of King. The request was granted, and the Pope sent a rich crown to the holy King. The prelate who brought the crown from Rome anointed and crowned St. Stephen King in the year 1000.

The devotion of St. Stephen toward the Blessed Virgin Mary was such that he placed all his dominions under her special patronage. In war, which he never undertook without necessity, he was always victorious, nor was he ever the aggressor. His time was divided between the duties of religion and those of his station; he kept his soul constantly recollected in God, and in the midst of the world he practiced great mortification and humility. He died August 15, 1038.

PRAYER Almighty God, Your Church flourished through the efforts of St. Stephen when he reigned on earth. Grant that she may now be defended by him dwelling gloriously in heaven. Amen.

ST. HYACINTH, Priest

August 17

THIS Saint was a native of Silesia, which then belonged to Poland. He studied at Cracow, Prague, and Bologna, receiving the degrees of doctor of laws and divinity. On his return home, the Bishop of Cracow gave him a stipend in the cathedral and employed his assistance in the administration of the diocese.

After the resignation of the pious Bishop Vincent, Yvo, the uncle of St. Hyacinth, was appointed to fill the See. Going to Rome, he took with him his two nephews, Hyacinth and Ceslas. St. Dominic was then (1218) in Rome, and Hyacinth, being greatly impressed, joined his institute, together with Ceslas and two German gentlemen, receiving the habit from St. Dominic himself in the convent of Santa Sabina. They made their vows by special dispensation after a novitiate of only six months and returned to Poland, St. Hyacinth being appointed superior of their mission. On their way they preached the Gospel in many places, received new members into their Order, and finally, after a lengthy period, arrived in Poland, where they were received with the greatest joy.

The preaching of St. Hyacinth effected an entire change of morals in the city of Cracow. He carried the Gospel to the idolatrous countries of the North: in Prussia, Pomerania, along the Baltic, in Denmark, Sweden, and Norway. He labored in Russia, traveling as far as the Black Sea and the Aegean, and returned to Cracow in 1231; but after two years he set out again to visit the convents he had founded, and penetrated among the Tartars, going even to China.

He again arrived at Cracow in 1257, the seventy-second and last year of his life. He died on August 15 of the same year. Ecclesiastical historians call him the Apostle of the North and the Thaumaturgus of his age, on account of his numerous miracles. He was,canonized in 1594 by Pope Clement VIII.

PRAYER God, You willed to send St. Hyacinth to enlighten many peoples. Through his intercession, grant that we may walk in the light of Your truth. Amen.

ST. JANE FRANCES DE CHANTAL, Religious

August 18

BORN at Dijon in 1572, into a prominent family, St. Jane Frances received an excellent education. In 1592, she married the Baron de Chantal, an officer in the army of Henry IV. After eight happy years, she was left a widow with four little children when the Baron was killed in a hunting accident. In 1604, she heard St. Francis de Sales preach and placed herself under his spiritual direction.

After providing for the welfare of her children, St. Jane Frances went to Annecy and established the Congregation of the Visitation in 1610. For many years she suffered great interior trials with the utmost resignation, while she labored to extend her Congregation and promote God's glory. Eighty-six houses were established before her death which took place in 1641. She was canonized in 1767 by Pope Clement XIII.

PRAYER God, You endowed St. Jane Frances with admirable qualities in various walks of life. Through her intercession help us to be true to our vocation and never fail to bear witness to the light You give us. Amen.

ST. HELENA, Widow

***The Same Day*—August 18**

IT IS generally believed by ecclesiastical historians of England that St. Helena was born in that country, and according to Leland, she was the daughter of Coel, a British King who lived in friendship with the Romans. Constantius, at that time an officer in the Roman army in Britain, married her. Constantine, his eldest son, received his education under her eyes.

In 293, Constantius was honored by the Empire with the title of Caesar, obtaining the government of Gaul and Britain. In return for this honor he was obliged to divorce St. Helena and marry Theodora, the daughter-in-law of the Emperor Maximian. St. Helena was not at that time a Christian, but after the accession of her son Constantine and his miraculous victory, she embraced the Christian Faith and the most heroic practices of Christian perfection. Her dutiful son proclaimed her Empress and struck medals in her honor.

In spite of this new dignity she assisted with the people at the Divine Office in modest attire, and employed her wealth in charity to the poor and the building of churches. When the Emperor determined to erect a church on Mount Calvary, St. Helena, although eighty years of age, undertook to see the work executed, and started for Jerusalem hoping to find the Holy Cross. Excavations were made and three crosses were discovered. The title which lay near one of the crosses, and perhaps the marks of the nails by which it had been attached, seemed to indicate which was the Cross of our Savior.

St. Helena built two magnificent churches, one on Mount Calvary, the other on Mount Olivet. After traveling through the East, where she beautified the city of Drepanum in honor of St. Lucian, so that Constantine afterward gave it the name of Helenopolis, she returned to Rome. Her journey had been marked by the most illustrious deeds of virtue and by innumerable charities. She died at Rome in August, 328 or 326, in the twentieth year of her son's reign. Constantine caused her obsequies to be performed with the utmost magnificence, and erected a statue to her memory.

PRAYER Lord, You willed to enrich Your Church through St. Helena with a treasure beyond price and so revealed to her the hiding place of Your Cross. Through her intercession, grant that the ransom paid on that life-giving wood may win the rewards of everlasting life for us. Amen.

ST. JOHN EUDES, Priest

August 19

ST. JOHN EUDES was born in France, November 14, 1601. An exemplary youth, he was extolled as one of the most brilliant students ever to attend the Jesuit College at Caen.

As a priest he was full of zeal for the salvation of souls. He worked valiantly among his countrymen and became known as one of the greatest missionaries of his day. Traveling throughout France, he taught the great truths of the Faith and succeeded in making a host of conversions.

He founded the Congregation of the "Priests of Jesus and Mary" and the Congregation of "Sisters of Our Lady of Charity." The main purpose of the former was the direction of seminaries and the religious instruction of the people through missions. He died on August 19, 1680.

Pope Leo XIII recognized St. John Eudes as the author of the liturgical devotion to the Sacred Hearts of Jesus and Mary, and Pope Pius XI canonized him in 1925.

PRAYER God, You wonderfully chose St. John, Your Priest, to announce the unsearchable riches of Christ. Help us to grow in the knowledge of You through his example and counsels and so to live faithfully according to the light of the Gospel. Amen.

ST. BERNARD, Abbot and Doctor of the Church

August 20

ST. BERNARD was born of noble parentage in Burgundy, France, in the castle of Fontaines near Dijon. Under the care of his pious parents he was sent at an early age to a college at Chatillon, where he was conspicuous for his remarkable piety and spirit of recollection. At the same place he entered upon the studies of theology and Holy Scripture. After the death of his mother, fearing the snares and temptations of the world, he resolved to embrace the newly established and austere institute of the Cistercian Order, of which he was destined to become the greatest ornament. He also persuaded his brothers and several of his friends to follow his example.

In 1113, St. Bernard, with thirty young noblemen, presented himself to the holy Abbot, St. Stephen, at Cîteaux. After a novitiate spent in great fervor, he made his profession in the following year. His superior soon after, seeing the great progress he had made in the spiritual life, sent him with twelve monks to found a new monastery, which afterward became known as the celebrated Abbey of Clairvaux. St. Bernard was at once appointed Abbot and began that active life which has rendered him the most conspicuous figure in the history of the 12th century.

He founded numerous other monasteries, composed a number of works and undertook many journeys for the honor of God. Several Bishoprics were offered him, but he refused them all. His reputation spread far and wide; even the Popes were governed by his advice.

He was commissioned by Pope Eugene III to preach the second Crusade. In obedience to the Sovereign Pontiff he traveled through France and Germany, and aroused the greatest enthusiasm for the holy war among the masses of the population. The failure of the expedition raised a great storm against the Saint, but he attributed it to the sins of the Crusaders. St. Bernard was eminently endowed with the gift of miracles. He died on August 20, 1153, and was canonized in 1174 by Pope Alexander III.

PRAYER God, You blessed Your Church with St. Bernard, a man full of zeal for Your house, radiating brightness and ardent love. Through his intercession, grant that we may be animated by the same spirit and always walk as children of light. Amen.

ST. PIUS X, Pope

August 21

ON June 2, 1835, Giuseppe Sarto saw the light of earth at Riesi, Province of Treviso, in Venice; on August 20, 1914, he saw the light of heaven; and on May 29, 1954, he who had become the 259th Pope was canonized St. Pius X.

Two of the most outstanding accomplishments of this saintly Pope were the inauguration of the liturgical renewal and the restoration of frequent communion from childhood. He also waged an unwavering war against the heresy and evils of Modernism, gave great impetus to Biblical studies, and brought about the codification of canon law. His overriding concern was to renew all things in Christ.

Above all, his holiness shone forth conspicuously. From St. Pius X we learn again that "the folly of the Cross," simplicity of life, and humility of heart are still the highest wisdom and the indispensable conditions of a perfect Christian life, for they are the very source of all apostolic fruitfulness.

His last will and testament bears the striking sentence: "I was born poor, I have lived in poverty, and I wish to die poor."

PRAYER God, to preserve the Catholic Faith and renew all things in Christ, You filled Pope St. Pius with heavenly wisdom and apostolic fortitude. Grant that we may follow his direction and example and be rewarded with eternal life with You. Amen.

QUEENSHIP OF MARY

August 22

ON October 11, 1954, His Holiness, Pope Pius XII, in his encyclical letter, *Ad Caeli Reginam*, decreed and instituted the feast of the Queenship of the Blessed Virgin Mary to be celebrated throughout the world every year. He declared that the Church has believed in Mary's Queenship from the earliest centuries and that this belief rests on Holy Scripture and tradition.

Mary is Queen of all "since she brought forth a Son, Who at the very moment that He was conceived, was, by reason of the hypostatic union of the human nature with the Word, even as man,

King and Lord of all things." Further, "as Christ is our Lord and King by a special title because He redeemed us, so the Blessed Virgin (is our Lady and Queen) because of the unique way in which she has cooperated toward our redemption by giving of her own substance, by offering Him willingly for us, and by desiring, praying for, and bringing about our salvation in a singular manner."

PRAYER God, You have given us the Mother of Your Son to be our Mother and Queen. Through her intercession, grant that we may attain the glory destined for Your adopted sons in Your heavenly Kingdom. Amen.

ST. ROSE OF LIMA, Virgin

August 23—*Patroness of South America*

ISABEL DE FLORES Y DEL OLIVA, called Rose by her mother because of her red cheeks and confirmed with that name by St. Turibius de Mogrovejo, was the first person in the Americas to be canonized as a Saint. Born at Lima, Peru, in 1586, she worked long and hard to help support her family, growing flowers and doing embroidery and other needlework.

Having taken a vow of virginity early in life, she consistently refused to marry and at twenty years of age became a Dominican Tertiary, and lived in a summerhouse in the garden of her home. Here she practiced extreme penance and mortification, modeling her life after that of St. Catherine of Siena.

St. Rose bore her many and great adversities with heroic patience and consoled the sick and suffering among the poor, Indians, and slaves. Consequently, she is regarded as the originator of social service in Peru. She died in 1617 at thirty-one years of age and was canonized in 1671 by Pope Clement X.

PRAYER God, You filled St. Rose with love for You and enabled her to leave the world and be free for You through the austerity of penance. Through her intercession, help us to follow her footsteps on earth and enjoy the torrent of Your delights in heaven. Amen.

ST. BARTHOLOMEW, Apostle

August 24—*Patron of Plasterers*

MANY Scripture scholars identify (reasonably but not conclusively) St. Bartholomew with Nathaniel who was conducted to Christ by St. Philip. The name of Bartholomew signifies son of Tolmai, and it was given to the Saint in the same sense that "Bar Jonah" was attached to St. Peter. He was chosen by our Lord Himself to be one of the Twelve Apostles.

According to Eusebius and other ancient writers, he preached the Gospel in the most barbarous countries of the East, penetrating as far as India. Eusebius relates that when St. Pantaenus, in the 3rd century, went to India, he still found the knowledge of Christ in that country, and a copy of the Gospel of St. Matthew in Hebrew was shown to him, which he was told had been brought there by St. Bartholomew.

St. John Chrysostom declares that St. Bartholomew brought the Faith to the people of Lycaonia. According to St. Gregory of Tours, the last field of his labors was Great Armenia, where, preaching in a place obstinately addicted to the worship of idols, he suffered martyrdom. By some it is said that he was flayed alive; by others that he suffered crucifixion—both these opinions being reconcilable. The relics of the Saint are preserved in the church of St. Bartholomew on the island in the Tiber River near Rome.

PRAYER Lord, strengthen in us that Faith by which Your Apostle St. Bartholomew adhered to Your Son with sincerity of mind. Through his intercession, grant that Your Church may become a sacrament of salvation for all nations. Amen.

ST. LOUIS, King of France

August 25—*Patron of Tertiaries*

ST. LOUIS, the ninth of his name, was born at Poissy, France, in 1214. His father was Louis VIII, and his mother was Blanche, daughter of Alfonso VIII of Castile. At the age of twelve he lost his father, and his mother became regent of the kingdom. From his tenderest infancy she had inspired him with a love for holy things.

In 1234, he married Margaret, the virtuous daughter of Raymond Berenger, Count of Provence, and two years later he took the reins of government into his own hands. In 1238, he headed a crusade, in which he fell a prisoner among the Mohammedans, but a truce was concluded and he was set free and he returned to France. In 1267, he again set out for the East at the head of a crusade, but he never again beheld his native land. In 1270, he was stricken by the pestilence at the siege of Tunis, and after receiving the Last Sacraments, he died.

PRAYER God, You transferred St. Louis from the cares of an earthly throne to the glory of the heavenly Kingdom. Grant, through his intercession, that we may seek Your eternal Kingdom by carrying out our earthly duties. Amen.

ST. JOSEPH CALASANZ, Priest

The *Same Day,* August 25—*Patron of Students*

BORN at Peralta de la Sal in Aragon, Spain, in 1556, St. Joseph Calasanz became a priest. His reputation for sanctity inspired the Bishop of Lerida to appoint him as his confessor, theologian, and synodal examiner.

In 1592, he went to Rome and became theologian to Cardinal Marc-Antonio Colonna. Here he joined the Confraternity of Christian Doctrine.

He became so convinced of the necessity of imparting religious instruction to children at an early age that he began this work alone in the Trastevere, where he rented several rooms in which he opened a little school, teaching the children reading, writing, and arithmetic. After some time several companions joined him in the good work and he began to lead a community life with them. Thus he laid the foundations of a congregation which in the course of time grew to be that of the "Clerics Regular of the Poor Schools of the Mother of God."

During the life of the holy founder his Order spread throughout Italy and afterward to other countries. By a brief of 1622 Pope Gregory XV approved the constitutions and appointed the holy founder General of the Order. The virtuous and austere life of this great servant of God came to an end on August 25, 1648. He was canonized in 1767 by Pope Clement XIII.

PRAYER God, You adorned St. Joseph Your Priest with excelling love and patience so that he might labor for the formation of Christian youth. Grant that as we honor this teacher of wisdom we may follow his example in working for truth. Amen.

ST. CAESARIUS OF ARLES, Bishop

August 26—*Patron of the Unmarried*

BORN at Chalon-sur-Saone in 470 of a good Gallo-Roman family, St. Caesarius entered the monastery of Lerins at the age of twenty and in 503 he was chosen Bishop of Arles. While retaining the kind of austere life he had adopted as a monk, this devout Bishop played a prominent role in the ecclesiastical administration of southern Gaul and established the claim of Arles to be the primatial See in Gaul.

St. Caesarius organized his diocese, reestablished and formed the clergy, and zealously defended the Church against heresy. He fought Arianism strenuously and was largely instrumental in securing the cooperation of Semi-Pelagianism at the Council of Orange in 529 (one of several over which he presided by order of the Pope).

He was a celebrated preacher, stressing brevity and clarity of language, as is shown by his Sermons which have come down to us. This dynamic pastor also wrote a Rule for his sister's nunnery, which he had founded, and it has for a long time remained the frame of life for a great number of religious. The modernity of this Rule can be seen in its provisions that every nun learn to read and write and that the nuns should have the right to choose their abbess. He died in 543.

PRAYER God, Light and Shepherd of souls, You established St. Caesarius as Bishop in Your Church to feed Your flock by his word and form it by his example. Help us through his intercession to keep the Faith he taught by his word and follow the way he showed by his example. Amen.

ST. MONICA, Widow

August 27—*Patroness of Mothers and Widows*

ST. MONICA came into the world in the year 333. As soon as she was old enough she was married to Patricius, a pagan citizen of Tagaste. Although Patricius was a man of high temper, she bore all trials with great patience. Her example and gentle conduct exercised such an influence over him that he was finally converted to Christianity. He died the year after his baptism.

The great cross of her life was the conduct of her son, Augustine, who was seventeen years of age when his father died in 371. His mother prayed long and fervently for his conversion. When he left her in Africa to go to Italy, she followed him and found him at Milan, where the words of St. Ambrose had already convinced him of the falsehood of Manichean doctrines, which he abandoned without being entirely converted.

In August, 386, St. Monica had the long-coveted happiness of seeing her son return to God. He was baptized by St. Ambrose on Easter eve the following year and soon after, with his mother and some friends, he set out for Africa. But St. Monica's work was done; her son was converted; the sinner had become a Saint. She fell sick on the road and died at Ostia, from where they were to embark, in 387.

PRAYER God, Comforter of the afflicted, You accepted St. Monica's tears to bring about the conversion of her son St. Augustine. Through their intercession, grant that we may have contrition for our sins and experience the grace of Your pardon. Amen.

ST. AUGUSTINE,
Bishop and Doctor of the Church

August 28

Patron of Theologians

ST. AUGUSTINE was born on November 13, 354, at Tagaste (modern Algeria) in Africa. In spite of the piety of his holy mother, St. Monica, he fell at an early age into the greatest disorders, and even at a later period became a heretic of the sect of the Manicheans. Unfortunately, his father, Patricius, was then an idolater, so that the youth met with little or no restraint on his side.

In the beginning of 370 he continued his studies at Carthage and the following year his father died, after being converted to Christianity. Some time later, St. Augustine took up his abode at Carthage and opened a school of rhetoric. Later he went to Rome and then to Milan, where he also began to teach rhetoric. Here God's grace and the prayers of his mother, who had followed him to Italy, as well as the instructions of saintly friends, particularly of St. Ambrose, effected his conversion. He abandoned the sect of the Manicheans, and after some time gave himself entirely to God. St. Ambrose administered to him the Sacrament of Baptism on Easter eve, 387.

On his return to Africa, the Saint lost his mother at Ostia in the same year, and in 388 he arrived at Carthage. At Tagaste he began to live a community life with some of his friends. He was ordained in 390 and moved to Hippo where he established another community with several of his friends who had followed him. Five years later he was consecrated Bishop and made coadjutor to Valerius, Bishop of Hippo, whom he succeeded in the following year.

From this period until his death his life was one of ceaseless activity. He governed his church, preached to his people, and wrote voluminous works that have received the admiration of the ages. His humility prompted him to write his *Confessions* about the year 397, and from this work we have a detailed account of his early years.

He exerted his zeal against the various errors of his day, and showed himself as intrepid a defender of the Faith as he had been its ignorant enemy. The Manicheans, Priscillianists, Origenists, Donatists and Pelagians all came in for a share of his zeal. Shortly before his death the Vandals under Genseric invaded Africa, and the Saint was witness of the desolation that followed in their tracks. This multi-faceted religious genius and devout servant of God died on August 28, 430.

PRAYER Lord, renew in Your Church the spirit which You inspired in St. Augustine, Your Bishop. Filled by this spirit, may we thirst after You as the true Source of wisdom. Amen.

BEHEADING OF ST. JOHN THE BAPTIST

August 29—*Patron of Farriers*

ST. JOHN, faithful to the inspiration of Divine grace, spent most of his life in the wilderness, and became the model of the many anchorites who later served God in the same manner. When thirty years old, he appeared before the world on the banks of the Jordan, as a preacher of penance, the precursor of Jesus Christ and "the voice of one crying in the wilderness." He had the honor of baptizing his Divine Master and pointing Him out as the Lamb of God.

The occasion of dying a martyr for his duty soon presented itself. Herod Antipas, son of Herod the Great, the slayer of the Innocents, was then ruler, or tetrarch, of Galilee. He is the same one whom our Lord called a "fox," and by whom the Savior was sent to Pilate. On a visit to Rome he had made the acquaintance of Herodias, the wife of his brother Philip, and he took her as his wife. His own spouse, the daughter of Aretas, an Arabian King, fled to her father, and a war in which the army of Herod was defeated resulted. St. John boldly denounced this adulterous and incestuous marriage, and as a result was thrown into prison. But Herodias wanted greater revenge: nothing but the head of her enemy, John the Baptist, could satisfy her.

On the occasion of the anniversary of Herod's birth, a feast was given in which Salome, the daughter of Herodias, pleased him exceedingly by a graceful dance. He swore that he would grant whatever she asked. The girl consulted her mother, who advised her to request the head of St. John. Herod was grieved by this request, for he esteemed the Baptist; yet he had the weakness to yield and to abide by his impious oath. An officer was dispatched to the prison, and St. John was beheaded to satisfy the revenge of a voluptuous woman. The death of St. John occurred about a year before that of our Lord.

PRAYER God, You chose St. John the Baptist to be the forerunner of Your Son Who was born and died for us. Grant that, as St. John was martyred for truth and justice, so we may energetically profess our Faith in You. Amen.

ST. MEDERICUS (OR MERRY), Abbot

***The Same Day*—August 29**

BORN at Autun in the 7th century, Medericus (or Merry) as a young man entered a local monastery, which was very likely St. Martin's in Autun. He was chosen Abbot and became a model of virtue for his subjects and a paragon of sanctity for the populace of the whole city.

After some time, Medericus' desire for greater solitude with God led him to resign his office and withdraw to a forest four miles away. There he lived from the fruits of his manual labor.

However, his reputation continued to draw crowds to him. Despite his preference for solitude, the Saint still found time to minister to their needs. In time, the holy monk fell ill and was obliged to return to the monastery.

In his old age, Medericus undertook to make a pilgrimage to the shrine of St. Germanus of Paris. Arriving in Paris, he set up a cell next to a chapel dedicated to St. Peter. After two years and some months of a lingering illness, Medericus was called to join the Lord Whom he had served so well during life. This took place about the year 700.

PRAYER Lord, amid the things of this world, let us be wholeheartedly committed to heavenly things in imitation of the example of evangelical perfection You have given us in St. Medericus the Abbot. Amen.

ST. FIACRE, Hermit

August 30—*Patron of Gardeners and Cabdrivers*

ST. FIACRE was born in Ireland around the beginning of the 7th century and traveled to Europe in the wake of St. Columban. He was accorded a kind reception by St. Faro, Bishop of Meaux, France, who provided him with a plot of land for a hermitage, and the humble man of God began to lead the religious life he had led in Ireland.

Soon, the people of the surrounding regions began coming in droves to learn about the Christian Faith from this man of God. Seeing their plight far from their homes and without shelter, Fiacre had compassion on them and determined to help them. With the aid of another grant of land from St. Faro, the saintly hermit himself chopped down trees to build a hospice to shelter them and cleared the soil in order to grow corn and vegetables to feed them.

His dedication and self-sacrifice brought about the conversion of the whole surrounding district and he was held in high esteem for his work with the spade. After his holy death about 675, St. Fiacre's cult grew steadily and reached its height in the 17th century, a thousand years later, when his shrine was famous for miraculous cures.

The name Fiacre was given to the four-wheeled cab because when it first came into use (in Paris, 1640) its stand was close to the St. Fiacre Hotel so that it might take the pilgrims on the first stage of the journey to St. Fiacre's shrine.

PRAYER Lord God, You alone are holy and no one is good without You. Through the intercession of St. Fiacre help us to live in such a way that we may not be deprived of a share in Your glory. Amen.

ST. ARISTEDES, Lay Apologist

August 31

EARLY in the 4th century, the celebrated Church historian Eusebius of Caesarea stated: "Aristedes also, a faithful disciple of our religion, has left an *Apology of the Faith* dedicated to Hadrian (about 124). His writing has also been kept by many, even to the present time." This writing was lost from that time until 1899 when it was discovered and made available to modern Christians.

Aristedes introduces himself as an Athenian philosopher and then develops a thesis based on the idea of God, which is given as a criterion of the truth of the Christian religion. He urges the Emperor to cease persecuting Christians and to be converted to their teaching. Recent critics think this Emperor was not Hadrian but Antoninus Pius (about 140).

Though lacking in style and literary devices, this writing of St. Aristedes reveals a penetrating and steadfast intelligence and is founded on an exalted idea of God. Its author, like St. Justin, retained the status and garb of a philosopher even after his conversion, and also has a Sermon on St. Luke 23:43 to his credit. More importantly, he is listed among the ranks of the Saints by the Church.

PRAYER Lord God, You endowed St. Aristedes with heavenly doctrine. Through his help, may we faithfully keep that teaching and profess it in our conduct. Amen.

ST. GILES, Abbot

September 1—*Patron of Cripples*

ST. GILES is said to have been a 7th century Athenian of noble birth. His piety and learning made him so conspicuous and an object of such admiration in his own country that, dreading praise and longing for a hidden life, he left his home and sailed for France. At first he took up his abode in a wilderness near the mouth of the Rhone, afterward near the river Gard, and, finally, in the diocese of Nimes.

He spent many years in solitude, conversing only with God. The fame of his miracles became so great that his reputation spread throughout France. He was highly esteemed by the French King, but he could not be prevailed upon to forsake his solitude. He admitted several disciples, however, to share it with him, founded a monastery, and established an excellent discipline therein. In succeeding ages it embraced the rule of St. Benedict. St. Giles died probably in the beginning of the 8th century, about the year 724.

PRAYER Lord, amid the things of this world, let us be wholeheartedly committed to heavenly things in imitation of the example of evangelical perfection You have given us in St. Giles the Abbot. Amen.

ST. INGRID OF SWEDEN, Virgin

September 2

BORN in Kanninge, Sweden, in the 13th century, St. Ingrid lived under the spiritual direction of Peter of Dacia, a Dominican priest. She was the first Dominican nun in Sweden and in 1281 she founded the first Dominican cloister there, called St. Martin's in Kanninge. She died in 1282 surrounded by an aura of sanctity.

Miracles obtained through her intercession followed and led to a popular cult of this Saint. In 1405, a canonization process was begun and the Swedish Bishops introduced her cause at the Council of Constance. An inquest was held in

Sweden in 1416-1417 and the results were inconclusive. In 1497, the cause was reactivated and in 1507 her relics were solemnly translated, and a Mass and Office were composed—but formal canonization seems never to have occurred. During the Reformation, her cult came to an end and her convent and relics were destroyed.

PRAYER Lord God, You showered heavenly gifts on St. Ingrid the Virgin. Help us to imitate her virtues during our earthly life and enjoy eternal happiness with her in heaven. Amen.

ST. GREGORY THE GREAT,
Pope and Doctor of the Church
September 3—*Patron of Teachers*

ST. GREGORY, born at Rome about the year 540, was the son of Gordianus, a wealthy senator, who later renounced the world and became one of the seven deacons of Rome. After he had acquired the usual thorough education, Emperor Justin the Younger appointed him, in 574, Chief Magistrate of Rome, though he was only thirty-four years of age.

After the death of his father he built six monasteries in Sicily and founded a seventh in his own house in Rome, which became the Benedictine Monastery of St. Andrew. Here he himself assumed the monastic habit in 575, at the age of thirty-five.

After the death of Pelagius, St. Gregory was chosen Pope by the unanimous consent of priests and people. Now began those labors which have merited for him the title of Great. His zeal extended over the entire known world, he was in contact with all the Churches of Christendom and, in spite of his bodily sufferings and innumerable labors, he found time to compose a great number of works. Known above all for his magnificent contributions to the liturgy of the Mass and Office, he is one of the four great Doctors of the Latin Church. He died March 12, 604.

PRAYER God, You look upon Your people with compassion and rule them with love. Through the intercession of Pope St. Gregory, give wisdom to the leaders of Your Church.

ST. ROSALIA, Virgin

September 4—*Patroness of Palermo*

ST. ROSALIA, daughter of Sinibald, Lord of Roses and Quisquina, was a descendant of the great Charlemagne. She was born at Palermo in Sicily. In her youth, her heart turned from earthly vanities to God. She left her home and took up her abode in a cave, on the walls of which she wrote these words: "I, Rosalia, daughter of Sinibald, Lord of Roses, and Quisquina, have taken the resolution to live in this cave for the love of my Lord, Jesus Christ." She remained there entirely hidden from the world.

Rosalia practiced great mortifications and lived in constant communion with God. Afterward she transferred her abode to Mount Pellegrino, about three miles from Palermo, in order to triumph entirely over the instincts of flesh and blood, in sight of her paternal home. She is said to have appeared after death and to have revealed that she spent several years in a little excavation near the grotto. She died alone, in 1160, ending her strange and wonderful life unknown to the world. Her body was discovered in 1625, during the pontificate of Pope Urban VIII.

PRAYER Lord God, You showered heavenly gifts on St. Rosalia, Your Virgin. Help us to imitate her virtues during our earthly life and enjoy eternal happiness with her in heaven. Amen.

ST. BERTIN, Religious

September 5

ST. BERTIN was born about the beginning of the 7th century near Constance, France, and received his religious formation at the Abbey of Luxeuil, at that time the model abbey for the rather strict Rule of St. Columban. About 639, together with two other monks, he joined St. Omer, Bishop of Thérouanne, who had for two years been evangelizing the pagan Morini in the low-lying marshy country of the Pas-de-Calais.

In this almost totally idolatrous region, these holy missionary monks founded a monastery which came to be called St. Mommolin after its first Abbot. After eight more arduous years of preaching the Faith for Christ, they founded a second monastery at Sithiu dedicated to St. Peter. St. Bertin ruled it for nearly sixty years and made it famous; accordingly, after his death it was called St. Bertin and gave birth to the town of St. Omer.

St. Bertin practiced the greatest austerities and was in constant communion with God. He also traveled much and trained disciples who went forth to preach the Faith to others. Among others, he selected St. Winnoc to found a monastery at Wormhoudt, near Dunkirk, and this Saint figures in many medieval English calendars. At an age past 100, this zealous preacher of Christ died, surrounded by his monks.

PRAYER God, You built up Your Church by means of the religious zeal and apostolic care of St. Bertin. Grant by his intercession that she may ever experience a new increase of Faith and holiness. Amen.

BLESSED BERTRAND OF GARRIGUES,
Priest
September 6

BORN at Garrigues in the Comtat Venaissin, France, in the latter part of the 12th century, Blessed Bertrand was educated by the Cistercian nuns and learned by first-hand experience of the dangers posed by the Albigensian heresy flourishing at the time. Accordingly, he became a priest and joined a Cistercian group that was laboring zealously in the Midi to counteract the evil effected by the heretics.

However, in 1208, the Cistercian legate was assassinated and the crusade of Simon de Montfort was let loose, leaving Bertrand without a peaceful means by which to keep combating the heresy. Shortly afterward, he met St. Dominic who was doing this very thing—combating the heresy by prayer, fasting and preaching. In 1215, Bertrand was one of six preachers who formed the nucleus for the Order of Preachers begun by St. Dominic, and became one of his close companions.

Appointed Prior Provincial of Provence, one of the eight provinces of the Dominican Order, he spent the last nine years of his active life preaching the Faith throughout southern France, and founded the great Priory of Marseille. After his death, it was written that by his watchings, fasting, and other penances, he succeeded in imitating his beloved Father so closely as to invite the words: "The disciple is like the master; there goes the image of St. Dominic!"

PRAYER Almighty, eternal God, You dedicated the joy of this day to the glorification of Blessed Bertrand. Mercifully grant that we may always strive to retain and complete by our works that Faith which he continually proclaimed. Amen.

ST. REGINA, Virgin and Martyr

September 7

THE LIFE of this Saint is shrouded in obscurity; all that we know about her is found in the Acts of her martyrdom which are considered rather unreliable in their details. She was born in the 3rd century in Alise, the ancient Alesia where two hundred years earlier Vercingetorix had fought so valiantly against Caesar. Her mother died at her birth, and her father, a prominent pagan citizen, entrusted the child to a Christian nurse who baptized her.

When he learned of this fact, the father flew into a rage and repudiated his own daughter. Regina then went to live with her nurse who possessed little means. The girl helped out by tending sheep, where she communed with God in prayer and meditated on the lives of the Saints.

In 251, at the age of fifteen, she attracted the eye of a man called Olybrius, the prefect of Gaul, who determined to have her as his wife. He sent for the girl and discovered that she was of noble race and of the Christian Faith. Chagrined, he attempted to have her deny her Faith, but the saintly maiden resolutely refused and also spurned his proposal of marriage. Thereupon, Olybrius had her thrown into prison.

Regina remained incarcerated, chained to the wall, while Olybrius went to ward off the incursions of the barbarians. On his return, he found the Saint even more determined to preserve her vow of virginity and to refuse to sacrifice to idols. In a rage, he had recourse to whippings, scorchings, burning pincers, and iron combs—all to no avail as the grace of God sustained the Saint. She continued to praise God and defy Olybrius. In the end, her throat was severed and she went forth to meet her heavenly Bridegroom.

PRAYER Lord God, You showered heavenly gifts on St. Regina. Help us to imitate her virtues during our earthly life and enjoy eternal happiness with her in heaven. Amen.

BIRTH OF MARY

September 8

MORE than nineteen hundred years ago there dwelt in the little Galilean village of Nazareth a holy couple of the royal race of David, whose names were Joachim and Ann. They were already far advanced in years, and had almost ceased to hope that God would bless them with a child, when the long-felt desire of their hearts was gratified by the birth of a daughter, who would be forever blessed among women and make the names of Joachim and Ann known and honored through all future ages. This child was called Mary, the chosen one of Adam's race, destined to be the Mother of Jesus Christ, Who became her Child, to redeem and save the world.

The Feast of September 8 in honor of the Blessed Virgin Mary originated at Jerusalem, as did the Solemnity of August 15. It is a case of the Feast of the basilica known at the end of the 5th century as the basilica "of holy Mary where she was born," and now known as the basilica of St. Ann.

On this feast the Church unites in spirit with the Patriarchs and Prophets of the Old Law, with all who during long centuries of expectation watched and prayed for the coming of the Just One, Whose advent and work of redemption had their beginning in the birth of His Immaculate Mother.

PRAYER God, give Your servants heavenly grace, so that as the Birth of the Blessed Virgin marked the beginning of salvation, this feast of her Nativity may serve to obtain peace for the world. Amen.

ST. PETER CLAVER, Priest

September 9—*Patron of the Black Missions*

ST. PETER CLAVER was born at Verdu, Catalonia, Spain, in 1580, of impoverished parents descended from ancient and distinguished families. He studied at the Jesuit College of Barcelona, entered the Jesuit novitiate at Tarragona in 1602 and took his final vows on August 8, 1604. While studying philosophy at Majorca, the young religious was influenced by St.

Alphonsus Rodriguez to go to the Indies and save "millions of those perishing souls."

In 1610, he landed at Cartagena (modern Colombia), the principal slave market of the New World, where a thousand slaves were brought every month. After his ordination in 1616, he dedicated himself to the service of the Black slaves—a work that was to last for thirty-three years. He labored unceasingly for the salvation of the slaves and the abolition of the slave trade, and the love he lavished on them was something that transcended the natural order.

Boarding the slave ships as they entered the harbor, he would hurry to the revolting inferno of the hold, and offer whatever poor refreshments he could afford; he would care for the sick and dying, and instruct the slaves through Black catechists, before administering the sacraments. Through his efforts three hundred thousand souls entered the Church. Furthermore, he did not lose sight of his converts when they left the ships, but followed them to the plantations to which they were sent, encouraged them to live as Christians, and prevailed on their masters to treat them humanely. He died in 1654 and was canonized in 1888 by Pope Leo XIII.

PRAYER God, You conferred on St. Peter Claver a remarkable love and patience to help Your enslaved people and bring them to a knowledge of Your Name. Through his intercession, help us to seek equality for all races. Amen.

ST. NICHOLAS OF TOLENTINE, Priest

September 10—*Patron of Mariners*

BORN at St. Angelo, a town near Fermo in Italy, in the year 1245, St. Nicholas was blessed by innocence and the practice of more than ordinary virtue from his early infancy. While he was still a young student, his extraordinary merit caused him to be appointed to a canonry in the Church of Our Savior, a position that was extremely pleasing to him, as it gave him the opportunity of being constantly employed in God's service. A sermon preached by an Augustinian friar, on the vanity of the world, persuaded him to enter religion. This was not a passing emotion, but a firm resolution, which he executed by entering the Augustinian Order at Tolentine, a small town in the Papal States.

From this town, where he spent the greater part of his life, he obtained his surname. He made his profession before he had completed his eighteenth year. Then he began to run the giant race of sanctity, in which he soon excelled, distinguishing himself especially by the virtues of humility and meekness. He was sent successively to several convents of his Order, and in that of Cingole he was ordained priest at the hands of the Bishop of Osimo. From that time he was employed in the works of the ministry, preaching, and hearing confessions.

The last thirty years of his life he spent at Tolentine. His zeal for the salvation of souls produced the most wonderful fruit. God favored the Saint with many heavenly gifts, and the time he could spare from his labors he spent in prayer and contemplation. He had also much to suffer from various painful diseases. He died happily on September 10, 1306, and was canonized in 1446 by Pope Eugenius IV.

PRAYER Almighty, eternal God, You dedicated the joy of this day to the glorification of St. Nicholas. Mercifully grant that we may always strive to retain and complete by our works that Faith which he continually proclaimed with unwearying zeal. Amen.

ST. ADELPHUS, Bishop

September 11

ST. ADELPHUS, Bishop of Metz, lived during the 5th century. According to a *Life* which appeared in the 9th century and is generally regarded to be apocryphal and legendary, he was born of a noble Burgundian family. A little while before his birth, an angel appeared in a dream to his mother Beatrice and greeted her with the words: "Hall, beloved of God." He then continued: "Rejoice, because you will conceive and bring forth a new Paul, the Bishop Adelphus."

The *Life* then continues, narrating the birth of Adelphus, his youth, and finally the fulfillment of the prophecy with his election as Bishop. He was the tenth Bishop of Metz.

PRAYER God, You made St. Adelphus an outstanding exemplar of Divine love and the Faith that conquers the world, and added him to the role of saintly Pastors. Grant by his intercession that we may become sharers of his glory. Amen.

BLESSED APOLLINARIS AND COMPANIONS, Martyrs

September 12

BETWEEN 1617 and 1632 a fierce anti-Christian persecution raged in Japan which produced two hundred and five martyrs for the

Christian Faith. In this number were eighteen First Order Franciscans and twenty-seven Third Order Franciscans.

The leader of the Franciscan martyrs was Apollinaris Franco, the Commissary Provincial of the Order of Japan. Defying an imperial decree condemning to death all who proclaimed themselves as Christians, Apollinaris upon landing in Japan openly announced himself as a disciple of Christ. He was soon cast into Omura prison where he spent five years catechizing and baptizing his fellow prisoners. On September 12, 1622, he and several other Franciscans were burned alive. They were beatified in 1867 by Pope Pius IX.

PRAYER Lord, we devoutly recall the sufferings of Blessed Apollinaris and his companions. Give success to our joyful prayers and grant us also constancy in our Faith. Amen.

ST. JOHN CHRYSOSTOM, Bishop and Doctor of the Church

September 13—*Patron of Sacred Orators*

SAINT JOHN, named Chrysostom (golden-mouthed) on account of his eloquence, came into the world of Christian parents, about the year 344, in the city of Antioch. His mother, a widow at the age of twenty, was a model of virtue. He studied rhetoric under Libanius, a pagan, the most famous orator of the age.

In 374, he began to lead the life of an anchorite in the mountains near Antioch, but in 386 the poor state of his health forced him to return to Antioch, where he was ordained priest.

In 398, he was elevated to the See of Constantinople and became one of the greatest lights of the Church. But he had enemies in high places and some were ecclesiastics, not the least being Theophilus, Patriarch of Alexandria, who repented of this before he died. His most powerful enemy, however, was the Empress Eudoxia, who was offended by the apostolic freedom of his discourses. Several accusations were brought against him in a pseudo-council, and he was sent into exile.

In the midst of his sufferings, like the Apostle St. Paul whom he so greatly admired, he found the greatest peace and happiness. He had the consolation of knowing that the Pope remained his friend, and did for him what lay in his power. His enemies were not satisfied with the sufferings he had already endured, and they banished him still further, to Pythius, at the very extremity of the Empire. He died on his way there on September 14, 407.

PRAYER God, You are the strength of those who hope in You. You gave Your Church St. John Chrysostom, Your Bishop, who was endowed with great eloquence and was able to withstand great sufferings. Let us learn from his teaching and be inspired by the example of his patience. Amen.

TRIUMPH OF THE CROSS

September 14

WHEN the Sacred Body of Jesus was taken down from the Cross and carried to the grave on Calvary, the Cross on which He died was thrown into a ditch or well, and covered over with stones and earth, so that the followers of the Crucified Redeemer might not find it. Almost three hundred years later (312 A.D.), Constantine the Great, not yet a Christian, while battling with Maxentius for the throne of the Roman Empire, prayed to the God of the Christians to aid him in his struggle.

In answer to his prayer, a luminous cross or monogram of Christ appeared in the heavens bearing the inscription: "In This Sign You Will Conquer." In gratitude for victory, under this banner, over Maxentius at the Milvian Bridge, on October 28, 312, Constantine had the Sign of Christianity placed on the Roman standards and on the shields of his soldiers. Then came the finding of the True Cross at Jerusalem by St. Helena in 326, commemorated by a feast on May 3.

In the year 614, Chosroes II, King of Persia, invaded Syria and Palestine; he took and sacked Jerusalem, carrying off with other treasures the great relic of the True Cross. The Emperor Heraclius of Constantinople, at the head of a large army, invaded Persia, and forced the Persians to sue for peace and to restore the Sacred Cross, which Heraclius piously brought back to Jerusalem in 629. When he reached the city gate on the way that led to Calvary, the Emperor laid aside every robe and mark of royalty, and, clothed in sackcloth of penance and barefoot, carried the Cross up the ascent of Calvary and restored it to its place in the Church of the Holy Sepulcher. This event is commemorated by the Church on September 14 in the feast of the Triumph of the Holy Cross.

PRAYER God, You willed that Your only Son should undergo crucifixion to bring about the salvation of the human race. Grant that we who have known His mystery on earth may deserve to reap the rewards of redemption in heaven. Amen.

OUR LADY OF SORROWS

September 15

THE object of this feast is to remind the faithful of the spiritual martyrdom of the Mother of God, and her compassion with the sufferings of her Divine Son. The seven great events of sorrow in her life were: Prophecy of Simeon, Flight into Egypt, Three Days' Loss of Jesus, Meeting Jesus on the Way to Calvary, Mary at the Foot of the Cross, Jesus Taken Down from the Cross, and the Burial of Jesus.

There was between Jesus and His Mother all that union and interchange of kinship and tender love which exists between a fond mother and her child. Added to this was the intense love with which she loved Him as her God, so that we may truly say there never could be a love between a human soul and God greater than the love between Jesus and Mary.

To what shall we compare, to what shall we liken, the sorrows and sufferings of this Virgin daughter of Zion? Truly, her heart was filled with the reproaches and the revilings of those who upbraided, scoffed at, and blasphemed her Son as she stood beneath His Cross of shame. "Come, all who pass by the way, look and see whether there is any suffering like my suffering" (Lamentations 1:12).

PRAYER God, You willed that the compassionate Mother of Your Son should stand near the Cross on which He was glorified. Grant that Your Church, having shared in Christ's Passion, may also participate in His Resurrection. Amen.

STS. CORNELIUS, Pope, **AND CYPRIAN,** Bishop, Martyrs

September 16

ST. CORNELIUS had scarcely been elected Pope, when Novatian also claimed the Papacy. After convoking a synod in Italy, in which he gained the support of sixty Bishops, he established himself as the lawful Pope. His correspondence with St. Cyprian in regard to reception of apostates in the Decian persecution remains as an early witness for the primacy of the Roman See. He died a martyr, in 253.

Thascius Cyprianus was born at Carthage in Africa, where his father was one of the principal senators. His proficiency in study was such that he became public professor of rhetoric in his native city. After a rather dissolute life, he was converted through the influence of a priest named Caecilian, and was formed at his school. He led a retired penitential life, gaining renown for his virtue and being raised to the priesthood. In 248, he was appointed to succeed Donatus as Bishop of Carthage and became a model pastor.

In a short span of ten years he led his flock through a two-year persecution under Decius, defended the unity of the Church against two schismatical movements, was the soul of the city's morale during a devastating plague, and experienced exile during which he kept up the spirits of his people by constant correspondence. In 258, this saintly man fell victim to a new persecution that erupted under Valerian.

PRAYER *God, You gave Your people Sts. Cornelius and Cyprian as zealous Priests and courageous Martyrs. Through their intercession, let us be strengthened in faith and persistence so that we may work strenuously for the unity of the Church. Amen.*

ST. ROBERT BELLARMINE

Bishop and Doctor of the Church

Sept. 17

Patron of Canonists

BORN at Montepulciano, Italy, on October 4, 1542, St. Robert Bellarmine was the third of ten children. His mother, Cinzia Cervini, a niece of Pope Marcellus II, was dedicated to almsgiving, prayer, meditation, fasting, and mortification of the body.

Robert entered the newly formed Society of Jesus in 1560 and after his ordination went on to teach at Louvain (1570-1576) where he became famous for his Latin sermons. In 1576, the Saint was appointed to the chair of controversial theology at the Roman College, becoming Rector in 1592; he went on to become Provincial of Naples in 1594 and Cardinal in 1598.

This outstanding scholar and devoted servant of God defended the Apostolic See against the anti-clericals in Venice and against the political tenets of James I of England. He composed an exhaustive apologetic work against the prevailing heresies of his day. In the field of church-state relations, he took a position based on principles now regarded as fundamentally democratic—authority originates with God, but is vested in the people, who entrust it to fit rulers.

This Saint was the spiritual father of St. Aloysius Gonzaga, helped St. Francis de Sales obtain formal approval of the Visitation Order, and in his prudence opposed severe action in the case of Galileo. He has left many important writings, including works of devotion and instruction, as well as controversy. He died in 1621.

PRAYER God, in order to vindicate Your Faith You endowed St. Robert, Your Bishop, with wondrous erudition and virtues. Through his intercession, grant that Your people may ever rejoice in the integrity of his Faith. Amen.

ST. JOSEPH OF CUPERTINO, Priest

September 18—*Patron of Aviators*

ST. JOSEPH was born at Cupertino, in the diocese of Nardo in the Kingdom of Naples, in

1603. After spending his childhood and adolescence in simplicity and innocence, he finally joined the Franciscan Friars Minor Conventual. After his ordination to the holy priesthood he gave himself up entirely to a life of humiliation, mortification, and obedience. He was most devoted to the Blessed Virgin Mary and promoted devotion to her among all classes of people.

It is said that the life of this Saint was marked by ecstasies and levitations. The mere mention of God or a spiritual matter was enough to take him out of his senses; at Mass he frequently floated in the air in rapture. Once as Christmas carols were being sung he soared to the high altar and knelt in the air, rapt in prayer.

The people flocked to him in droves seeking help and advice in the confessional, and he converted many to a truly Christian life. However, this humble man had to endure many severe trials and terrible temptations throughout his life. He died on September 18, 1663, and was canonized in 1767 by Pope Clement XIII.

PRAYER God, You willed that Your only-begotten Son should draw all things to Himself when He was lifted up above the earth. May the merits and example of St. Joseph, Your Priest, help us to rise above all earthly desires so that we may come to Jesus. Amen.

ST. JANUARIUS (GENNARO),

Bishop and Martyr

September 19—*Patron of Naples*

ST. JANUARIUS, born about 275, was Bishop of Benevento when the persecution of Diocletian broke out. Sosius, deacon of Misenum; Proculus, deacon of Puzzuoli; Euthyches and Acutius, eminent laymen, were imprisoned for the Faith at Puzzuoli, by order of Dracontius, Governor of Campania. St. Januarius, who was a special friend of Sosius, hearing of this, determined to pay the confessors a visit, in order to encourage them.

The keepers, being aroused to suspicion, gave information that an eminent person from Benevento had visited the prisoners. Timothy, who had succeeded Dracontius, gave orders that St. Januarius should be brought before him at Nola, the usual place of his residence. Festus, his deacon, and Desiderius, a lector of his church, were also apprehended and they shared in his sufferings.

Some time after, when the Governor went to Puzzuoli, the three confessors, loaded with irons, were made to walk before his chariot to that town, where they were thrown into the same prison in which the four other martyrs were detained. They had been condemned, by an order of the Emperor, to be torn to pieces by wild beasts. The day after the arrival of St. Januarius, they were all exposed in the amphitheater, but none of the animals touched them. The people imputed this to magic and the martyrs were condemned to be beheaded. The sentence was executed near Puzzuoli, about 305. The relics of St. Januarius were later translated to Naples, of which city he became the patron.

St. Januarius has become famous for the liquefaction of his blood, a dark solid mass in a sealed vial, which becomes liquid when held near a relic, believed to be his head. This usually happens on September 19, the first Sunday of May (the day of the transferal of his relics to Naples), and on December 16 (the anniversary of Naples' deliverance from Vesuvius through the intercession of St. Januarius). Scientists have for a long time been seeking a natural explanation for this well-attested phenomenon but have never done so.

PRAYER God, You enable us to venerate the memorial of Your Martyr, St. Januarius. Grant that we may also enjoy his company in eternal beatitude. Amen.

STS. ANDREW KIM TAEGON,
Priest and Martyr,
PAUL CHONG HASANG, and COMPANIONS,
Martyrs
September 20

THE evangelization of Korea began during the 17th century through a group of lay persons. A strong vital Christian community flourished there under lay leadership until missionaries arrived from the Paris Foreign Mission Society.

During the terrible persecutions that occurred in the 19th century (in 1839, 1866, and 1867), one hundred and three members of the Christian community gave their lives as martyrs. Outstanding among these witnesses to the Faith were the first Korean priest and pastor, Andrew Kim Taegon, and the lay apostle, Paul Chong Hasang.

Among the other martyrs were a few bishops and priests, but for the most part lay people, men and women, married and unmarried, children, young people, and the elderly. All suffered greatly for the Faith and consecrated the rich beginnings of the Church of Korea with their blood as martyrs.

Pope St. John Paul II, during his trip to Korea, canonized these martyrs on May 6, 1984, and inserted their feast into the Calendar of the Universal Church.

PRAYER O God, You have created all nations and You are their salvation. In Korea You called a people of adoption to the Catholic Faith and nurtured their growth by the blood of Andrew, Paul, and their Companions. Grant us strength through their martyrdom and their intercession so that we too may remain faithful to Your commandments even until our death. Amen.

ST. MATTHEW, Apostle and Evangelist

September 21—*Patron of Bankers*

ST. MATTHEW, one of the twelve Apostles, is the author of the first Gospel. This has been the constant tradition of the Church and is confirmed by the Gospel itself. He was the son of Alpheus and was called to be an Apostle while sitting in the tax collector's place at Capernaum. Before his conversion he was a publican, i.e., a tax collector by profession. He is to be identified with the "Levi" of Mark and Luke.

His apostolic activity was at first restricted to the communities of Palestine. Nothing definite is known about his later life. There is a tradition that points to Ethiopia as his field of labor; other traditions make mention of Parthia and Persia. It is uncertain whether he died a natural death or received the crown of martyrdom.

St. Matthew's Gospel was written to fill a sorely-felt want for his fellow countrymen, both believers and unbelievers. For the former, it served as a token of his regard and as an encouragement in the trial to come, especially the danger of falling back to Judaism; for the latter, it was designed to convince them that the Messiah had come in the Person of Jesus, our Lord, in Whom all the promises of the Messianic Kingdom embracing all people had been fulfilled in a spiritual rather than in a carnal way: "My Kingdom is not of this world." His Gospel, then, answered the question put by the disciples of St. John the Baptist, "Are You He Who is to come, or shall we look for another?"

Writing for his countrymen of Palestine, St. Matthew composed his Gospel in his native Aramaic, the "Hebrew tongue" mentioned in the Gospel and the Acts of the Apostles. Soon afterward, about the time of the persecution of Herod Agrippa I in 42 A.D., he took his departure for other lands. Another tradition places the composition of his Gospel either between the time of this departure and the Council of Jerusalem, i.e., between 42 A.D. and 50 A.D., or even later. Definitely, however, the Gospel itself, depicting the Holy City with its altar and temple as still existing, and without any reference to the fulfillment of our Lord's prophecy, shows that it was written before the destruction of the city by the Romans (70 A.D.), and this internal evidence confirms the early traditions.

PRAYER God, You chose St. Matthew the Publican to become an Apostle. By following his example and benefiting by his prayers, may we always follow and abide by Your will. Amen.

ST. THOMAS OF VILLANOVA, Bishop

September 22—*Patron of Valencia*

ST. THOMAS was born in the Kingdom of Castile, Spain, in 1488, but he was called "of Villanova" after the town where he was educated. From his pious parents he learned that charity for the poor which distinguished his later life and which he practiced from his earliest childhood. After years of innocence and virtue, at the age of fifteen he was sent to the University of Alcalà, which had recently been founded by Cardinal Ximenez. The Cardinal gave him a place in the College of St. Ildefonso. After eleven years of edifying conduct, having obtained the degree of master of arts, he became professor of philosophy.

From Alcalà he moved to Salamanca, where he taught moral philosophy for two years. In 1518, he took the habit of the Augustinian Order in that city, about the same time that Luther was leaving it in Germany. After his novitiate he was ordained a priest in 1520 and began to devote himself to the work of the ministry. His zeal was such that he was soon known as "the Apostle of Spain." At the same time, he taught theology in the Augustinian College at Salamanca, allowing himself no relaxation in his Rule. After filling several honorable positions in his Order, he was prevailed upon to become Archbishop of Valencia in 1544.

In the episcopacy he lived as a poor man, giving an example worthy of the first ages, and enjoying the confidence of his brother Bishops. His health prevented him from assisting at the Council of Trent, at which he was represented by the Bishop of Huesca. Finally his life of self-denial drew to a close and he expired in 1555.

PRAYER God, You made St. Thomas an outstanding exemplar of Divine love and the Faith that conquers the world, and added him to the roll of saintly pastors. Grant by his intercession that we may persevere in Faith and love and become sharers of his glory. Amen.

ST. CONSTANTIUS

September 23

ACCORDING to St. Gregory the Great, St. Constantius, a layman, was sacristan of the famous Cathedral of St. Stephen at Ancona, Italy. In monastic garb, he attended to his duties with a great spirit of perfection which belied his slight stature. He was known as a wonder-worker, and one of his deeds consisted in keeping the lamps of the church lighted even with water or oil in them. Word of his holiness and extraordinary powers spread far and wide, prompting many to ask spiritual favors of him.

The character of the Saint is best illustrated by a story told about him. One day a rude fellow happened into the church and at the sight of the Saint on a ladder attending to the lamps refused to believe in his sanctity. Instead, he began to insult and ridicule the man of God, calling him a liar and a man full of pride; St. Constantius, hearing this tirade, ran to the man and embraced and kissed him in gratitude for having seen him as he was and telling him so. As St. Gregory remarked, he thus gave conclusive proof that he was as great in humility as in miracles.

PRAYER God, through the intercession of St. Constantius, grant that we may overcome all feelings of pride. May we always serve You with that humility which pleases You, through his merits and example. Amen.

ST. PACIFIC OF SAN SEVERINO, Priest

September 24

BORN in 1653, St. Pacific was orphaned when he was quite young and was raised by an uncle. At the age of seventeen he entered the Franciscan Order and after his ordination he was assigned to minister to the Apennine mountain villages of Italy. After a successful apostolate of some seven years, he was stricken with an incapacitating illness and resigned himself to thirty years as a semi-invalid. He transformed these years into an intense apostolate of prayer and became famous for his patience, austerity, and gift of prophecy.

PRAYER God, the giver of all gifts, You adorned St. Pacific with the virtue of unusual patience and with the love of solitude. Through his intercession, may we walk in his footsteps and obtain a like reward. Amen.

ST. FINBAR (BARRY), Bishop

September 25

FINBAR was born in the latter part of the 6th century to a lady of the Irish royal court and an artisan. At Baptism he was given the name Lochan but received the name Fionbarr ("Whitehead") from his educators, the monks of Kilmacahill, Kilkenny, on account of his light hair. He is reported to have visited St. David in Pembrokeshire in southern Wales and to have accompanied him to Rome. Pope St. Gregory is said to have wanted to make Finbar a Bishop but to have been deterred by a vision notifying him that God had reserved that honor to himself.

St. Finbar preached the Gospel throughout southern Ireland and founded a number of churches. He then went to live the life of a hermit on a small island in Gouganebarra. Later, he founded a monastery at Lough Eirc, marshland at the mouth of the Lee River, called Corcaghmer from which Cork is derived.

Soon candidates for the monastery began arriving in ever-increasing numbers and its school began to extend its influence over the whole of southern Ireland. Out of the desert arose the great city of Cork, and Finbar is regarded as its founder and first Bishop. He died about 633.

PRAYER God, You made St. Finbar an outstanding exemplar of Divine love and the Faith that conquers the world, and added him to the roll of saintly pastors. Grant by his intercession that we may persevere in Faith and love and become sharers of his glory. Amen.

BLESSED HERMAN THE CRIPPLE, Religious

***The Same Day*—September 25**

A hopeless cripple from his birth in 1013 at Althausen in Suabia, Herman was sent at the age of seven to the Monastery of Reichenau, on an island in Lake Constance. With the aid of gifted instructors, he was able to make use of the gifts of his fine mind and noble soul. He took monastic vows in 1043 and developed into a master of arithmetic, geometry, astronomy, history, poetry, and music. He produced the first medieval chronicle, a monument of erudition, and brilliantly-conceived fraction tables as well as some of the Church's finest hymns, for example, the *Alma Redemptoris Mater* ("Benign Mother of Our Redeeming Lord") and probably the *Salve Regina* ("Hail to the Queen"). He died in 1054.

PRAYER God, by Your help Blessed Herman strove to imitate the poor and humble Christ. Through his intercession grant that we may faithfully pursue our vocation and attain that perfection which You held out to us in Your Son. Amen.

STS. COSMAS AND DAMIAN, Martyrs

September 26—*Patrons of Druggists*

STS. COSMAS and DamIan were brothers, born in Arabia, who had become eminent for their skill in the science of medicine. Being Christians, they were filled with the spirit of charity and never took money for their services. At Egaea in Cilicia, where they lived, they enjoyed the highest esteem of the people.

When the persecution under Diocletian broke out, their very prominence rendered them marked objects of persecution. Being apprehended by order of Lysias, Governor of Cilicia, they underwent various torments and were finally beheaded about the year 283.

PRAYER Lord, may the devout memorial of Sts. Cosmas and Damian render praise to You. For in Your ineffable providence You conferred eternal glory on them and a duty on us. Amen.

ST. VINCENT DE PAUL, Priest

September 27

Patron of Charitable Societies

ST. VINCENT was born of poor parents in the Village of Pouy in Gascony, France, about 1580. He enjoyed his first schooling under the Franciscan Fathers at Acqs. Such had been his progress in four years that a gentleman chose him as a tutor for his children, and he was thus enabled to continue his studies without being a burden to his parents. In 1596, he went to the University of Toulouse for theological studies, and there he was ordained priest in 1600.

In 1605, on a voyage by sea from Marseilles to Narbonne, he fell into the hands of African pirates and was carried as a slave to Tunis. His captivity lasted about two years, until Divine Providence enabled him to effect his escape. After a brief visit to Rome he returned to France, where he became tutor in the family of Emmanuel de Gondy, Count of Joigny, and general of the galleys of France. In 1617, he began to preach missions, and in 1625 he laid the foundations of a congregation which afterward became the Congregation of the Mission, or Lazarists, so named on account of the Priory of St. Lazarus, which the Fathers began to occupy in 1633.

It would be impossible to enumerate all the works of this servant of God. Charity was his predominant virtue. It extended to all classes of persons, from forsaken childhood to old age. The Sisters of Charity also owe the foundation of their congregation to St. Vincent. In the midst of the most distracting occupations his soul was always intimately united with God. Though honored by the great ones of the world, he remained deeply rooted in humility. The Apostle of Charity, the immortal Vincent de Paul, breathed his last in Paris at the age of eighty, September 27, 1660. He was canonized in 1737 by Pope Clement XII.

PRAYER God, You gave St. Vincent de Paul apostolic virtues for the salvation of the poor and the formation of the clergy. Grant that, endowed with the same spirit, we may love what he loved and act according to his teaching. Amen.

STS. LAWRENCE RUIZ AND COMPANIONS,
Martyrs
September 28

FROM 1633 to 1637 sixteen martyrs shed their blood out of love for Christ in the city of Nagasaki, Japan. They included members and associates of the Order of Preachers: nine priests, two religious, two virgins, and three lay people, one of whom was Lawrence Ruiz, the father of a family from the Philippine Islands. All had, at different times and under varying circumstances, preached the Christian Faith in the Philippines, Formosa, and Japan. They manifested the universality of the Christian religion and sowed the seed of future missionaries and converts.

The list of these martyrs is as follows: Dominic Ibañez de Erquicia, priest; James Kyushei Gorobioye Tomonaga, priest; Luke Alonso, priest; Hyacinth Ansalone, priest; Thomas Hioji Rokuzayemon Nishi, priest; Anthony Gonzalez, priest; William Courtet, priest; Michael de Aozaraza, priest; Vincent Schiwozuka, priest; Francis Shoyemon, religious; Matthew Kohioye, religious; Madeline of Nagasaki, virgin; Marina of Omura, virgin; Lawrence Ruiz, husband and father; Michael Kurobioye, layman; and Lazarus of Kyoto, layman. They were canonized in 1987 by Pope St. John Paul II.

PRAYER Lord God, You are the strength of all the Saints. You called Sts. Lawrence Ruiz and Companions to eternal life through the cross. Grant us, through their intercession, perfect fidelity to keep the Faith until our death. Amen.

ST. WENCESLAUS, Martyr

The Same Day*, September 28—*Patron of Bohemia

THE father of St. Wenceslaus, Vratistlas, Duke of Bohemia, was a Christian; but his mother Drahomira, a pagan, was a wicked and cruel woman. Fortunately for St. Wenceslaus, he was educated under the care of his saintly grandmother, St. Ludmilla, with whose efforts he fully corresponded. At Budweis, about sixty miles from Prague, he went to a college where he made great progress in learning. His father died while he was still young, and Drahomira, assuming the title of Regent, gave vent to her hatred of Christianity by a cruel persecution.

At the advice of his grandmother, St. Wenceslaus finally took the government into his own hands; but to prevent disputes between him and his brother, Boleslaus, the people divided the territory between them, giving to Boleslaus a considerable share. The latter, who had been under the influence of his mother, had acquired her hatred of the Christian religion. The pious St. Wenceslaus led the life of a Saint in the midst of his court, distinguishing himself by his devotion to the Blessed Sacrament.

His piety and his severity against the oppressions of the nobility caused some to join the faction of his mother. Being treacherously invited to the court of Boleslaus after the festivities, he went at midnight to pray in the church. The assassins found him there and the mortal blow was given him by his own brother, Boleslaus. His death occurred in 929.

PRAYER God, You taught St. Wenceslaus to prize the Kingdom of heaven more than his earthly reign. Grant, through his prayers, that we may deny ourselves and cling to You with our whole heart. Amen.

STS. MICHAEL, GABRIEL, RAPHAEL,
Archangels

September 29—*(St. Michael) Patron of Policemen (St. Gabriel) Patron of Communications Workers (St. Raphael) Patron of Travelers*

ANGELS are spirits without bodies, who possess superior intelligence, gigantic strength, and surpassing holiness. They enjoy an intimate relationship to God as His special adopted children, contemplating, loving, and praising Him in heaven. Some of them are frequently sent as messengers to men from on high.

This feast celebrates three Angels who were sent by God to man over the course of the ages: Michael, Gabriel, and Raphael. They are termed Archangels, the second of nine choirs of Angels, which are in descending order: Seraphim, Cherubim, Thrones, Dominations, Virtues, Powers, Principalities, Archangels, and Angels.

The name MICHAEL signifies "Who is like to God?" and was the war cry of the good Angels in the battle fought in heaven against Satan and his followers. Holy Scripture describes St. Michael as "one of the chief princes," and as leader of the forces of heaven in their triumph over the powers of hell. He has been especially honored and invoked as patron and protector by the Church from the time of the Apostles. Although he is always called "the Archangel," the Greek Fathers and many others place him over all the Angels—as Prince of the Seraphim.

The name GABRIEL means "man of God," or "God has shown Himself mighty." It appears first in the prophecies of Daniel in the Old Testament. This Angel announced to Daniel the prophecy of the seventy weeks (Daniel 9:21-27). His name also occurs in the apocryphal book of Henoch. He was the Angel who appeared to Zechariah to announce the birth of St. John the Baptizer (Luke 1:11). Finally, he announced to Mary that she would bear a Son Who would be conceived of the Holy Spirit, Son of the Most High, and the Savior of the world (Luke 1:26).

The name RAPHAEL means "God has healed." This Angel first appears in Holy Scripture in the Book of Tobit. He acts as a guide to young Tobiah on his journey to Rages, a city in the country of the Medes, east of Nineveh, to collect a debt owed to his father. The Angel binds the demon Asmodeus in the desert of Egypt, helps Tobiah to find a wife and recover the debt, and heals Tobit from his blindness. He then reveals his identity: "I am the Angel Raphael, one of the seven who stand before the throne of God."

PRAYER God, with great wisdom You direct the ministry of Angels and men. Grant that those who always minister to You in heaven may defend us during our life on earth. Amen.

ST. JEROME, Priest and Doctor of the Church

September 30

Patron of Librarians

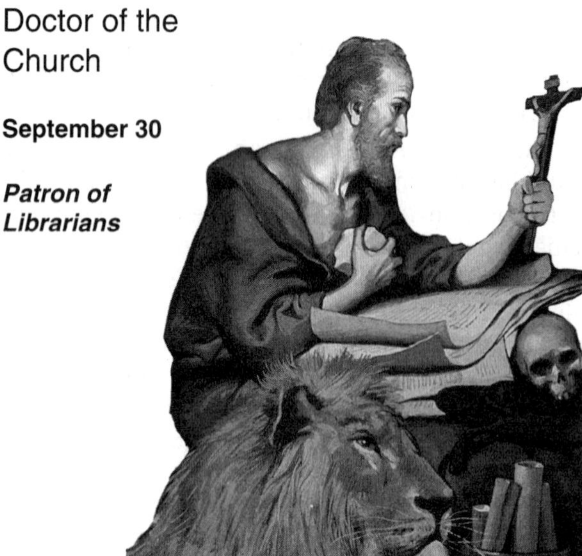

STRIDONIUM, a small town on the border of Dalmatia, was the place where St. Jerome first beheld the light. In Rome he studied Latin and Greek, devoted himself to oratory, and finally pleaded at the bar. For a time he gave himself up to the world, but his piety returned to him after he began to travel. Having made a tour of Gaul, he went again to Rome, where he received Baptism, which at that time was frequently deferred until a mature age. Whether this sacrament was administered before or after his journey to Gaul is not certain. From Rome, he journeyed to the East, and visited the Anchorites and other persons of sanctity. After sojourning a while at Antioch, he took up his abode in the desert of Chalcis in Syria, with the holy Abbot Theodosius. Here he spent four years of prayer and study; and here, temptations in the form of recollections of the past assailed him. To distract his mind from these he began the study of Hebrew.

At Antioch he received Holy Orders about the year 377, under the stipulation that he should not be obliged to serve in the ministry. After traveling in Palestine, he visited Constantinople, where St. Gregory Nazianzen was then Bishop. Again returning to Palestine, he departed for Rome, where he filled for some time the office of secretary to Pope St. Damasus.

After the death of St. Damasus, he returned to the East, in 385. On his way he visited St. Epiphanius at Cyprus, and arrived at Jerusalem in the winter, leaving soon after for Alexandria to improve himself in sacred learning. Returning to Palestine, he retired to Bethlehem. His wanderings were now at an end, and his solitary life at Bethlehem began that career of study which has immortalized him.

His scriptural works, above all, have been unparalleled in the history of the Church. Besides this branch of sacred learning, he attacked, like the other Fathers of that age, the various errors of his day. The fame of St. Jerome spread far and wide, and people came to consult him from all sides. He also governed and directed the monastery of nuns founded by St. Paula. Finally, after a long life of prayer, penance, and labor, St. Jerome died at Bethlehem in 420.

PRAYER God, You gave St. Jerome a great love for Holy Scripture. Let Your people feed more abundantly on Your word and find in it the source of life. Amen.

ST. THERESA OF THE CHILD JESUS,

Virgin and Doctor of the Church

October 1

Patroness of the Missions

BORN at Alençon in Normandy, France in 1873, Marie Frances Theresa Martin entered the Carmel of Lisieux in 1889, at the age of fifteen years, and on September 30, 1897, she winged her flight to heaven. She was canonized in 1925

by Pope Pius XI, and made the third woman Doctor of the Church by Pope St. John Paul II.

The story of those nine years is faithfully told in the *Autobiography* which she wrote under obedience. Every line is marked by the artless simplicity of a literary genius, so that even when translated from its musical euphonious French into mechanical, clanking English, it still reads with the rhythm of a prose poem.

She took for her motto the well-known words of the great Carmelite mystic St. John of the Cross: "Love is repaid by love alone." With these thoughts ever present in her mind, her heart found courage to endure hours and days of bitterness that few Saints have been privileged to undergo. She understood deeply the meaning of those mysterious words of St. Paul: "Far be it from me to glory save in the Cross of my Lord Jesus Christ, by which I am crucified to the world and the world is crucified to me. I fill up those things that are wanting in the sufferings of Christ for His members."

Love of God as a Father, expressed in childlike simplicity and trust, and a deep understanding of the mystery of the Cross were the basic principles of her "little way."

There is just one other doctrine that needs to be mentioned to complete the picture of her soul's surrender—her vivid realization of the spiritual Motherhood of Mary, the Mother of God, and heaven's Queen, and our own loving

Mother. She had learned the meaning of the strong phrase of St. Augustine, written fifteen hundred years ago, that we were all begotten with Jesus in the womb of Mary as our Mother.

The Little Flower is a faithful inheritor of all the loving tradition of the greatest Saints and Doctors of the Church in honoring Mary Immaculate. It is doubtful if that harpist of Mary, St. Bernard, could compose anything more beautiful, tender, and theological than the very last poem St. Theresa wrote, entitled, *Why I Love You, Mary* and written almost when the agony of death was upon her. In it she sings:

"O you who came to smile on me
At the dawn of life's beginning,
Come once again to smile on me . . . Mother!
The night is nigh.
I fear no more your majesty,
So far removed above me,
For I have suffered much with you;
Now hear me, Mother mild!
Oh let me tell you, face to face,
Dear Mary, how I love you;
And say to you forevermore:
I am your little child."

PRAYER God our Father, You destined Your Kingdom for Your children who are humble. Help us to imitate the way of St. Theresa, so that, by her intercession, we may attain the eternal glory which You promised. Amen.

THE GUARDIAN ANGELS

October 2

THE Angels are pure spirits endowed with a natural intelligence, will power, and beauty far surpassing the nature, faculties, and powers of man. They offer continuous praise to God and serve Him as messengers and ministers, and as guardians of men on earth. They are divided into three hierarchies: Seraphim, Cherubim, and Thrones; Dominations, Principalities, and Powers; Virtues, Archangels, and Angels.

Those blessed spirits who are appointed by God to be protectors and defenders of men are called Guardian Angels. Faith teaches us that each individual has a Guardian Angel who watches over him during the whole course of his life. It is also a generally accepted teaching that communities, the Church, dioceses, and nations also have their tutelary Angels.

The Guardian Angels defend those of whom they have charge against the assaults of the demons, endeavoring to preserve them from all evils of soul or body, particularly from sin and the occasions of sin. They strive to keep us in the right path: if we fall they help us to rise again, encourage us to become more and more virtuous, suggest good thoughts and holy desires, offer our prayers and good actions to God, and, above all, assist us at the hour of death.

PRAYER God, in Your Providence, You saw fit to send Your Angels to watch over us. Grant that we may always be under their protection and one day enjoy their company in heaven. Amen.

ST. GERARD OF BROGNE, Abbot

October 3

A nobleman by his birth which occurred about 895, Gerard was brought up in a military atmosphere and assigned to the household of Berengarius, the ruling Count of Namur, Belgium. However, amid the countless privileges, pleasures, and pursuits of his noble way of life, Gerard felt called to the religious life—but not in the lax monasteries of his milieu. While on an important mission on behalf of his sovereign to the court of France in 918 he caught a glimpse of the life led by monks of St. Denis and was greatly attracted to it. After settling all his temporal affairs, he returned to the monastery and became a member with wholehearted joy.

In time, St. Gerard was ordained, though only after wrestling with his sense of total inadequacy, and he helped reform the monastery. After eleven years he was sent by his Abbot to found a monastery on his estate at Brogne, so that his countrymen who desired to be monks might have a place to go to. As its Abbot, Gerard formed a well-nigh model monastery, and its fame spread far and wide. Duke Gislebert of Lorraine saw his work and commissioned him to reform the Abbey of St. Ghislain near Mons, where the holy monk established the Rule of St. Benedict. And herein he discovered his true vocation.

Over the course of the next twenty years, St. Gerard labored zealously in this work, restoring Benedictine rule and discipline in some eighteen monasteries, as far as Flanders, Lorraine, and Champagne. Finally, advanced in age and slowed down by his extensive labors for God, he retired to Brogne and passed his last few years in solitude and prayer, before being born to his heavenly life on October 3, 959.

PRAYER Lord, amid the things of this world, let us be wholeheartedly committed to heavenly things in imitation of the example of evangelical perfection which You have given us in St. Gerard the Abbot. Amen.

ST. FRANCIS OF ASSISI

October 4—*Patron of Catholic Action*

FRANCIS BERNARDONE, the founder of the three Franciscan Orders, was born at Assisi, Italy in 1181. His father was a wealthy merchant of the town. During a year's imprisonment at Perugia due to his participation as a knight in an unsuccessful campaign against that town, and again during a prolonged severe illness, Francis

became aware of a vocation to a life of extraordinary service to the Church of Christ.

Inspired at the age of twenty-five by the Scripture passage of Matthew commanding the disciples to evangelize the world without possessions, Francis abandoned his affluent way of life and began to live a life of radical poverty. Disinherited by his father, Francis went away penniless "to wed Lady Poverty" and to live a life that was poorer than the poor whom he served. His example soon drew followers to his way of life.

Three years later, in 1210, when his companions numbered twelve, he sought and received approval of Pope Innocent III to lead a life according to the Rule of the Holy Gospel, and they became a band of roving preachers of Christ in simplicity and lowliness. Thus began the "Friars Minor," or "Lesser Brothers." Up and down the extent of Italy the brothers summoned the people to faith and penitence; they refused even corporate ownership of property, human learning, and ecclesiastical preferment. St. Francis himself never became a priest out of humility, and at first only some of his band were in Holy Orders.

Francis' practice of evangelical poverty and devotion to the humanity of Christ warmed the hearts of a "world growing cold" and soon a vast Franciscan movement was sweeping through Europe. By 1219, over five thousand Franciscans gathered at Assisi for the famed Chapter of Mats. To accommodate this religious revival, Francis founded a Second Order through St. Clare of Assisi for cloistered nuns and a Third Order for religious and laity of both sexes.

Francis' devotion to the Passion of Christ prompted him to make a missionary journey to the Holy Land. Worn out by his tremendous apostolic efforts, pained by the stigmata he had received in 1224, and blinded by eye disease, Francis died at sunset, October 3, 1226, while singing the eighth verse of Psalm 142: "Lead me forth from prison that I may give thanks to Your Name." He was canonized two years later by Pope Gregory IX.

Francis of Assisi has captured the heart and imagination of men of all religious persuasions by his love for God and man, as well as all God's creatures, by his simplicity, directness, and single-mindedness, and by the lyrical aspects of his multifaceted life. However, he was far more than an inspired individualist. He was a man possessed of vast spiritual insight and power; a man whose all-consuming love for Christ and redeemed creation burst forth in everything he said and did.

PRAYER God, You enabled St. Francis to imitate Christ by his poverty and humility. Walking in St. Francis' footsteps, may we follow Your Son and be bound to You by a joyful love. Amen.

ST. FLORA, Virgin

October 5

BORN in France about the year 1309, St. Flora was a very devout child and later resisted all attempts on the part of her parents to find a husband for her. In 1324, she entered the Priory of Beaulieu of the Hospitaller nuns of St. John of Jerusalem. Here she was beset with many and diverse trials, fell into a depressed state, and was made sport of by some of her religious sisters.

However, she never ceased to find favor with God and was granted many unusual and mystical favors. One year on the feast of All Saints she fell into an ecstasy and took no nourishment until three weeks later on the feast of St. Cecilia. On another occasion, while meditating on the

Holy Spirit she was raised four feet from the ground and hung in the air in full view of many onlookers. She also seemed to be pierced with the arms of our Lord's Cross, causing blood to flow freely at times from her side and at others from her mouth.

Other instances of God's favoring of His servant were also reported, concerning prophetic knowledge of matters which she could not naturally know. Through it all, St. Flora remained humble and in complete communion with her Divine Master, rendering wise counsel to all who flocked to her because of her holiness and spiritual discernment. In 1347, she was called to her eternal reward and many miracles were worked at her tomb.

PRAYER God, You showered heavenly gifts on St. Flora. Help us to imitate her virtues during our earthly life and enjoy eternal happiness with her in heaven. Amen.

BLESSED MARIE ROSE DUROCHER, Virgin

October 6

BORN on October 6, 1811, at St. Antoine in Quebec, Canada, Eulalie Durocher was the youngest of ten children. After her education at the hands of the Sisters of Notre Dame, she helped her brother, a parish priest, and in the process established the first Canadian parish Sodality for young women.

In 1843, she was invited by Bishop Bourget to found a new congregation of women dedicated to Christian education. Accordingly she founded the Sisters of the Holy Names of Jesus and Mary and took the religious name of Marie Rose. Under her saintly and wise leadership, her community flourished in spite of all kinds of obstacles, including great poverty and unavoidable misunderstandings. She remained unswerving in her concern for the poor.

Worn out by her many labors, Marie Rose was called to her heavenly reward on October 6, 1849, at the age of 38. She was declared Blessed by Pope St. John Paul II on May 23, 1982.

PRAYER O Lord, You enkindled in the heart of Blessed Marie Rose Durocher the flame of an ardent charity and a burning desire to collaborate, as a teacher, in the mission of the Church. Inspire our hearts with that same charity so that we may lead our brothers and sisters to the bliss of eternal life. Amen.

ST. BRUNO, Priest

***The Same Day*, October 6—**
Patron of Those Possessed

ST. BRUNO, the founder of the illustrious Carthusian Order, was born at Cologne about the year 1033, and educated under the eyes of St. Cunibert, Bishop of that city. He became Canon of the Cathedral, but afterward went to France to continue his studies at Rheims. He was ordained about 1056 and taught theology at Rheims for twenty years. His abilities so impressed Gervasius, Archbishop of that city, that he shared with him the government of his diocese.

After the death of Gervasius, Manasses, the simoniacal intruder into the See, was deposed and all eyes turned to St. Bruno, but he positively refused the archiepiscopal dignity, and determined to put into execution a project of retreat he had some time before conceived. Together with ten friends, he presented himself to St. Hugh, Bishop of Grenoble, to ask his advice. The holy Bishop pointed out to them the desert of Chartreuse as their abode. There they went and there they began to imitate the lives of the early solitaries, laying the foundations of the Carthusian Order, the mother house of which still exists upon the very same spot.

After spending six years in this retreat, St. Bruno was summoned to Rome by Pope Urban II, who had been his pupil at Rheims. He spent some time at Rome, but having succeeded in obtaining leave to retire, he went to Calabria, where he founded a second monastery. Here the Saint spent the remainder of his life. He died at the Monastery of La Torre on October 6, 1101.

PRAYER God, You called St. Bruno to serve You in solitude. Through his intercession, grant that amidst the many affairs of this world we may always have time for You. Amen.

OUR LADY OF THE ROSARY

October 7

ON OCTOBER 7, the first Sunday of October in the year 1571, Don Juan of Austria gained his famous naval victory over the Turks at Lepanto. In thanksgiving for this event, which he attributed to the intercession of the Blessed Virgin through the recitation of the Holy Rosary, St. Pius V instituted an annual feast under the title of Our Lady of Victory. His immediate successor, Gregory XIII, changed the title to that of the Rosary, and granted its Office to all churches in which there was an altar dedicated to Our Lady of the Rosary.

In 1716, the army of Emperor Charles VI, under Prince Eugene, gained a remarkable victory over the Turks near Belgrade, on the Feast of Our Lady of the Snows, at a time when the members of the Society of the Holy Rosary were offering solemn prayers in Rome. Soon after, the Turks were forced to raise the siege of Corcyra. Clement XI, in memory of this, extended the feast of the Most Holy Rosary to the Universal Church. Benedict XIV caused an account of all this to be inserted into the Roman Breviary, and Leo XIII raised the feast to the rank of a feast of the second class. He also added to the Litany of Loreto the invocation: "Queen of the Most Holy Rosary, pray for us." In 1961, the title of this feast became: Our Lady of the Rosary.

According to a venerable tradition, the devotion of the Holy Rosary was revealed to St. Dominic by the Blessed Virgin.

PRAYER God, fill us with Your grace. We know the Incarnation of Your Son by the message of an Angel. Through the intercession of Mary may we obtain the glory of resurrection through Christ's Passion and Cross. Amen.

ST. PELAGIA, Virgin and Martyr

October 8

OUT of a maze of lengendary tales connected with this name we can ascertain that the historical St. Pelagia was a devout Christian who lived in Antioch at the end of the 3rd century and the beginning of the 4th. About the year 305, when she was fifteen, the local persecutor of the Church learned of her Christian Faith and sent a group of soldiers to bring her to him for examination.

Despite her tender years, St. Pelagia was well aware of the outrages to which Christ's virgins were subjected in such cases. Therefore, when the soldiers reached her home, she declared that she had to put on her bravest apparel and excused herself from the room. Instead, she swiftly made her way to the roof of her house and flung herself headlong to the ground below in order to preserve her richest prize—the virginity she had vowed to Jesus.

The learned and saintly Doctors, St. Ambrose and St. John Chrysostom, both knew of her action and both concurred that it was a noble example of love of chastity. She is thus classified as a Virgin and Martyr by the Church.

PRAYER All-powerful and ever-living God, You choose the weak in this world to confound the powerful. As we celebrate the martyrdom of St. Pelagia, may we like her remain constant in Faith. Amen.

STS. DENIS, Bishop and Martyr, **AND HIS COMPANIONS,** Martyrs

October 9

ABOUT the middle of the 3rd century, six Bishops were sent to preach the Faith in Gaul by Pope St. Fabian. One of these was St. Denis who brought the Faith to Lutetia Parisiorum (the present Paris) and organized a church. In carrying out his duties as the first Bishop of Paris, he was aided by a priest named Rusticus and a deacon called Eleutherius. So effective were these holy men in converting the people to Christ that the pagan priests became alarmed over their loss of followers. At their instigation, the Roman governor arrested the missionaries, and after a long imprisonment the three servants of God suffered martyrdom together at a place called Vicus Catulliacus, the present St. Denis, during the persecution of Decius (250) or Valerian (258). The site of their death provided the foundation for the Abbey of St. Denis which went on to become the burial place for the Kings of France.

PRAYER *God, You sent St. Denis and his Companions to proclaim Your glory to the nations and strengthened them with the virtue of constancy in their passion. Help us, after their example, to despise worldly prosperity and adversity. Amen.*

ST. JOHN LEONARDI, Priest

***The Same Day*—October 9**

ST. JOHN LEONARDI was born in 1541 at Decimi in Lucca, Italy, and from childhood he manifested a desire to seek solitude and give himself to prayer and meditation. At the age of thirty-two he became a priest and guided many youths in the way of perfection. To convert sinners and restore Church discipline in Italy, he founded the Clerks Regular of the Mother of God.

A contemporary of St. Philip Neri and St. Joseph Calasanz, he labored zealously for the defense of the Faith and in 1603, together with Cardinal Vivès, he founded the College of the Propaganda. He died at Rome on October 9, 1609, while caring for the victims of the great plague, and was canonized in 1938 by Pope Pius XI.

PRAYER *God, the Giver of all good things, You had the Gospel preached to the people through St. John Your Priest. Grant, through his intercession, that the true Faith may spread always and everywhere. Amen.*

ST. GHISLAIN (GISLENUS), Abbot

October 10

THIS 7th century follower of Christ initially led the life of a hermit in a forest of Hainault, Belgium. In 650, realizing that others were also desirous of serving God in this way, he founded a monastery in honor of Sts. Peter and Paul and spent the rest of his life directing those who flocked to this manner of life.

For thirty years St. Ghislain was the model of sanctity and prudence in his role of Abbot. No problem was too great and no difficulty too small for him; he was a bulwark of strength and a bearer of Christ for every member of his community.

At the same time, this towering figure was a source of wise counsel and unwavering encouragement for all who came into contact with him. It was St. Ghislain who encouraged St. Waldetrudis to found a convent at Mons where he himself had had his first hermitage. And it was this same Saint who was responsible for the fact that her sister St. Aldegondis established a convent at Maubeuge. In 680, worn out by a lifetime of labors in God's service, this saintly man ended his stay on earth and went to his heavenly reward.

PRAYER Lord, amid the things of this world, let us be wholeheartedly committed to heavenly things in imitation of the example of evangelical perfection You have given us in St. Ghislain the Abbot. Amen.

ST. FIRMINUS, Bishop

October 11

THE dates of birth and death of St. Firminus are not known, but we do know that he was the third Bishop of Uzès, Gaul, followed by St. Ferreolo, and he enjoys a cult that goes back to ancient times. In 541 he was already a Bishop and took part in the Council of Orleans, and in 552 he was present at the Council of Paris. He was a friend and disciple of St. Caesarius of Aries and together with other Bishops signed his *Rule for Holy Virgins*. Then after St. Caesarius' death in 543, he wrote the first book of his *Life* in conjunction with Cyprian of Toulon and others.

About the year 544, the Roman poet Arator praised St. Firminus in the following terms:

"The venerable priest Firminus
is able to feed his people with the gold of dogma;
his praise reaches to the ends of Italy
and his name possesses a glory outside his own country."

PRAYER *God, Light and Shepherd of souls, You established St. Firminus as Bishop in Your Church to feed Your flock by his word and form it by his example. Help us through his intercession to keep the Faith he taught by his word and follow the way he showed by his example. Amen.*

ST. WILFRID, Bishop of York

October 12

BORN in Northumberland in 634, St. Wilfrid was educated at Lindisfarne and then spent some time in Lyons and Rome. Returning to England, he was elected Abbot of Ripon in 658 and introduced the Roman rules and practices in opposition to the Celtic ways of Northern England. In 664, he was the architect of the definitive victory of the Roman party at the Conference of Whitby. He was appointed Bishop of York and after some difficulty finally took possession of his See in 669. He labored zealously and founded many monasteries of the Benedictine Order, but he was obliged to appeal to Rome in order to prevent the subdivision of his diocese by St. Theodore, Archbishop of Canterbury.

While waiting for the case to be decided, he was forced to go into exile, and he worked hard and long to evangelize the heathen south Saxons until his recall in 686. In 691, he had to retire again to the midlands until Rome once again vindicated him. In 703, he resigned his post and retired to his monastery at Ripon where he spent his remaining time in prayer and penitential practices, until his death in 709.

St. Wilfrid was an outstanding personage of his day, extremely capable and possessed of unbounded courage, remaining firm in his convictions despite running afoul of civil and ecclesiastical authorities. He helped bring the discipline of the English Church into line with that of Rome. He was also a dedicated pastor and a zealous and skilled missionary; his brief time spent in Friesland in 678-679 was the starting point for the great English mission to the Germanic peoples of continental Europe.

PRAYER God, You built up Your Church by means of the religious zeal and apostolic care of St. Wilfrid. Grant by his intercession that she may ever experience a new increase of Faith and holiness. Amen.

ST. GERALD OF AURILLAC

October 13

ST. GERALD of Aurillac led a saintly life in the world at a particularly decadent and disordered period. Born in 855, he succeeded his noble father as Count of Auvergne and owner of considerable estates. Filled with love of God and neighbor, he gave away much of his revenue to the poor, avoided all extravagance and worldly pomp, and lived a simple and prayerful life. He conscientiously fulfilled all the duties of a wealthy nobleman and was careful to deal with everyone fairly and justly.

This Saint delighted in studies, prayer, and meditation instead of the worldly pursuits of the noble classes. Rising at two o'clock every morning, he devoutly recited the first part of the Divine Office and heard Mass; the rest of the day was then divided according to a rule, with much of it set aside for communing with God and reading.

About 890, on returning from a pilgrimage to Rome, St. Gerald founded a Benedictine monastery at Aurillac which went on to attain widespread fame. He himself pondered joining the monastery but St. Gausbert, Bishop of Cahors, helped him realize that his true vocation lay in working in the world for the glory of God. Seven years before his death, he was afflicted with blindness, which he bore with Christian resignation. He died in 909 and became known throughout France as a result of a biography written by St. Odo of Cluny.

PRAYER Lord God, You alone are holy and no one is good without You. Through the intercession of St. Gerald, help us to live in such a way that we may not be deprived of a share in Your glory. Amen.

ST. CALLISTUS I, Pope and Martyr

October 14

A Roman by birth, St. Callistus was a slave of a Christian master early in life. After inadvertently losing some of his master's money, he panicked, fled, and was cast into a dungeon when captured. Later, his master freed him in the hope that this honest and intelligent slave would be able to make some money and give back what he had lost. In trying to obtain money from some who had cheated him, the Saint was accused as a Christian and condemned to the Sardinian mines.

Fortunately for him, the kindly Marcia, a favorite of the Emperor, obtained his release, and he was taken into the service of Pope Victor who was impressed by the Saint's constancy in misfortune and devotion to the Sardinian martyrs. He became a deacon and later secretary to Pope Zephyrinus, who put him in charge of the Christian cemetery on the Appian Way which still bears his name. When Zephyrinus died in 217, Callistus was chosen to be Pope and he governed the Church for five years and two months.

Throughout his brief reign which coincided with the rather peaceful reign of Emperor Alexander Severus during which Christians began to build churches for the public exercise of their religion, this Pope displayed the qualities of a wise, firm, and compassionate shepherd. He instituted the fast on Ember Days, decreed that ordinations should be held during the Ember Weeks, and established the practice of absolution of all sins, including those which rigorists considered irremissible. He also founded the Church of St. Mary Beyond the Tiber and provided for the burial of martyrs. He himself was martyred in 222, probably at the hands of a mob.

PRAYER Lord, graciously hear the prayers of Your people. Let us be aided by the merits of Pope St. Callistus, at whose passion we rejoice. Amen.

ST. TERESA OF AVILA,

Virgin and Doctor of the Church

October 15—*Patroness for Headache-Sufferers*

ST. TERESA was born on March 28, 1515, in Avila, Spain. Her mother died when she was twelve and her father placed her in a convent of Augustinian nuns. When she returned home, she determined to enter religion. She became a nun in the Carmelite Convent of the Incarnation, near Avila, and made her profession in November, 1534.

Though for many years in the convent she led a good religious life, certain faults still adhered to her; but the moment of grace came at last and the noble heart of St. Teresa began to soar upward to perfection. Inspired by the Holy Spirit and acting under the direction of enlightened men, among whom was St. Peter of Alcantara, she undertook the superhuman task of reforming her Order and restoring its primitive observance.

Assisted by St. John of the Cross, she succeeded in establishing the Reform of the Discalced Carmelites, for both the brethren and the sisters of her Order. Before her death in 1582, thirty-two monasteries of the Reformed Rule had been established, among which seventeen were convents of nuns. She was canonized in 1622 by Pope Gregory XV.

St. Teresa received great gifts from God. She also wrote many books on Mystical Theology considered by Popes Gregory XV and Urban VII to be equal to those of a Doctor of the Church. Accordingly, on September 27, 1970, Pope St. Paul VI added her to the roll of the Doctors of the Church.

PRAYER God, You raised up St. Teresa by Your Spirit so that she could manifest to the Church the way to perfection. Nourish us with the food of heaven, and fire us with a desire for holiness. Amen.

ST. HEDWIG, Religious

October 16

BORN in Bavaria in 1174, Hedwig was the daughter of the Duke of Croatia. In 1186, she was married to Henry I of Silesia and Poland to whom she bore seven children; after the birth of her last child, she and her husband vowed continence. She is best remembered for her great zeal for religion and her penitential mortifications, which led her to live like a hermit amidst her husband's court. She donated her entire fortune to the Church and the poor, and after her husband's death she entered the Cistercian convent of Trebnitz, which she had founded, among many others. She died in October, 1243, and was canonized in 1266 by Pope Clement IV.

PRAYER Almighty God, may the venerable intercession of St. Hedwig obtain heavenly aid for us, for her life constitutes a wonderful example of humility for all. Amen.

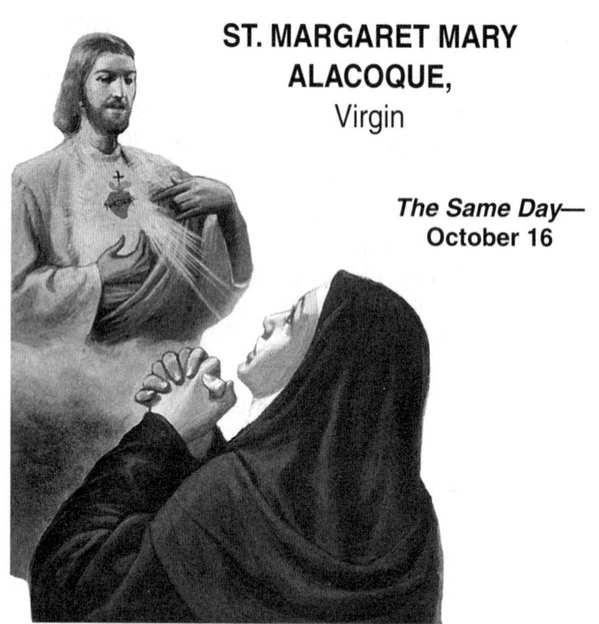

ST. MARGARET MARY ALACOQUE,

Virgin

The Same Day—
October 16

BORN in the diocese of Autun, France, St. Margaret Mary Alacoque consecrated her heart, while yet a child, to the Most Sacred Heart of Jesus.

In order to dedicate herself wholly to her Divine Spouse, she joined the Visitation Order of nuns at twenty-three years of age at Paray-le Monial in Charleroi. She was subjected to many trials and sufferings, but she underwent all for the love of Jesus. In 1675, she was chosen by God to reveal to the Christian World the devotion to the Sacred Heart of Jesus. St. Margaret and St. Claude de la Colombiere, S.J., were the chief instruments of the Feast of the Sacred Heart. She died in 1690 and was canonized in 1920 by Pope Benedict XV.

PRAYER Lord, pour out upon us the spirit with which You enriched St. Margaret Mary. Help us to know the love of Christ which is too great for human knowledge and to be filled with the fullness of God. Amen.

ST. GERARD MAJELLA,
Religious

The Same Day,
October 16—
Patron of Expectant Mothers

GERARD was born at Muro, Italy, in 1726 and joined the Redemptorists at the age of twenty-three, becoming a professed lay brother in 1752. He served as sacristan, gardener, porter, infirmarian, and tailor. However, because of his great piety, extraordinary wisdom, and his gift of reading consciences, he was permitted to counsel communities of religious women.

This humble servant of God also had the faculties of levitation and bi-location associated with certain mystics. His charity, obedience, and selfless service as well as his ceaseless mortification for Christ made him the perfect model of lay brothers. He was afflicted with tuberculosis and died in 1755 at the age of twenty-nine. He was canonized in 1904 by Pope St. Pius X.

This great Saint is invoked as a patron of expectant mothers as a result of a miracle effected through his prayers for a woman in labor.

PRAYER God, by Your grace St. Gerard persevered in imitating Christ in His poverty and humility. Through his intercession, grant that we may faithfully follow our vocation and reach that perfection which You held out to us in Your Son. Amen.

ST. IGNATIUS OF ANTIOCH, Bishop and Martyr

October 17

ST. IGNATIUS was a convert to the Faith and a disciple of St. John the Evangelist. St. John Chrysostom says that St. Peter appointed him Bishop of Antioch, which See he governed for forty years. The Saint longed to shed his blood for Christ, but the opportunity was not granted him during the persecution under Domitian.

While the short reign of Nerva lasted the Church was at peace, but under Trajan persecution broke out anew. In the year 107 the Emperor came to Antioch. St. Ignatius was seized and brought before him. Having confessed Christ, he was condemned to be taken in chains to Rome, there to be exposed to the wild beasts. During this last journey he was welcomed by the faithful of Smyrna, Troas, and other places along the way.

He arrived in Rome just as the public spectacles in the amphitheater were drawing to a close. The faithful of the city came out to meet him. He was at once hurried to the amphitheater, where two fierce lions immediately devoured him. He ended his saintly life by a glorious death, exclaiming, "May I become agreeable bread to the Lord." His remains were carried to Antioch, where they were interred. In the reign of Theodosius they were transferred to a church within the city. At present they are venerated in Rome.

During his long journey he addressed seven epistles to various congregations, in which, as a disciple of the Apostles, he testifies to the dogmatic character of Apostolic Christianity.

PRAYER Almighty and ever-living God, You adorn the body of Your holy Church with the witness of Your Martyrs. Grant that the sufferings of St. Ignatius on this day which brought unending glory to him may bring us perpetual protection. Amen.

ST. LUKE,
Evangelist

October 18—*Patron of Doctors and Painters*

ST. LUKE was born at Antioch, Syria, according to the Church historian Eusebius. He was a Gentile by birth and a physician by profession. According to a legend of the 6th century he was also a painter.

He was one of the earliest converts to the Faith and later became the missionary companion of St. Paul, whom he accompanied on part of his second and third missionary journeys, and attended during his Caesarean and Roman captivities. Little is known with certainty of his subsequent life.

The unanimous tradition of the Church ascribes the third Gospel to St. Luke. Allusions to and citations from the Gospel are most frequent in early Christian writings, and even heretics made diligent use of this inspired book. The Gospel itself shows that its author was a person of literary powers, a physician, and a companion of St. Paul. Early Christian tradition ascribes the Gospel and its companion volume, The Acts of the Apostles, to approximately 75 A.D.

Little is known with certainty about the place of composition. Some of the ancient authors suggest Achaia (Greece); some of the manuscripts mention Alexandria or Macedonia; while modern writers also defend Caesarea, Ephesus or Rome. As an artist, St. Luke shows his skill in portraying living characters, and he has remained an inspiration to painters for centuries. As a historian, he is comparable with the great Greek and Latin writers. In his Gospel there is a steady movement of events from Nazareth to Jerusalem, whereas in the Acts it is from Jerusalem to Rome.

PRAYER God, You chose St. Luke to reveal in preaching and writing Your love for the poor. Grant that those who already glory in Your Name may persevere in one heart and one mind, and that all people may hear Your Good News of salvation. Amen.

STS. ISAAC JOGUES, JOHN DE BREBEUF, Priests, AND COMPANIONS, Martyrs

October 19

STS. ISAAC JOGUES, John de Brebeuf, Charles Garmier, Anthony Daniel, Gabriel Lallemant, Noel Chabanel, John de Lalande and René Goupil, French Jesuits, were among the missionaries who preached the Gospel to Huron and Iroquois Indians in the United States and Canada. They were martyred by the Iroquois Indians in the years 1642, 1648, and 1649. Pope Pius XI beatified them on June 21, 1925, and in 1930 they were canonized by the same Pope.

St. Isaac Jogues, in particular, is outstanding. In the course of his labors preaching the Gospel to the Mohawks in Canada he penetrated to the eastern entrance of Lake Superior, one thousand miles inland and became the first European to do so. In 1642, he was taken captive by the Iroquois and imprisoned for thirteen months. During this time, he underwent cruel tortures and ultimately lost the use of his hands. After being rescued by the Dutch, he returned to Canada two years later, and in 1646 he visited Auriesville, New York, to negotiate peace with the Iroquois. He is said to be the first Catholic priest to have set foot on Manhattan Island.

On a third visit to the Iroquois, the Bear clan, which believed that he was a sorcerer, blamed him for an outbreak of sickness and the failure of their crops. Accordingly, he was seized, tortured, and beheaded.

PRAYER God, You consecrated the spread of the Faith in North America by the blood of St. Isaac Jogues and his companions who were preaching the Faith to the Indians. Through their intercession let more people everywhere respond to the Good News of salvation. Amen.

ST. PAUL OF THE CROSS,
Priest

October 20

ST. PAUL of the Cross was born at Ovada in the Republic of Genoa, January 3, 1694. His infancy and youth were spent in great innocence and piety. He was inspired from on high to found a congregation; in an ecstasy he beheld the habit which he and his companions were to wear. After consulting his director, Bishop Gastinara of Alexandria in Piedmont, he reached the conclusion that God wished him to establish a congregation in honor of the Passion of Jesus Christ.

On November 22, 1720, the Bishop vested him with the habit that had been shown to him in a vision, the same that the Passionists wear at the present time. From that moment the Saint applied himself to prepare the Rules of his institute; and in 1721 he went to Rome to obtain the approbation of the Holy See. At first he failed, but finally succeeded when Benedict XIV approved the Rules in 1741 and 1746. Meanwhile St. Paul built his first monastery near Obitello. Some time later he established a larger community at the Church of Sts. John and Paul in Rome.

For fifty years St. Paul remained the indefatigable missionary of Italy. God lavished upon him the greatest gifts in the supernatural order, but he treated himself with the greatest rigor, and believed that he was a useless servant and a great sinner. His saintly death occurred at Rome in the year 1775, at the age of eighty-one. He was canonized in 1867 by Pope Pius IX.

PRAYER Lord, may the prayers of St. Paul who loved the Cross with a singular love gain Your grace for us. May we be inspired by his example and embrace our own cross with courage. Amen.

BLESSED ADELINE, Abbess

***The Same Day*—October 20**

THE sister of St. Vitale, Abbot of Savigny, Blessed Adeline was introduced to the religious life by him. She rose to become the first Abbess of the monastery founded at Mortain in 1105 or 1115 by Count William of Mortain. The

Rule followed by this religious house was that of St. Benedict together with a few observances drawn from the Cistercian tradition.

Because of the color of their habit the religious came to be called the "White Ladies." After a life dedicated to prayer, mortification, and charitable works, Blessed Adeline was called to her reward in 1125. Such was her reputation for sanctity that shortly afterward she began to be honored as one of the Blessed and her remains were solemnly transferred together with those of her brother and other religious of Savigny.

PRAYER God, You inspired Blessed Adeline to strive for perfect charity and so attain Your Kingdom at the end of her pilgrimage on earth. Strengthen us through her intercession that we may advance rejoicing in the way of love. Amen.

ST. CELINE, Mother of St. Remigius

October 21

WE have very few details about the life of this Saint who is best known as the mother of St. Remigius, Bishop of Rheims at the time of the conversion of the people of Gaul under Clovis. St. Celine miraculously gave birth to St. Remigius when she was already at an advanced age. Immediately after giving birth, about 438, she also gave sight to the hermit Montanus who had three times foretold the birth of the saintly Bishop.

After a holy life filled with good works and assiduous prayer, this saintly woman attained the rewards of heaven about the year 458. She was buried near Lyons, probably at Cerny, where she had lived. Unfortunately her relics were destroyed during the French Revolution.

PRAYER God, You inspired St. Celine to strive for perfect charity and so attain Your Kingdom at the end of her pilgrimage on earth. Strengthen us through her intercession that we may advance rejoicing in the way of love. Amen.

ST. SALOME, Mother of the Apostles James and John

October 22—*Patroness of Veroli*

ST. SALOME, whose name in Hebrew evokes prosperity and peace and corresponds to the Greek Irene, is thought to be a sister or cousin of Mary, the Mother of Jesus, mentioned by St. John as being one of the three women standing at the foot of the Cross. St. Mark calls this woman Salome and St. Matthew characterizes her as "the mother of the sons of Zebedee."

Mark also mentions her as one of the same three as they came to anoint the body of Jesus in the tomb early on Easter morning.

It was this holy woman who asked Jesus to give her two sons, James and John, a place of honor in His Kingdom. In His reply, Jesus addressed the two Apostles and lovingly directed them to the life of sacrifice, abnegation, and imitation of His sufferings. Their reward would come beyond the boundaries of time.

She is venerated as Patroness of the Church of Veroli, Italy, to which city an ancient tradition says she came, with two companions called Blase and Demetrius, and proclaimed the Faith. Then at an advanced age she closed out her days in peace there, while her two companions bore witness to the Faith with their lives.

PRAYER God, You alone are holy and without You no one is good. Through the intercession of St. Salome, grant that we may so live as not to be deprived of Your glory. Amen.

ST. JOHN OF CAPISTRANO, Priest

October 23—*Patron of Jurists*

ST. JOHN was born at Capistrano, Italy in 1385, the son of a former German knight of that city. He studied law at the University of Perugia and practiced as a lawyer in the courts of Naples. King Ladislas of Naples appointed him governor of Perugia.

During a war with a neighboring town he was betrayed and imprisoned. Upon his release he entered the Franciscan community at Perugia in 1416. He and St. James of the March were fellow students under St Bernardine of Siena, who inspired him to institute the devotion to the Holy

Name of Jesus and His Mother. John began his brilliant preaching apostolate while a deacon in 1420. After his ordination he traveled throughout Italy, Germany, Bohemia, Austria, Hungary, Poland, and Russia preaching penance and establishing numerous communities of Franciscan renewal.

When Mohammed II was threatening Vienna and Rome, St. John, at the age of seventy, was commissioned by Pope Callistus II to preach and lead a crusade against the invading Turks. Marching at the head of 70,000 Christians, he gained victory in the great battle of Belgrade against the Turks in 1456. Three months later he died at Illok, Hungary and was canonized in 1724.

PRAYER Lord, You raised up St. John to console Your people in their distress. Grant that we may always be safe under Your protection and preserve Your Church in unending peace. Amen.

ST. ANTHONY MARY CLARET, Bishop

October 24

BORN in Sallent, Spain, in 1807, the son of a weaver, St. Anthony was ordained a priest in 1835. After five years, he began to give missions and retreats all over Catalonia. Seeing their success and the people's need for them, he founded (in 1849) the Congregation of the Missionary Sons of the Immaculate Heart of Mary (Claretians) to continue this work on a wider scale.

In that same year, he was consecrated Bishop of Santiago de Cuba. Finding the diocese in a deplorable spiritual condition, he quickly initiated vigorous reform measures, one of which was the establishment of the Teaching Sisters of Mary Immaculate.

In 1857, he was recalled to Spain and made the chaplain of Queen Isabella II. This position made it possible for him to continue his mission work by preaching and publishing. He established a museum, library, schools, and a laboratory, also helping to revive the Catalan language. He spread devotion to the Blessed Sacrament and the Immaculate Heart of Mary, and after the revolution of 1868 ended his life in exile with the Queen in 1870. He was canonized in 1950 by Pope Pius XII.

PRAYER God, You strengthened St. Anthony Mary with wondrous love and patience in evangelizing the people. Through his intercession, enable us to seek those things which are Yours, and to labor in Christ for the good of our fellowmen. Amen.

ST. GAUDENTIUS OF BRESCIA, Bishop

October 25

BORN at Brescia, Italy about the middle of the 4th century, St. Gaudentius was educated under St. Philastrius, Bishop of Brescia, whom he terms his "father." After earning a reputation for sanctity, he traveled to the East where he gained even more fame. In his absence, he was elected Bishop by the people on the death of St. Philastrius; though he felt unworthy to receive such an honor, he was influenced to accept it by the Eastern Bishops, and in 387 he was consecrated by St. Ambrose.

He was a powerful preacher and ten of his twenty-one Sermons have survived, offering ample testimony to this fact. He governed his See with prudence and humility, inspiring his flock to imitate the Divine Master constantly.

In 405, he was sent with two others by Pope Innocent I and the Emperor Honorius to the East to defend St. John Chrysostom before Arcadius. However, the party was prevented from reaching Arcadius and never formally interceded for John; the three men were shipped back home on a vessel so unseaworthy that it almost sank and had to be left at Lampsacus. Subsequently, St. John wrote St. Gaudentius a letter of thanks for his efforts even though they had not borne fruit. This saintly man died about 410 and was called by Rufinus: "the glory of the doctors of the age in which he lives."

PRAYER God, Light and Shepherd of souls, You established St. Gaudentius as Bishop in Your Church to feed Your flock by his word and form it by his example. Help us through his intercession to keep the Faith he taught by his word and follow the way he showed by his example. Amen.

ST. DEMETRIUS, Martyr

October 26

ALL that we know for certain about St. Demetrius is that he was martyred during the persecution of Diocletian at Sirmium in Dalmatia. Afterward a prefect of Illyria named Leontius introduced his cult to Salonika, transferred some of his relics there, and built a temple in his honor in both cities. From the 5th century on, Salonika was the great center of the cult of St. Demetrius, and his imposing church was destroyed only in 1917.

According to a legendary history, St. Demetrius was a citizen of Salonika who was arrested for proclaiming the Faith. He was then slain without a trial as he was being detained in a room of the public baths. Other accounts make him a proconsul and a warrior-saint, and in this latter capacity he almost equaled the popularity of the great legendary figure St. George. Both of these Saints were adopted as patrons by the crusaders and a story says that they were seen in their ranks at the Battle of Antioch in 1098.

St. Demetrius is still very popular in the East and his feast is celebrated with solemnity in the Eastern Liturgy.

PRAYER Almighty and ever-living God, You enabled St. Demetrius to fight for justice even unto death. Through his help, grant that we may tolerate all adversity and hasten with all our might to You Who alone are life. Amen.

BLESSED EMILINA, Lay Sister

October 27

BORN about 1115, Blessed Emilina lived as a solitary lay sister in the Cistercian Abbey of Boulancourt, located in the commune of Longeville, in Haute-Marne. She led a life of great penitence: fasting from food and liquids three days a weeks, wearing a hair shirt and a pointed iron chain, and going barefoot both in winter and in summer. She also led a wondrous life of prayer, constantly communing with God and frequently reciting the Psalms.

The fame of her sanctity spread quickly and people came to consult her from all around, especially when they heard of her gift of prophecy.

The Saint received them with patience and humility, counseling them wisely and bringing about the conversion of many. Finally, worn out by her lifelong labors and penances, the saintly woman went on to her eternal reward in 1178. Such was her renown that an eternal light was placed at her grave.

PRAYER *God, You gladden us each year by the feast of Blessed Emilina. Grant that as we honor her in such festivities we may also imitate her example in our conduct. Amen.*

STS. SIMON AND JUDE,
Apostles

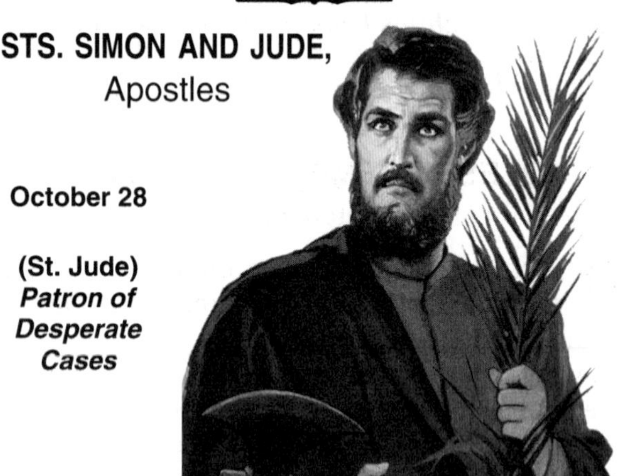

October 28

(St. Jude)
Patron of Desperate Cases

ST. SIMON is surnamed the Canaanean and also the Zealot, to distinguish him from St. Peter and from St. Simeon, the brother of St. James the Less. The Syro-Chaldaic expression Canaanean means the same as the Greek *Zelotes,* a title that is said to have been given to him on account of his great zeal, but, according to others, from his belonging to a sect (among the Jews) called Zealots. It is supposed that he suffered martyrdom in Persia.

ST. Jude, known as Thaddaeus, was a brother of St. James the Less, and a relative of our Savior. Ancient writers tell us that he preached the Gospel in Judea, Samaria, Idumaea, Syria, Mesopotamia, and Libya. According to Eusebius, he returned to Jerusalem in the year 62, and assisted at the election of his brother, St. Simeon, as Bishop of Jerusalem. He is the author of an Epistle to the Churches of the East, particularly the Jewish converts, directed against the heresies of the Simonians, Nicolaites, and Gnostics. This Apostle is said to have suffered martyrdom in Armenia, which was then subject to Persia. The final conversion of the Armenian nation to Christianity did not take place until the 3rd century of our era.

PRAYER God, You made Your Name known to us through the Apostles. By the intercession of Sts. Simon and Jude, let Your Church continue to grow with an increased number of believers. Amen.

ST. NARCISSUS, Bishop of Jerusalem

October 29

IT MAY be inferred that the average reign of the early Bishops of Jerusalem was short indeed, for St. Simeon, the second incumbent, died in 116, and St. Narcissus who died toward the close of the same century, was its thirtieth Bishop. St. Narcissus was born toward the end of the 1st century. He was almost eighty years of age when he ascended the episcopal throne of Jerusalem. More than a century had then elapsed since the city had been destroyed by the Romans, and it had since been rebuilt as Aelia Capitolina by the Emperor Hadrian.

In 195, St. Narcissus, together with Theophitus, Bishop of Caesarea in Palestine, presided over a Council held by the Bishops of Palestine in the last-named city, and it was decreed that Easter is always to be kept on a Sunday and not with the Jewish Passover. According to Eusebius, the holy Bishop wrought several miracles. Notwithstanding his sanctity, the holy man was basely calumniated by certain members of his own flock, but God soon made his innocence known and the imprecations with which the calumniators had sought to confirm their words were terribly verified in their case.

The holy man left Jerusalem and retired into solitude, where he spent several years. Three Bishops governed the See in succession during his absence. On his return to his diocese, the faithful besought him to resume the administration, which he did; but, bending under the weight of extreme old age, he made Alexander his coadjutor. He continued to serve his flock and other churches by his assiduous prayers and his earnest exhortations to unity and concord. He died in his hundred and seventh year. Eusebius testifies that he once changed water into oil to supply the lamps of the church on the Vigil of Easter.

PRAYER God, You made St. Narcissus an outstanding exemplar of Divine love and the Faith that conquers the world, and added him to the roll of saintly pastors. Grant by his intercession that we may persevere in Faith and love and become sharers of his glory. Amen.

ST. MARCELLUS THE CENTURION, Martyr

October 30

IN THE year 298, the birthday of the Emperor Maximian was celebrated with extraordinary solemnity. St. Marcellus, a Christian centurion in one of the legions then stationed in Spain, refused to take part in the sacrifices offered to the gods, and declared himself a Christian. He threw down his arms and the vine-branch, which was the mark of his dignity.

Anastasius Fortunatus, the Prefect of the legion, having learned the fact, commanded St. Marcellus to be cast into prison. After the feast, the prisoner was brought before the Prefect, who asked the reason for his conduct. St. Marcellus replied that it was his religion. Hereupon the Prefect declared that he would have to lay his case before Maximian and Caesar Constantius.

The latter ruled over Gaul and Spain, and he was most favorable to the Christians. However, St. Marcellus was sent under a strong guard to Aurelian Agricolus, vicar to the Prefect of the praetorium, who was then at Tangier in Africa. When St. Marcellus admitted the truth of the accusation, he was condemned to death for the desertion and impiety. Cassian, the notary of the court, refused to write the sentence, which he declared to be unjust. In consequence of this, he, too, was condemned to death. St. Marcellus was beheaded on October 30, and St. Cassian suffered death on the 3rd of the following December.

PRAYER Almighty, ever-living God, You enabled St. Marcellus to fight to the death for justice. Through his intercession enable us to bear all adversity and with all our strength hasten to You Who alone are life. Amen.

ST. WOLFGANG, Bishop of Ratisbon

October 31

BORN in Suabia about 925, St. Wolfgang went on to become one of the outstanding men of his day. He studied at the Abbey of Reichenau in Lake Constance, which was at that time a noted center of learning, and then taught at the cathedral schools of Wurzburg and Trier. In the latter capacity, he joined the monk Ramhold in reforming the dioceses for their mutual friend, Henry the Archbishop.

When Henry died, St. Wolfgang entered the Benedictine monastery of Einsiedeln in Switzerland, where his learning, piety, and overall ability soon came to the fore. Named director of the Abbey school, he made it the finest in the country. He was then ordained a priest and with a group of monks set out to evangelize the Magyars in Pannonia. However, their zealous efforts bore little outward fruit, and he was named Archbishop of Ratisbon, despite his honest protestations to the contrary.

Though his heart longed for solitude, this saintly man remained in his post for the rest of his days and brought to his work all his zeal and capabilities. He restored canonical life among his clergy, reformed monasteries, preached tirelessly, and discharged his duties as spiritual shepherd with exemplary fidelity, earning the love of his flock and the esteem of the royal court. He died about 994, and such was his reputation for holiness and the miracles he effected that he was canonized in 1022 by Pope Benedict VIII.

PRAYER God, Light and Shepherd of souls, You established St. Wolfgang as Bishop in Your Church to feed Your flock by his word and form it by his example. Help us through his intercession to keep the Faith he taught by his word and follow the way he showed by his example. Amen.

ALL SAINTS

November 1

THIS feast dates back to the 7th century, and the occasion of its introduction was the conversion of the ancient Pantheon at Rome into a Christian church. This famous temple, which possibly existed in the time of the Republic, is generally considered to have been built by Marcus Agrippa in his third consulate in the year 27 B.C., but it is not improbable that he merely restored and added to it. Historians do not agree as to the origin of its name, but Pliny tells us that Agrippa dedicated it to Jupiter the Avenger. It was afterward repaired by Septimus Severus and his son Caracalla.

In the beginning of the 7th century, the Emperor Phocas gave it to Pope Boniface IV, who converted it into a church and dedicated it to the Blessed Virgin and all the saints, about the year 608. The feast of this dedication was kept on May 13, and before that event the feast of all the Apostles had been celebrated on the first of the same month.

About the year 731, Pope Gregory III consecrated a chapel in St. Peter's Church in honor of all the saints, and since then the feast of All Saints has been celebrated in Rome. Gregory IV, while in France in 837, greatly encouraged the celebration of this feast in that country. The

Greeks celebrate the feast of All Saints on the Sunday after Pentecost.

PRAYER God, You allow us to honor all Your Saints in one common festival. Through the prayers of so many intercessors grant us an abundance of Your merciful favors which we so greatly desire. Amen.

ALL SOULS

November 2

ON November 2, the Church commemorates all the Faithful Departed. The white vestments of All Saints' day are laid aside, and the dark robes and emblems of mourning are worn to indicate the sympathy of Mother Church for her children, who are being purified in the sufferings of purgatory.

The reason for the commemoration of all the Faithful Departed is the doctrine and belief that all who die in venial sin, or have not fully atoned for other past transgressions, are detained in purgatory, and that the faithful on earth can help them through their temporal punishment and hasten their admission to the joys of heaven by prayers and alms, and especially by the Holy Sacrifice of the Mass. The memorial day of the dead comes down to us from the first Christians, and, in the course of centuries, November 2 was selected for the annual commemoration of all the Faithful Departed in churches of the Latin rite.

In every land and in every Christian soul resound the mournful tones of prayer for the dead: "Eternal rest grant to them, O Lord, and let perpetual light shine upon them. May they rest in peace."

Since August 10, 1915, every priest is allowed to offer three Masses on All Souls' day: one for all the Faithful Departed, one for the intention of the Pope, and one for the intention of the priest himself. Since it is impossible to offer a Mass for the particular intention or intentions of each individual on All Souls' day, or during the month of November, in many dioceses of the United States and other countries there is a custom by which a collection is made of money offerings by the people. Masses are then offered on All Souls' day, and, in some places, on other days during November, for the intentions of all the people. In churches where there are several priests, each offers a Mass or Masses, according to the custom of the diocese for the All Souls' day intentions.

PRAYER Merciful God, graciously hear our prayers. As we believe that Your Son rose from the dead, so strengthen our faith in the resurrection of all Your servants. Amen.

ST. MARTIN DE PORRES,

Religious

November 3
Patron of Hairdressers

ST. Martin de Porres was born at Lima, Peru, in 1579. His father was a Spanish gentleman and his mother an Indian woman from Panama. At fifteen, he became a lay brother at the Dominican Friary at Lima and spent his whole life there—as a barber, farm-laborer, almoner, and infirmarian among other things.

Martin had a great desire to go off to some foreign mission and thus earn the palm of martyrdom. However, since this was not possible, he made a martyr out of his body, devoting himself to ceaseless and severe penances. In turn, God endowed him with many graces and wondrous gifts, such as aerial flights and bilocation.

St. Martin's love was all-embracing, shown equally to humans and animals, including vermin, and he maintained a cats' and dogs' hospital at his sister's house. He also possessed spiritual wisdom, demonstrated in his solving his sister's marriage problems, raising a dowry for his niece inside of three days' time, and resolving theological problems for the learned of his Order and for Bishops. A close friend of St. Rose of Lima, this saintly man died on November 3, 1639 and was canonized on May 6, 1962, by Pope St. John XXIII.

PRAYER God, You led St. Martin by the way of humility to heavenly glory. Help us to follow the example of his holiness and so become worthy to be exalted with him in heaven. Amen.

ST. CHARLES BORROMEO, Bishop

November 4—*Patron of Seminarians*

ST. CHARLES, of the noble family of Borromeo, was born in 1538 on the banks of Lake Maggiore, Italy. He studied at Milan and afterward at the University of Pavia, where he received his doctorate in civil and canon law in 1559. His uncle, the Cardinal de Medici, having in the same year been elected Pope under the title of Pius IV, sent for him and created him Cardinal, and a short time afterward nominated him Archbishop of Milan, though he was only twenty-two years of age.

At the same time he was detained at Rome by the Pope and he began to labor diligently in the interests of the Church. There he founded the Vatican Academy for literary work. As Papal Secretary of State he was instrumental in reassembling the Council of Trent in 1562. He was active in enforcing its reforms and in composing the Roman Catechism, containing the teachings of the Council.

After receiving priestly ordination, he also accepted the office of grand penitentiary. For merely honorary or lucrative positions he had no ambition. He assisted at the deathbed of the Pope in 1564, and on the election of Pius V he went to reside at Milan.

In 1572, he concurred in the election of Gregory XIII. In the great plague at Milan, in 1575, he showed himself the true shepherd by his self-sacrificing charity and heroism. This great light in the firmament of the Church was extinguished in 1584. He was canonized in 1610 by Pope Paul V.

PRAYER God, maintain in Your people that spirit with which You inspired Your Bishop, St. Charles, so that Your Church may be constantly renewed, conforming itself to Christ and manifesting Christ to the world. Amen.

ST. SYLVIA, Mother of St. Gregory the Great

November 5

THE Church venerates the sanctity of Sylvia and Gordian, the parents of St. Gregory the Great, as well as his two aunts, Tarsilla and Emiliana. St. Sylvia was a native of the region of Sicily while St. Gordian, her husband, came from the vicinity of Rome. They had two sons: Gregory and another whose name has not survived the ages.

Gordian died about 573 and Gregory converted his paternal home into a monastery. Sylvia therefore retired to a solitary and quasi-monastic life in a little abode near the Church of St. Saba on the Aventine. It became her custom frequently to send fresh vegetables to her son on a silver platter. One day, when Gregory found himself with nothing to give a poor beggar, he presented him with the platter.

St. Sylvia is thought to have gone on to her heavenly reward between 592 and 594. After her death, the holy Pontiff had a picture of both his parents depicted in the Church of St. Andrew. In the 16th century, Pope Clement VIII had St. Sylvia inscribed in the Roman Martyrology.

PRAYER God, You gladden us each year by the feast of St. Sylvia. Grant that as we honor her in such festivities we may also imitate her example in our conduct. Amen.

ST. BERTILLE, Religious

November 6

ST. BERTILLE was born in the territory of Soissons, France, during the reign of Dagobert I. She embraced the religious state in 630, in a monastery of nuns at Jouarre, about twelve miles from Meaux. In this abode of virtue her prudence appeared so perfect that though she was still young, the care of entertaining strangers, and the charge of the sick and of the children that were educated in the monastery, were successively committed to her. She gave such satisfaction in these various offices that she was chosen Prioress, to assist the Abbess in her administration.

Her example exercised the most salutary influence upon the entire community. St. Bathildis, wife of Clovis II, having refounded the Abbey of Chelles, which St. Clotildis had originally established, desired the Abbess of Jouarre to send over a small colony to lead the novices in the practice of monastic perfection. St. Bertille was chosen to lead the colony, and she became the first Abbess of Chelles, about the year 646.

Her reputation for sanctity and the good discipline of her monastery drew to it several foreign princesses, among whom was Hereswith, Queen of the East Angles, who had been the wife of the good King Annas. Queen Bathildis herself took the monastic habit in this house in 665, so that St. Bertille became the superior of two Queens. Yet, she seemed the most humble of all her Sisters. She governed her monastery for forty-six years, increasing daily in virtue, and in her old age redoubling rather than diminishing her fervor. Her happy death occurred in the year 692.

PRAYER God, You showered heavenly gifts on St. Bertille. Help us to imitate her virtues during our earthly life and enjoy eternal happiness with her in heaven. Amen.

STS. CARINA AND HER COMPANIONS,

Martyrs

November 7

NOTHING is known about this Saint (also called Cassina) apart from the Acts of her martyrdom. In the year 360, at the time of Emperor Julian the Apostate in the city of Ankara, she and her husband Antonius as well as her thirteen-year-old son Melasippus were arrested on account of their Christian Faith.

The local authorities, as was the custom in such matters, endeavored to sway them from their devotion to the true God by means of cruel and inhuman tortures. But, aided by grace from on high, the three Christians remained unswerving in their allegiance and steadfast in their Faith. They thus attained the crown of martyrdom and went on to receive their heavenly reward from our Lord and Savior Jesus Christ Whom they had so closely followed on earth.

PRAYER God, You surround and protect us by the glorious confession of St. Carina and her Companions. Help us to profit from their example and be supported by their prayers. Amen.

ST. GODFREY (GEOFFREY),

Bishop of Amiens

November 8

BORN near Soissons, France, in 1065, St. Godfrey became a monk and priest and was chosen Abbot of Nogent in Champagne, a rapidly declining religious house. Its membership had been drastically reduced, its outer appearance was completely dilapidated, and its religious life was floundering in sad disarray. However, such was the force of Godfrey's personality and spirituality that he soon had this same house flourishing in every way.

As a result, he was offered the great Abbacy of Saint-Remi at Rheims but turned it down, in favor of running his own house. In 1104, however, he was constrained to accept the episcopacy of Amiens. Here he showed himself to be a true religious in his conduct as well as in his administration—putting an end to simony, strenuously enforcing celibacy, and endorsing the establishment of communes.

In time the unbending, severe, and rigorously exact attitude of this Saint provoked the opposition of some and led to his withdrawal to a Carthusian monastery in 1114. Ordered to return to his diocese by a council, he died before he could do so in 1115 at St. Crispin's Abbey, Soissons.

PRAYER God, You made St. Godfrey an outstanding exemplar of Divine love and the Faith that conquers the world, and added him to the roll of saintly pastors. Grant by his intercession that we may persevere in Faith and love and become sharers of his glory. Amen.

DEDICATION OF ST. JOHN LATERAN

November 9

THIS is the oldest and ranks first among the four greater or patriarchal churches of Rome. It was originally the palace of Constantine, adapted and dedicated under the title "Our Savior" to serve as the church of the Pope. The present archbasilica was built later, on the site of the original church, and is known as St. John Lateran, having been dedicated to St. John the Baptist.

The other patriarchal basilicas of Rome are St. Peter's, St. Mary Major, and St. Paul's which is situated outside of the walls of the ancient city. These four basilicas represent the four great patriarchates, or ecclesiastical provinces, of the world. There are a number of churches in Rome and elsewhere which rank in honor as lesser basilicas, but do not possess the special privileges of the greater basilicas.

PRAYER God, out of living and chosen stones You prepare an eternal dwelling for Yourself. Multiply in Your Church the spirit of grace which You have given her, so that Your people may ever grow into that building which is the heavenly Jerusalem. Amen.

ST. LEO THE GREAT, Pope and Doctor of the Church

November 10

ST. LEO the Great was born in Tuscany. As deacon, he was dispatched to Gaul as a mediator by Emperor Valentinian III. He reigned as Pope between 440 and 461. He persuaded Emperor Valentinian to recognize the primacy of the Bishop of Rome in an edict in 445. The doctrine of the Incarnation was confirmed by him in a letter to the Patriarch of Constantinople, who had already condemned Eutyches. At the Council of Chalcedon this same letter was confirmed as the expression of Catholic Faith concerning the Person of Christ.

All secular historical treatises eulogize his efforts during the upheaval of the 5th-century barbarian invasion. His encounter with Attila the Hun, at the very gates of Rome, persuading him to turn back, remains a historical memorial to his great eloquence. When the Vandals under Genseric occupied the city of Rome he persuaded the invaders to desist from pillaging the city and harming its inhabitants. He died in 461, leaving many letters and writings of great historical value.

PRAYER God, You established Your Church on the solid rock of the Apostles and You will never allow the powers of hell to dominate her. Grant that she may persevere in Your truth and enjoy continual peace through the intercession of Pope St. Leo. Amen.

ST. MARTIN OF TOURS, Bishop

November 11—*Patron of Soldiers*

THIS great and renowned Saint was born in Pannonia (Hungary) about 317. The son of pagan parents, he early became a catechumen and served in the Roman army until, after he had given half his cloak to a beggar at Amiens, a vision of Christ (about 339) impelled him to Baptism and the religious life.

He was ordained an exorcist by St. Hilary, Bishop of Poitiers, and spent the ensuing years in various places, for some time leading the life of a hermit off the Italian coast. He had the happiness of converting his mother and also was flogged for offering public opposition to the Arians. Upon St. Hilary's return from exile, St. Martin rejoined him and built a monastery at Ligugé where he lived until being chosen Bishop of Tours in 371.

In his new dignity he continued to lead the same humble and mortified life as before. At first he lived in a little cell near the church, but he afterward laid the foundations of the celebrated monastery of Marmoutier, which then consisted only of a series of grottoes in the rock, or of wooden cells, in which the holy Bishop and his disciples dwelt and performed their exercises of piety. A number of disciples flocked to his monastic standard, and he thus became the founder of monasticism in Gaul, as St. Anthony had been in Egypt and St. Hilarion in Palestine. This monastery also became a nursery of Bishops, such was the reputation of the disciples of St. Martin.

The zealous labors of the Saint succeeded in extirpating idolatry from the diocese of Tours and the neighboring parts of Gaul. Although in the midst of the heresies of his time, he was a staunch adherent of the Catholic Faith. He, as well as St. Ambrose, energetically protested against those who would put heretics to death. The life of this great Saint was one of constant prayer. His virtues were also rewarded by an extraordinary gift of miracles. After a long life of more than eighty years, he died peacefully in the year 397.

PRAYER God, Your Bishop St. Martin glorified You by both his life and his death. Renew in us Your grace, so that neither death nor life can separate us from Your love. Amen.

ST. JOSAPHAT, Bishop and Martyr

November 12

JOSAPHAT Kuncewicz was born in Poland of noble parents in 1580 and went on to become the first great leader of the Ruthenian Catholics, or Uniates, the former schismatics who had returned to the Church through the treaty of Brest Litovsk in 1595. Entering the Order of St. Basil at twenty years of age, he thoroughly reformed it, giving it a more active character.

So well-known did his wisdom and knowledge become that he was recommended to the Pope by his own people to rule over them as Archbishop of Polotsk in 1617. In this office, he campaigned intensively for the conversion of schismatics and for the reform of his own clergy, who were commonly ignorant and venal. Through his boundless charity and powerful preaching, he established the ascendancy of the Uniate

Church, but was soon marked for destruction by the schismatics. He was slain by Orthodox fanatics in 1623, at Vitebsk, and was canonized in 1687 by Pope Innocent XI.

PRAYER God, stir up in Your Church the Spirit which strengthened St. Josaphat to be able to lay down his life for his sheep. May we be strengthened by the same Spirit so that through Josaphat's intercession we may be ready to lay down our lives for our brothers. Amen.

ST. FRANCES XAVIER CABRINI, Virgin

November 13—*Patroness of Immigrants*

FRANCES Xavier Cabrini was born in Lombardy, Italy, in 1850, one of thirteen children. At eighteen, she desired to become a Sister but poor health stood in her way. She helped her parents until their death, and then worked on a farm with her brothers and sisters.

One day a priest asked her to teach in a girls' school and she stayed for six years. At the request of her Bishop, she founded the Missionary Sisters of the Sacred Heart to care for poor children in schools and hospitals. Then at the urging of Pope Leo XIII she came to the United States with six Sisters in 1889 to work among the Italian immigrants.

Filled with a deep trust in God and endowed with a wonderful administrative ability, this remarkable woman soon founded schools, hospi-

tals, and orphanages in a strange land and saw them flourish in the aid of Italian immigrants and children. At the time of her death, in Chicago on December 22, 1917, her institute numbered houses in England, France, Spain, the United States, and South America. In 1946, she became the first American citizen to be canonized, when she was elevated to sainthood by Pope Pius XII.

PRAYER God, through the work of St. Frances Cabrini You brought comfort and love to the immigrants and those in need. May her example and work be continued in the lives of those dedicated to You. Amen.

ST. SIDONIUS, Abbot

November 14

A NATIVE of Ireland in the 7th century, St Sidonius came in contact with some monks from the Abbey of Jumièges (Normandy) who had been sent into Ireland to ransom Anglo-Saxon slaves. Impressed by their life, he journeyed to Jumièges and received the monastic habit about 664. Some ten years later, he was sent to the monastery of Herio and then to the monastery of Quincay; and in 674 he accompanied St. Audoenus to Rome.

About 685, Sidonius returned to Jumièges and at the request of St. Audoenus founded a monastery northeast of Rouen, which became known as Saint-Saens and was destroyed in 851 by the Normans. After the death of St. Audoenus, Sidonius was instrumental in founding still another monastery in that region. Thus, he played a leading role in the religious life of his age.

Like all pioneering religious, St. Sidonius weathered many storms both physical and spiritual by clinging steadfastly to trust in God. He was devoted to prayer and penance, and helped innumerable souls before his death.

PRAYER Lord, amid the things of this world, let us be wholeheartedly committed to heavenly things in imitation of the example of evangelical perfection You have given us in St. Sidonius the Abbot. Amen.

ST. ALBERT THE GREAT, Bishop and Doctor of the Church

November 15—*Patron of Scientists*

BORN in 1206 at Swabia, Germany, St. Albert the Great spent his youth under the spiritual tutelage of Blessed Jordan of Saxony, who inspired him to join the Order of Preachers. He studied and taught philosophy at Cologne and Paris, where he became one of the most famous philosophers of his day. At Cologne he was famous as the teacher of St. Thomas Aquinas. Named to the Bishopric of Ratisbon, he retired to dedicate his talents to writing and teaching. He died in Poland in 1280.

St. Albert the Great was a man of immense knowledge and erudition. His works are voluminous in bulk and encyclopedic in scope: they include—besides biblical and theological works and sermons—treatises on logic, metaphysics, ethics, and the physical sciences. His interests extended to physics, astronomy, chemistry, and biology, to human and animal physiology, to geography, geology and botany. This "Universal Teacher" stands out for his recognition of the autonomy of human reason in its own sphere and the validity of knowledge gained from sense-experience. Yet he never ceased to regard the Scriptures as the fount of man's spirituality or true wisdom. He was beatified in 1622 by Pope Gregory XV and was equivalently canonized by being declared a Doctor of the Church in 1931 by Pope Pius XI.

PRAYER God, You made St. Albert great by enabling him to combine human wisdom and Divine Faith. Help us so to adhere to his teaching that we may progress in the sciences and at the same time come to a deeper understanding and love of You. Amen.

ST. MARGARET OF SCOTLAND

November 16

A GRAND-NIECE of Edward the Confessor, St. Margaret was born in 1045 in Hungary, the daughter of an exiled Scottish nobleman (King Edward the Exile) and a Hungarian princess. Brought by her father to Scotland, she became the Queen of Malcolm III, about 1070. She was devoted to the spiritual perfection of her eight children, practiced austere self-denial, and possessed unflagging love for the poor.

As Queen, Margaret used her influence in the interests of the Faith; she convoked a synod which drew up regulations for the Lenten fast, Easter communion, and marriage laws. She founded several churches, and was constantly engaged in prayer and devout practices. After her death in 1093 she was continually venerated by the Scottish people and in 1673 Pope Clement X proclaimed her Patroness of Scotland.

PRAYER God, You endowed St. Margaret with a wonderful love for the poor. Through her inter-

cession and example, make us so generous that all people may see in us the image of Your goodness. Amen.

ST. GERTRUDE, Virgin

***The Same Day*—November 16**

Patroness of the West Indies

ST. GERTRUDE was born in 1256 at Eisleben in Saxony. At the age of five she was placed in the care of the Benedictine nuns at Helfta and later became a nun in the same abbey. There she delighted in the study of the Latin laguage and literature as well as music and painting.

At the age of twenty-five, she underwent a conversion to follow the Lord more closely. She began a life filled with humility, patience in suffering and care for others. She dedicated herself to the meditation of Scripture and liturgical texts and frequented the reading of the Fathers.

St. Gertrude had enjoyed a good education. She wrote and composed in Latin, and was versed in sacred literature. The life of this Saint, though not replete with stirring events and striking actions, was one of great mental activity. It was the mystic life of the cloister, a life hidden with Christ in God.

She was characterized by great devotion to the Sacred Humanity of our Lord in His Passion and in the Blessed Eucharist, and by a tender love for the Blessed Virgin. She died in 1302. Her feast was inserted in the Universal Calendar in 1677 by Pope Innocent XI.

PRAYER God, You prepared a pleasing abode for Yourself in the heart of St. Gertrude the Virgin. Through her intercession, mercifully lighten the darkness of our heart so that we may rejoice in the knowledge that You are present and working within us. Amen.

ST. ELIZABETH OF HUNGARY, Religious

November 17

ST. ELIZABETH was born in Hungary in 1207, the daughter of Alexander II, King of Hungary. At the age of four she was sent for her education to the court of the Landgrave of Thuringia, to whose infant son she was betrothed. As she grew in age, her piety also increased by leaps and bounds. In 1221, she married Louis of Thuringia and in spite of her position at court began to lead an austerely simple life, practiced penance, and devoted herself to works of charity.

Her husband was himself much inclined to religion and highly esteemed her virtue, encouraging her in her exemplary life. They had three children when tragedy struck—Louis was killed while fighting with the Crusaders. After his death, Elizabeth left the court, made arrangements for the care of her children, and in 1228 renounced the world, becoming a tertiary of St. Francis. She built the Franciscan hospital at Marburg and devoted herself to the care of the sick until her death at the age of twenty-four in 1231. She was canonized in 1235 by Pope Gregory IX.

PRAYER God, You taught St. Elizabeth to recognize and serve Christ in the poor. Grant, through her intercession, that we may always lovingly serve the needy and the oppressed. Amen.

ST. ROSE PHILIPPINE DUCHESNE, Virgin

November 18

BORN in Grenoble, France, in 1769, Rose joined the Society of the Sacred Heart. In 1818, when she was forty-nine, Rose was sent to the United States. She founded a boarding school for daughters of pioneers near St. Louis and opened the first free school west of the Missouri.

At the age of seventy-one, she began a school for Indians, who soon came to call her "the woman who is always praying." Her biographers have also stressed her courage in frontier conditions, her singlemindedness in pursuing her dream of serving Native Americans, and her self-acceptance.

This holy servant of God was beatified in 1940 by Pope Pius XII and canonized in 1988 by Pope St. John Paul II.

PRAYER Gracious God, You filled the heart of Philippine Duchesne with charity and missionary zeal and gave her the desire to make You known among all peoples. Fill us, who honor her memory today, with that same love and zeal to extend Your Kingdom to the ends of the earth. Amen.

DEDICATION OF THE CHURCHES OF STS. PETER AND PAUL, Apostles

***The Same Day*—November 18**

AMONG the sacred places venerated by Christians from ancient times, one of the most celebrated has always been the tomb of St. Peter, at Rome. The Emperor Constantine erected a splendid basilica over this tomb and another basilica on the Ostian Way at the place where St. Paul suffered martyrdom. Both were consecrated by St. Sylvester.

When the basilica of St. Peter was destroyed, it was rebuilt in a more imposing style and newly consecrated in 1626. The basilica of St. Paul, also destroyed by fire, was in turn rebuilt and newly consecrated by Pius IX in 1854, before an assemblage of Cardinals and Bishops who were in Rome to attend the ceremonies connected with the promulgation of the dogma of the Immaculate Conception. The anniversaries of both dedications are united and form the object of today's feast.

PRAYER God, give apostolic protection to Your Church, so that as she received the first revelation about You from the Apostles she may also receive through them an increase of heavenly grace until the end of time. Amen.

ST. MECHTILDE (MATHILDA)

November 19

AT THE age of seven, St. Mechtilde was entrusted to the nuns of Rodalsdorf, who shortly afterward elected her elder sister Gertrude as their Abbess. Mechtilde herself became a nun, and mistress of the school when the house moved to Helfta. In this capacity, it became her lot to train a five-year-old who entered the monastery in 1261 and went on to become St. Gertrude the Great. The pupil wrote of her mistress: “There has never been anyone like her in our monastery, and I am afraid there will never be again.”

In collaboration with another nun St. Gertrude wrote an account of Mechtilde’s spiritual teaching and mystical experiences entitled *The Book of Special Grace*, which was made public after her death on November 19, 1298.

PRAYER God, You prepared a pleasing abode for Yourself in the heart of St. Mechtilde the Virgin. Through her intercession mercifully lighten the darkness of our heart so that we may rejoice in the knowledge that You are present and working within us. Amen.

ST. BERNWARD, Bishop of Hildesheim

November 20

A SAXON by birth and an orphan at an early age, St. Bernward was brought up under the care of his uncle, Bishop Volkmar of Utrecht. Sent first to the Cathedral school of Heidelburg, he completed his studies at Mainz and was ordained a priest. After the death of his grandfather in 987, St. Bernward became an imperial chaplain and tutor of the child-emperor Otto III.

In 1003, he was elected Bishop of Hildesheim and remained in that position for twenty years. He built the church and monastery dedicated to St. Michael and administered his diocese with the utmost wisdom and understanding. He also dabbled in ecclesiastical art and he is especially remembered in connection with metal-work of every kind. He himself spent much time plying the arts of painting and metalworking and several very beautiful pieces of work at Hildesheim are attributed directly to him.

In an ecclesiastical dispute with St. Willigis, Archbishop of Mainz, Bernward conducted himself in a manner beyond reproach and lived to see his opponent publicly submit to the Holy See's decision in favor of the Bishop of Hildesheim. He died on November 20, 1022, and was canonized in 1193 by Pope Celestine III.

PRAYER God, Light and Shepherd of souls, You established St. Bernward as Bishop in Your Church to feed Your flock by his word and form it by his example. Help us through his intercession to keep the Faith he taught by his word and follow the way he showed by his example. Amen.

PRESENTATION OF MARY

November 21

THERE was a religious custom among the Jews, in former times, of promising to dedicate children to God's service in the temple, even before the children were born. The child, before its fifth year had passed, was taken to the temple at Jerusalem and committed to the care of the priest who offered it to the Lord, and, sometimes, the child remained in the temple to be educated and trained to serve the sanctuary and sacred ministers by making vestments and ornaments, assisting at the services, and contributing to the worship of God in the various liturgical offices.

Tradition tells us that the Blessed Virgin Mary was vowed to God by her parents, St. Joachim and St. Ann, and taken by them to the temple when she was three years old. This offering and dedication of the Blessed Virgin to the Lord, the Church commemorates by the feast of the Presentation on November 21. In some religious communities the day is observed with special devotion as a patronal feast.

PRAYER Today we celebrate the glorious memory of the most holy Virgin Mary. Grant, Lord, that through her intercession we too may receive many graces from Your superabundant bounty. Amen.

ST. CECILIA, Virgin and Martyr

November 22—*Patroness of Musicians*

ACCORDING to her legendary Acts, Cecilia was a native of Rome. At an early age she made a vow of virginity, but her parents forced her to marry a nobleman named Valerian. She converted him to the Faith of Christ, and, by the Providence of God, preserved her virginity. She also converted Tiburtius, the brother of Valerian. Both these men suffered martyrdom for the Faith, and St. Cecilia died the same glorious death a few days after. Their death occurred probably in the reign of Marcus Aurelius or of Commodus, between the years 161 and 192.

The name of St. Cecilia has always been most illustrious in the Church, and since the primitive ages it has been mentioned in the Canon of the Mass (First Eucharistic Prayer). She is honored as the patroness of ecclesiastical music.

PRAYER Lord, hear our requests. Through the intercession of Cecilia, please grant what we ask. Amen.

ST. CLEMENT I, Pope and Martyr

November 23—*Patron of Marble-Workers*

A ROMAN of Jewish extraction, St. Clement owed his conversion to Sts. Peter and Paul. He was ordained Bishop by St. Peter. After the martyrdom of Sts. Peter and Paul, St. Linus became Bishop of Rome, and, after governing for eleven years, was succeeded by St. Cletus. Upon the death of the latter, about the year 91, St. Clement became Pope.

Clement wrote a classic Epistle to the Christians at Corinth. He died a martyr about the year 100.

PRAYER Almighty and ever-living God, You show forth Your glory in the strength of Your saints. Help us to be filled with joy in the annual celebration of St. Clement who by his death bore witness to the death of Jesus, which he proclaimed and which he commemorated in the sacrifice of the Mass. Amen.

ST. COLUMBAN, Abbot

***The Same Day*—November 23**

BORN in the province of Leinster, Ireland, in 563, St. Columban has remained famous as a result of the numerous monasteries he established in Gaul, Switzerland, and Italy.

The monastic reform that he undertook with success can be seen in the rigors of his own penances and in his Rule, which was less balanced than that of St. Basil. After his death in 615, many of his Irish companions went on to become great founders in their own right and helped create a bulwark of faith against the onrush of paganism in the Dark Ages.

PRAYER God, in St. Columban You joined the gift of proclaiming the Gospel with a love for the monastic life. Through his intercession and ex-

ample, help us to seek You in all things and labor to increase the company of believers. Amen.

BLESSED MIGUEL AGUSTIN PRO,

Priest and Martyr

***The Same Day*—November 23**

MIGUEL Pro was born near Zacatecas, Mexico, on January 13, 1891. In 1911, he entered the Society of Jesus; his studies took him to the United States, Spain, and Belgium, where he was ordained in 1926.

On his return to Mexico, he carried out his priestly ministry in secret because of the religious persecution. Eventually, his zeal attracted the attention of the authorities; he was arrested on false charges and was condemned to death.

The sentence was carried out by shooting on November 23, 1927. Miguel was beatified on September 25, 1988 by Pope St. John Paul II.

PRAYER Lord, You gave Blessed Miguel the grace to seek Your glory and the salvation of souls. Through his prayers, may we serve and glorify You by faithfully performing our daily duties and helping our neighbor. Amen.

STS. ANDREW DUNG-LAC, Priest and Martyr, **AND COMPANIONS,** Martyrs

November 24

THROUGH the missionary efforts of various religious families beginning in the 16th century and continuing until 1866, the Vietnamese people heard the message of the Gospel, and many accepted it despite persecution and even death.

On June 19, 1988, Pope St. John Paul II from the great number of Vietnamese martyrs canonized 117 persons martyred in the 18th century. Among these are included 96 Vietnamese, 11 missionaries born in Spain and belonging to the Order of Preachers, and 10 French missionaries belonging to the Paris Foreign Mission Society. Among these Saints are 8 Spanish and French bishops, 50 priests (13 European and 37 Vietnamese), and 59 lay people of every state in life.

These martyrs gave their lives not only for the Church but for their country as well. They showed that they wanted the Gospel of Christ to take root in their people and contribute to the good of their homeland. On June 1, 1989, these holy martyrs were inscribed in the liturgical calendar of the Universal Church for November 24.

PRAYER God, the fount and origin of all fatherhood, You enabled the blessed Martyrs Andrew and his companions to be faithful to the Cross of Your Son even unto the shedding of their blood. Grant through their intercession that we may propagate Your love among our brothers and sisters and not only be called but really be Your children. Amen.

ST. CATHERINE LABOURÉ, Virgin

November 25

ST. CATHERINE LABOURÉ was born on May 2, 1806. At an early age she entered the community of the Daughters of Charity, in Paris, France. Three times in 1830 the Virgin Mary appeared to St. Catherine Labouré, who then was a 24-year-old novice.

On July 18, the first apparition occurred in the community's motherhouse. St. Catherine beheld a lady seated on the left side of the sanctuary. When St. Catherine approached her, the heavenly visitor told her how to act in time of trial and pointed to the altar as the source of all consolation. Promising to entrust St. Catherine with a mission which would cause her great suffering, the lady also predicted the anticlerical revolt which occurred at Paris in 1870.

On November 27, the lady showed St. Catherine the medal of the Immaculate Conception, now universally known as "The Miraculous Medal." She commissioned St. Catherine to have one made, and to spread devotion to this medal.

At that time, only her spiritual director, Father Aladel, knew of the apparitions. Forty-five years later, St. Catherine spoke fully of the apparitions to one of her superiors. She died on December 31, 1876, and was canonized on July 27, 1947, by Pope Pius XII.

PRAYER O Lord Jesus Christ, You were pleased to gladden the holy Virgin Catherine by the wonderful apparition of Your Immaculate Mother. Grant that we may follow the example of the same Saint in honoring Your most holy Mother with filial devotion and obtain the joy of eternal life. Amen.

ST. JOHN BERCHMANS, Religious

November 26—*Patron of Altar Boys*

THE son of a shoemaker, John Berchmans was born in Diest, Belgium in 1599. After studying for three years under a parish priest who prepared boys for the priesthood, he entered the newly-opened Jesuit College at Mechlin in 1615, and a year later joined their novitiate. In 1618 he journeyed to Rome on foot (in ten weeks) to continue his studies at the Roman College.

After studying philosophy for three years, he was selected by his superiors to take part in a public debate, but became ill before it had ended. As this model Jesuit Seminarian lay on what turned out to be his deathbed, he clasped his rosary, his crucifix, and his book of rules and said: "These are my three treasures; with these I shall gladly die." The very next day, August 13, 1621, he passed on to his heavenly reward. He was canonized in 1888 by Pope Leo XIII.

PRAYER God, You inspired St. John Berchmans to strive for perfect charity and so attain Your Kingdom at the end of his pilgrimage on earth. Strengthen us through his intercession that we may advance rejoicing in the way of love. Amen.

ST. MAXIMUS, Bishop

November 27

ST. MAXIMUS was born in Provence, France. From his earliest years he gave evidence of more than ordinary virtue. After living a saintly life in the world for some years, he finally retired to the famous monastery of Lerins, where he was kindly received by St. Honoratus, by whom it was governed. When the latter had become Archbishop of Aries in 426, St. Maximus was chosen second Abbot of Lerins.

The reputation of his sanctity drew crowds to the island, and the monastery prospered under his benevolent administration. He had governed it about seven years when the See of Riez in Provence became vacant. Finding that he was wanted to fill it, he fled to the coast of Italy; but he was overtaken, brought back, and forced to accept the new dignity. In this position, he continued to wear a hair shirt and to observe the monastic rule insofar as his duties allowed.

He assisted at the Council of Riez in 439, the first held in Orange in 441, and at that of Aries in 454. He died before the year 462.

PRAYER Almighty and ever-living God, You willed to make Bishop St. Maximus rule over Your people. Grant by his interceding merits that we may receive the grace of Your mercy. Amen.

ST. JAMES OF THE MARCH, Priest

November 28

JAMES GANGALA was born in 1391 in the March of Ancona, Italy, and was therefore surnamed "of the March." Though of humble origin he was able to attend the University of Perugia and won the laurels of Doctor of Laws. However, after a short stint at teaching, he renounced the world to become a Franciscan friar. He was ordained and for fifty years preached the Faith to thousands in season and out of season. Together with St. John of Capistrano he fought strenuously against the rigorist and heretical sects known as the Fraticelli, and helped reconcile the moderate Hussites to the Church at the Council of Basle.

Everywhere he went James stood as a luminous figure of sanctity and the Franciscan apostolate. Such was the fervor and power of his preaching that he is said to have converted fifty thousand heretics and countless sinners, including thirty-six harlots through a single sermon on St. Mary Magdalene. He traveled all over Europe as the ambassador of Popes and rulers, sleeping little and praying much.

His love for the poor led him to establish pawnshops where they might borrow money at low rates, a work which was made very popular by his protégé, St. Bernardine of Feltre. Despite a vigorous life schedule, rigorous penances, and never-ending activity, St. James died at the age of eighty-five on November 28, 1476.

PRAYER God, You made St. James an illustrious preacher of the Gospel to save souls and to bring back sinners from the mire of sin to the pathway of virtue. Through his intercession may we be cleansed from all sin and obtain eternal life. Amen.

ST. SATURNINUS, Bishop and Martyr

November 29—*Patron of Toulouse*

THE life of St. Saturninus is shrouded in mystery. However, a late tradition says that he was sent from Rome to Gaul by Pope Fabian, about the year 245, to preach the Faith to the people of that country. In the year 250, during the consulate of Decius and Gratus, he fixed his See at Toulouse, and converted a number of idolaters by his preaching and miracles.

One day, as he was passing the principal temple in the city, the priests seized him and dragged him into it, declaring that he should either appease the offended deities by offering sacrifices to them or die. On his positive refusal, they abused him and finally tied his feet to a wild bull which had been brought there for sacrifice. They then drove the beast from the temple and the martyr was dragged after it. He soon expired, but his body was literally torn to pieces. This probably happened under Valerian, in 257.

PRAYER God, You gave splendor to Your Church by granting St. Saturninus the victory of martyrdom. Grant that, as he imitated the Lord's Passion, so we may follow in his footsteps and attain everlasting joys. Amen.

ST. ANDREW, Apostle

November 30

Patron of Fishermen

ST. ANDREW, the brother of St. Peter, was a native of the town of Bethsaida in Galilee, and a fisherman by profession. Being first a disciple of St. John the Baptist, he later joined Jesus, and also brought to Him his brother Simon, with whom he became a member of the Apostolic College. After the dispersion of the Apostles, St. Andrew preached the Gospel in Scythia, as we learn from Origen; and, as Sophronius says, also in Sogdiana and Colchis.

According to Theodoret, St. Gregory Nazianzen, and St. Jerome, he also labored in Greece. It is even believed that he carried the Gospel as far as Russia and Poland, and that he preached at

Byzantium. He suffered martyrdom at Patras in Achaia, and, according to ancient authorities, by crucifixion on a cross in the form of an X.

The body of the Saint was taken to Constantinople in 357, and deposited in the Church of the Apostles, built by Constantine the Great. In 1270, when the city fell into the hands of the Latins, the relics were transported to Italy and deposited in the Cathedral of Amalfi.

PRAYER Lord, You raised up St. Andrew, Your Apostle, to preach and rule in Your Church. Grant that we may always experience the benefit of his intercession with You. Amen.

ST. FLORENCE, Laywoman

December 1

ST. FLORENCE was the daughter of a Roman colonist who was residing in Asia Minor on the road that led from Frigia to Seleucia. St. Hilary of Poitiers met her during a stop on his journey toward Seleucia where the Synod of 359 was to be held. Florence requested Baptism from the holy Bishop and followed him on his return to Poitiers the next year.

She then retired to Comblé, Vienne, France, where she led the life of a hermit. She communed with God day and night, practicing much penance and combating the assaults of the devil. Finally worn out by her labors, she died in 366 at twenty-nine years of age. Her relics were transferred to the Cathedral of Poitiers in the 11th century.

PRAYER God, You inspired St. Florence to strive for perfect charity and so attain Your Kingdom at the end of her pilgrimage on earth. Strengthen us through her intercession that we may advance rejoicing in the way of love. Amen.

ST. BIBIANA, Virgin and Martyr

December 2

OTHER than the name nothing is known for certain about this Saint. However, we have the following account from a later tradition.

In the year 363, Julian the Apostate made Apronianus Governor of Rome. St. Bibiana suffered in the persecution started by him. She was the daughter of Christians, Flavian, a Roman knight, and Dafrosa, his wife. Flavian was tortured and sent into exile, where he died of his wounds. Dafrosa was beheaded, and their two daughters, Bibiana and Demetria, were stripped of their possessions and left to suffer poverty. However, they remained in their house, spending their time in fasting and prayer.

Apronianus, seeing that hunger and want had no effect upon them, summoned them. Demetria, after confessing her Faith, fell dead at the feet of the tyrant. St. Bibiana was reserved for greater sufferings. She was placed in the hands of a wicked woman called Rufina, who in vain endeavored to seduce her. She used blows as well as persuasion, but the Christian virgin remained faithful.

Enraged at the constancy of this saintly Virgin, Apronianus ordered her to be tied to a pillar and beaten with scourges, laden with lead weights, until she expired. The Saint endured her torments with joy, and died under the blows inflicted by the hands of the executioner.

PRAYER Lord God, You showered heavenly gifts on St. Bibiana. Help us to imitate her virtues during our earthly life and enjoy eternal happiness with her in heaven. Amen.

ST. FRANCIS XAVIER, Priest

December 3—*Patron of Foreign Missions*

THE Apostle of the Indies was born at the castle of Xavier in Navarre, Spain, in 1506. He was of noble descent. At the age of eighteen he went to Paris to study philosophy. About four years later, St. Ignatius Loyola came to the same city and took up his abode in the College of St. Barbara, to which St. Francis belonged. At that time St. Francis was full of the world and ambition, but the company of St. Ignatius exercised such a beneficent influence upon him that he grew to be a changed man and became one of the first disciples of the Saint.

In 1536, he went to Venice with the first companions of St. Ignatius. After visiting Rome he was ordained a priest at Venice in 1537, and the

first Jesuits made their vows before the Pope's nuncio. Shortly after the Society had been established, St. Francis was sent to Portugal. In 1541, he set sail for India, which was to be the field of his labors for the rest of his life, and landed at Goa the following year. From that city, which he completely reformed, his apostolic labors extended to the coast of Malabar, to Travancor, Malacca, the Moluccas, and Ceylon, and in all these places he converted large numbers to Christianity.

In 1549, he carried the light of Faith to Japan, of which he became the first missionary, and where a flourishing Christian community soon arose. He remained in Japan two years and four months, and returned to India in 1551.

He then turned his eyes to China. After visiting Goa, he set sail, in 1552, to carry out his resolve, but God was satisfied with his will. On the twenty-third day after his departure from Malacca he arrived at Sancian. On November 20 a fever seized him, and, alone upon a foreign shore, he died on Friday, December 2, 1552, at the age of forty-six. He was canonized in 1602 by Pope Clement VIII.

PRAYER Lord, You won many peoples for Your Church through the preaching of St. Francis. Inspire the faithful today with the same zeal for spreading the Faith, so that everywhere the Church might rejoice in her many children. Amen.

ST. JOHN DAMASCENE,

Priest and Doctor of the Church

December 4

ST. JOHN was born about the year 676. He was famous for his great encyclopedic knowledge and theological method, which later was a source of inspiration to St. Thomas Aquinas.

He vigorously opposed the Iconoclast persecution of the Emperor of Constantinople, Leo the Isaurian, and he distinguished himself in the defense of the veneration of sacred images. He was condemned to have his right hand cut off, but lived to see it miraculously restored through the intercession of the Blessed Virgin. After continued persecutions he died in peace, toward the latter part of the 8th century.

PRAYER Grant, O Lord, that we may be aided by the prayers of St. John, Your Priest. May the true Faith which he taught with excellence be our constant light and strength. Amen.

ST. GERALD, Bishop of Braga

December 5

IN THE latter half of the 11th century, the Archbishop of Toledo named Bernard was delegated by the Pope to bring about an ecclesiastical reform in Spain. He called in various French clerics and monks, among whom was St. Gerald, Abbot of Moissac, who was appointed choir director of the Cathedral of Toledo.

So well did this saintly man fulfill his duties and so much did he influence the people for good that when the See of Braga became vacant, Gerald was selected by the clergy and people of that city to be their Bishop. Gerald visited his diocese, eradicating the abuses that had cropped up, especially that of the administering of ecclesiastical investiture by laymen.

This man of God was called to his heavenly reward on December 5, 1109, at Bornos, Portugal.

PRAYER God, Light and Shepherd of souls, You established St. Gerald as Bishop in Your Church to feed Your flock by his word and form it by his example. Help us through his intercession to keep the Faith he taught by his word and follow the way he showed by his example. Amen.

ST. NICHOLAS, Bishop

December 6—*Patron of Bakers and Pawnbrokers*

IT IS the common opinion that St. Nicholas was a native of Patara in Lycia, Asia Minor. He became a monk in the monastery of Holy Zion near Myra. Of this house he was made Abbot by the Archbishop, its founder. When the See of Myra, the capital of Lycia, fell vacant, St. Nicholas was appointed its Archbishop. It is said that he suffered for the Faith under Diocletian, and that he was present at the Council of Nice as an opponent of Arianism. His death occurred at Myra, in the year 342.

The characteristic virtue of St. Nicholas appears to have been his charity for the poor. It is also related that he was mortified and abstemious from his very infancy. St. Nicholas is regarded as the special patron of children, and our well-known Santa Claus is a derivative of St. Nicholas. The Emperor Justinian built a church in his honor at Constantinople in the suburb of Blacharnae, about the year 340.

He has always been honored with great veneration in the Latin and Greek Churches. The Russian Church seems to honor him more than any other Saint after the Apostles.

PRAYER We call upon Your mercy, O Lord. Through the intercession of St. Nicholas, keep us safe amid all dangers so that we may go forward without hindrance on the road of salvation. Amen.

ST. AMBROSE,

Bishop and Doctor of the Church

December 7—*Patron of Candlemakers*

ST. AMBROSE was born in Gaul, where his father exercised the office of Prefect of the Praetorium, about the year 340. His father died while he was still an infant, and with his mother he returned to Rome, where he enjoyed a good education, learned the Greek language, and became a good poet and orator. Later he moved to Milan with his brother.

Probus, Praetorian Prefect of Italy, appointed Ambrose Governor of Liguria and Aemilia. His virtues in this office, and the voice of a child who proclaimed him Bishop, marked him out to the people of Milan as their Bishop on the vacancy of the See. Both Catholics and Arians elected him to the first dignity in the diocese, a dignity which he reluctantly accepted. As he was only a catechumen, he received the Sacrament of Baptism, after which he was consecrated Bishop, in 374, at the age of thirty-four.

After giving his fortune to the Church and the poor, he applied himself to study the Scriptures and ecclesiastical writers, placing himself under the instruction of Simplicianus, a priest of the Church of Rome, who succeeded him in the Archbishopric of Milan. His warfare against the Arians was such that by the year 385 very few still professed that heresy in the diocese. In 381, he held a Council at Milan against the heresy of Apollinaris, and assisted at that of Aquileia; the next year, he assisted at one held in Rome.

When Maximus assumed the purple in Gaul, St. Ambrose was sent there, and he succeeded in concluding a treaty with the Emperor. But a second embassy, in 387, was not so successful: Maximus invaded Italy and was defeated by the Emperor Theodosius. St. Ambrose at a later date had occasion to reprehend Theodosius and did so with the greatest apostolical freedom.

He had the satisfaction of witnessing the conversion of the great St. Augustine, whom he baptized in 387. One of his last actions was the ordination of St. Honoratus. After a life of labor and prayer the holy Bishop of Milan died in 397.

PRAYER God, by Your grace St. Ambrose, Your Bishop, became a great teacher of the Catholic Faith and an example of apostolic fortitude. Raise up Bishops in Your Church today who will give strong and wise leadership. Amen.

IMMACULATE CONCEPTION OF THE BLESSED VIRGIN MARY

December 8—*Patroness of the United States*

MARY the Mother of God is venerated on December 8 as the Immaculate Conception. This feast commemorates the preservation of the Blessed Virgin from the stain of original sin from the first moment of her conception. It originated in the Eastern Church about the 8th century.

The doctrine of the Immaculate Conception was defined by Pope Pius IX on December 8, 1854. This dogma, in accord with the texts of Scripture—"I will put enmity between you and the woman, between your seed and her seed" (Gn 3:15); "Hail, full of grace" (Luke 1:28)—was clearly understood and accepted by tradition, by the writings of the Fathers and by feasts observed according to the general belief of the faithful long before it was officially defined by Pope Pius IX.

PRAYER God, through the Immaculate Conception of the Virgin, You prepared a worthy place for Your Son. In view of the foreseen Death of Your Son, You preserved her from all sin. Through her intercession grant that we may also reach You with clean hearts. Amen.

ST. JUAN DIEGO, Layman

December 9

LITTLE is known about the life of Juan Diego, to whom Our Lady of Guadalupe appeared on December 9, 1531. His given name was said to be "Cuauhtlatzin" (meaning "Talking Eagle" in his native language).

He was a member of the Chichimeca people, one of the more culturally advanced groups living in the Valley of Anahuac, as the area that is now Mexico City was once known. He was a leader of his own people and may have been involved in the area's textile industry.

After the apparitions of the Blessed Virgin Mary, according to tradition, Juan Diego received the Bishop's permission to live as a hermit in a small hut near the chapel that was built on Tepeyac. There he cared for the church and the first pilgrims who came to see the miraculous image and pray to the Mother of Jesus. His contemporaries were impressed with his holiness; parents used to bless their children with the wish, "May God make you like Juan Diego." He was canonized by Pope St. John Paul II on July 31, 2002.

PRAYER Lord God, through St. Juan Diego You made known the love of Our Lady of Guadalupe toward Your people. By his intercession, grant that we who follow the counsel of Mary, our Mother, may strive continually to do Your will. Amen.

ST. ROMARIC, Abbot

December 10

A MEROVINGIAN nobleman of the 7th century, St. Romaric was a courtier at the court of Clotaire II when he was converted to God by St. Amatus. Romaric granted freedom to the numerous serfs under him and entered the monastery of Luxeuil. In 620, he founded on his estates the Abbey of Remiremont (which means Romaric's hill) with St. Amatus as its first Abbot.

In a short time, however, the duties of Abbot were shifted to St. Romaric who went on to retain that position for thirty years. During this time, the fame of the monastery drew members in droves and made it possible to have the Divine Office sung without intermission by seven alternating choirs.

Perhaps the best illustration of the type of dedication possessed by St. Romaric is the fact that three days before his death he traveled all the way to Metz to prevent an attack on the young prince Dagobert. Such was the high regard in which he was held by all that the insurgents heard him out and treated him with respect before sending him back to his monastery. He died in 653.

PRAYER Lord, amid the things of this world, let us be wholeheartedly committed to heavenly things in imitation of the example of evangelical perfection You have given us in St. Romaric the Abbot. Amen.

ST. DAMASUS I, Pope

December 11

THE father of St. Damasus, either after his wife's death, or with her consent, had entered the priesthood and served the parish church of St. Lawrence in Rome. His son, St. Damasus, also entered the sacred ministry, being attached to the same church. Under Pope Liberius he obtained a great share in the government of the Church; and when Liberius died in 366, St. Damasus, then sixty years old, was elected Pope.

In 368, St. Damasus held a Council in Rome, another in the same city in 370, both directed against the Arians, and one in 374, in which the errors of Apollinaris were condemned. St. Jerome, who was a great admirer of St. Damasus, acted as his secretary during the last three years of the life of this holy Pontiff. The Pope encouraged St. Jerome in his studies, and the latter calls him "an incomparable person, learned in the Scriptures, a virgin doctor of the virgin Church, who loved chastity and heard its praises with pleasure."

The church, named to the present day St. Lawrence *in Damaso*, was repaired by the Saint, who also made other improvements in Rome. He was a poet and a man of genius who wrote with elegance. Ancient writers commend especially his zeal for the purity of the Faith, the innocence of his manners, his Christian humility, his compassion for the poor, and his piety. St. Damasus sat in the Chair of St. Peter for eighteen years and two months. He died in 384.

PRAYER Lord, grant that we may always celebrate the merits of Your Martyrs in imitation of St. Damasus who loved and venerated them. Amen.

OUR LADY OF GUADALUPE

December 12—*Patroness of the Americas*

THE Shrine of Our Lady of Guadalupe, near Mexico City, is one of the most celebrated places of pilgrimage in North America. On Dec. 9, 1531, the Blessed Virgin Mary appeared to an Indian convert, Juan Diego, and left with him a picture of herself impressed upon his cloak.

Later, the picture was placed in a magnificent shrine which the Roman Pontiffs ennobled by granting it a Chapter of Canons for the splendor of Divine Worship. There it became famous for the concourse of people and the frequency of miracles, exciting immeasurably the piety of the Mexican nation toward the Mother of God.

Therefore, the Archbishop of Mexico and the other Bishops of those regions as well as all classes of society regarded her as their most powerful Protectress in public and private calamities and elected her principal Patroness of Mexico.

Devotion to Mary under this title has continually increased and today she is the Patroness of the Americas. Because of the close link between the Church in Mexico and the United States this feast was placed on the American Calendar.

PRAYER God, in Your concern and love for Your people You favored the New World with the appearance of Mary, Mother of Jesus, at Guadalupe. Help the countries of this New World to live with one another in peace, unity, and brotherhood. Amen.

ST. LUCY, Virgin and Martyr

December 13—*Patroness of the Blind*

ST. LUCY, a native of Syracuse in Sicily, was from her cradle educated in the Faith of Christ under the care of her widowed mother, Eutychia. At an early age she secretly made a vow of virginity. She accompanied her long-suffering mother to the tomb of St. Agatha, and there her mother was cured of her disease. St. Lucy then disclosed to her mother the vow she had taken, and her mother, in gratitude for her recovery, left her free to follow her pious inclinations.

The young nobleman who had sought her in marriage was so enraged that he accused Lucy of being a Christian. She was imprisoned, but God gave her grace to overcome the tortures she was made to endure. About the year 304, during the fierce war waged against the Christians under Diocletian, St. Lucy met her death by the sword.

PRAYER Lord, may the intercession of Your Virgin and Martyr St. Lucy help us so that, as we celebrate her heavenly birthday on earth, we may contemplate her triumph in heaven. Amen.

ST. JOHN OF THE CROSS, Priest and Doctor of the Church

December 14

JOHN YEPEZ was born at Fontiberos in Old Castile, Spain, in 1542. From his tenderest infancy he evinced a marked devotion toward the Blessed Virgin, of whose Order he became one of the brightest ornaments. After studying in a Jesuit college, he took the Carmelite habit, in the monastery of that Order at Medina del Campo in 1563, and practiced the greatest austerities. In 1567 he was ordained priest.

Shortly after, he met St. Teresa of Avila at Medina del Campo, at which time she interested him in the work of reforming the Order. He entered heartily into her plans, and when the first monastery of Discalced Carmelite Friars was opened at Duruelo, John Yepez (who was to be St. John of the Cross) was its first member.

He successively filled the posts of superior, prior, vicar-general, and definitor. In the midst of his exterior labors his heart was always intimately united to God; he is known in the Church as one of the great contemplatives and teachers of mystical theology.

In his last illness he had a choice between two monasteries; one of them was a pleasant residence and its prior was his intimate friend, but he chose the other, the one of Ubeda, which was poor and where the prior was ill-disposed toward him. After much suffering, he died in 1591 and was canonized in 1726 by Pope Benedict XIII.

PRAYER God, Your Priest St. John became a model of perfect self-denial and showed us how to love the Cross. May we always imitate him and be rewarded with the eternal contemplation of Your glory. Amen.

ST. NINO, Virgin

December 15

CHRISTIANITY was first brought to Georgia, Iberia, at the end of the 3rd century, and ancient tradition attributes this fact to the witness and apostolate of St. Nino. Many legends were in time woven around this Saint (called simply "Christiana," "the Christian Woman," by the Roman Martyrology and Nino by the Georgians). But the most trustworthy account is still the most ancient and simplest one recorded, which Prince Bakur of Georgia gave to Rufinus of Aquileia, the 4th century Church historian.

Captured and brought to Georgia as a slave, Nino impressed the populace by her goodness and religious devotion, as well as by her power to cure disease in the name of Christ her God. Her prayers obtained the cure of a dying child, brought the Queen herself back from sickness, and enabled the King—when lost while hunting—to find his way again by calling on Christ. Both rulers received instruction and Baptism from Nino, and she was free to teach and preach.

Under her direction, a church was erected in such wondrous fashion that the people began to clamor to become Christians also. Hence, the King sent a legate to Emperor Constantine, asking for Bishops and priests to continue and extend St. Nino's work, and so the Faith came to this region along the Black Sea.

PRAYER God, through St. Nino, Your Virgin, You enabled those without the Faith to pass from darkness to the light of truth. Grant us through her intercession to stand fast in the Faith and remain constant in the hope of the Gospel which she preached. Amen.

ST. ADELAIDE, Queen

December 16—*Patroness of Prisoners*

BORN in 931 to a noble family of Burgundy, Adelaide was married at the age of sixteen to King Lothair of Italy. She was widowed after three years and suffered much at the hands of Berengarius II of Friuli who had taken over the kingdom. Liberated by King Otto the Great of Germany, she married him and bore him three sons, one of whom was the future Otto II.

St. Adelaide possessed great intellectual gifts and took part in the affairs of state. In 962, she and her husband were crowned by Pope John XII. After her husband's death in 973 she experienced a particularly difficult time because of the problems that arose between her and her son Otto II and his wife. From 983, and especially

991, onward she ruled in place of her minor grandson Otto III, showing rare prudence and understanding.

This saintly woman had a great love for the poor and interested herself in the reform of Cluny brought about by Sts. Majolus and Odilo. She built monasteries and churches and granted benefices to all who were worthy of them. Toward the end of her full life, she retired to a Benedictine monastery which she had founded near Strasbourg and prepared herself for a holy death, which took place on December 16, 999.

PRAYER God, You gladden us each year by the feast of St. Adelaide. Grant that as we honor her in such festivities we may also imitate her example in our conduct. Amen.

ST. OLYMPIAS, Widow

December 17

ST OLYMPIAS, a lady of illustrious descent and ample fortune, was born about the year 368. Educated under the care of Theodosia, sister of St. Amphilochius, she practiced eminent virtue at an early age. She was very young when she married Nebridius, treasurer of the Emperor, Theodosius the Great, but he died within days. She positively refused a second marriage, in spite of the pressure that was brought to bear upon her.

In Contantinople where she resided, her life was henceforth devoted to good works and charitable deeds. Her immense riches were entirely consecrated to the Church and the poor. Like all the saints of God, she also had to endure many afflictions, corporal infirmities, and persecutions on the part of the world. Nectarius, Patriarch of Constantinople, appointed her deaconess of the Church, an office which existed at that time. St. John Chrysostom, who became Patriarch in 398, also had the greatest respect for her virtue. Her fidelity to his cause when he was exiled in 404 drew upon her the persecution of his enemies, until she was finally obliged to leave the city (but she returned the next year).

Her correspondence with St. John Chrysostom was a great comfort and encouragement for her. In exchange for the direction received from the Saint, she sent plentiful supplies with which, in his dreary exile, he ransomed many captives. She survived St. John Chrysostom, for she was still living in the year 408. Her death occurred about the year 410.

PRAYER God, You inspired St. Olympias to strive for perfect charity and so attain Your Kingdom at the end of her pilgrimage on earth. Strengthen us through her intercession that we may advance rejoicing in the way of love. Amen.

ST. GATIAN, Bishop of Tours

December 18

ST. GATIAN came from Rome with St. Dionysius of Paris, about the middle of the 3rd century, and preached the Faith, principally at Tours in Gaul, where he fixed his episcopal See. In that portion of Gaul idolatry was strong, but the perseverance of the Saint gained a number of converts. He was often obliged to conceal himself from the fury of the heathen inhabitants of the place. He celebrated the Divine mysteries in caves and grottoes, where he assembled his little flock. He continued his labors amid many dangers for nearly fifty years, and died in peace.

PRAYER God, You made St. Gatian an outstanding exemplar of Divine love and the Faith that conquers the world, and added him to the roll of saintly Pastors. Grant by his intercession that we may persevere in Faith and love and become sharers of his glory. Amen.

BLESSED URBAN V, Pope

December 19

URBAN V is regarded as the best of the so-called Avignon Popes who ruled the Church for some one hundred and seventy years from Avignon in the 13th and 14th centuries. Born in Grisac, France in 1310, William of Grimoard became a noted Benedictine canonist and served as papal legate to Milan and Naples before being elected Pope in 1362.

The most important event of his reign was his abortive attempt to return the papacy to Rome which occurred in 1367. He restored the papal buildings and reconciled the Eastern Emperor

John V Palaeologus to the Church. He also concluded an alliance with Emperor Charles IV, founded the Universities of Cracow and Vienna, and aided the universities of Avignon, Toulouse, Orange, and Orléans.

However, political conflicts obliged him to return to Avignon in 1370. In June of that year he informed the Romans that he was leaving them for the good of the Church and on September 5 he sailed for France with a heavy heart. On December 19 he was dead, called by a contemporary "a light of the world and a way of truth; a lover of righteousness, fleeing from wickedness and fearing God."

PRAYER Almighty and eternal God, You willed to set Blessed Urban over your entire people and to go before them in word and example. By his intercession keep the pastors of Your Church together with their flocks and guide them in the way of eternal salvation. Amen.

STS. ABRAHAM, ISAAC, AND JACOB,

Patriarchs

December 20

ABRAHAM, son of Thare, left Ur of the Chaldees about 2,000 years before Christ and went to Haran, where his father died. At God's command he took up his abode in Canaan, the land promised to his posterity. Forced by famine into Egypt, he returned to Canaan and rescued his nephew Lot from the King of Elam. On his return he was met by Melchizedek, King of Salem, who blessed him.

God made a covenant with Abraham and promised that his descendants would be as numerous as the stars of the heavens. In accord with God's specific promise he and his wife Sarah had a son in their old age whom they called Isaac. Abraham's faith in God was tested by God's command to sacrifice his son in the manner of the surrounding peoples who practiced child sacrifice. After staying his hand, by means of an Angel, God revealed to Abraham the greatness of his posterity as a reward for his unbounded trust in his Creator. Abraham died at an advanced old age.

As the Divinely promised son of Abraham and Sarah after a long childless marriage, Isaac became the heir of the Messianic blessings. He was proclaimed the sole legal ancestor of God's chosen people, ousting Ishmael, another son of Abraham. He resided at Beersheba and married a member of his father's family, Rebekah, who had been brought from Mesopotamia. She bore him two sons, Esau and Jacob. During a famine Isaac sought the help of Abimelech, the King of the Philistines, at Gerar, where he became rich and powerful. Shortly before his death, when he wished to bless Esau, his favorite son, Rebekah frustrated his intention by a ruse and substituted Jacob.

After depriving his brother Esau of his birthright, Jacob fled to Haran, the dwelling place of his maternal uncle, Laban, who gave him his daughters, Leah and Rachel, as wives. Jacob had twelve sons who became the ancestors of the twelve tribes of the Hebrew people. At Bethel he received a vision and blessing which constitute one of the outstanding events of early Hebrew history. And at Peniel he wrestled all night with a mysterious Divine stranger and received the Divinely given name. In his old age he journeyed to Egypt to rejoin his son Joseph, taking his whole household with him and setting the stage for the Exodus centuries later.

PRAYER Lord God, You showered heavenly gifts on Sts. Abraham, Isaac, and Jacob. Help us to imitate them during our earthly life and enjoy eternal happiness with them in heaven. Amen.

ST. PETER CANISIUS, Priest and Doctor of the Church

December 21

THIS eminent Jesuit was born in Nijmegen, Holland (when it was part of Germany), May 8, 1521. At twenty-two years of age he joined the Society of Jesus and distinguished himself in studies and spiritual perfection. He was the second great Apostle of Germany, preacher, theologian, and leader of the Counter Reformation.

With astonishing clarity this devout man of God saw that in order to combat the Reformation the Church must first reform herself in her pastors and prepare generations of instructed laymen capable of defending their Faith. Of the many works which flowed from his pen, the most celebrated remains a Catechism which appeared in 1560 and went on to achieve two hundred editions before the turn of the century.

He died at Fribourg, Switzerland in 1597. Pope Pius XI canonized him on May 21, 1925, and proclaimed him a Doctor of the Church.

PRAYER God, You endowed Your Priest, St. Peter Canisius, with holiness and learning for the defense of the Church. Through his intercession, grant that those who seek the truth may joyfully find You and that the people of believers may ever persevere in bearing witness to You. Amen.

STS. CHAEREMON AND ISCHYRION,

Martyrs

December 22

IN THE year 247 St. Dionysius was chosen Bishop of Alexandria. Soon afterward, the people of Alexandria, incited by a pagan prophet and given further impetus by an edict of the Emperor Decius, began a fierce persecution of all Christians. St. Dionysius was himself hunted and escaped only through the aid and insistence of a wedding party of pagans.

St. Dionysius wrote an account of this persecution to Fabian, Bishop of Antioch. In it he states that many Christians fled into the desert and there perished from the elements, from hunger, thirst, and over-exposure, or from wild beasts and wild men. Others were captured and sold into slavery.

He especially mentions Chaeremon, Bishop of Nilopolis, a very old man who took refuge in the mountains with a companion. Although a search was made in the mountains of Arabia by the Christians, nothing was ever again heard or seen of either of them.

He also mentions St. Ischyrion who was the procurator of a magistrate in a city of Egypt—probably Alexandria. When ordered by his master to sacrifice to the gods, this holy man refused outright. He steadfastly persisted in this refusal in the face of both abuse and threats on the part of his master. Thereupon, the enraged magistrate had St. Ischyrion mutilated and impaled.

Both of these holy Martyrs are named in the Roman Martyrology on this date.

PRAYER May the prayers of Sts. Chaeremon and Ischyrion make us pleasing to You, Lord, and strengthen Your truth. Amen.

ST. JOHN OF KANTY, Priest

December 23

ST. JOHN was born in 1403 in a village, the name of which he bears, situated in the diocese of Cracow, Poland. His childhood was passed in innocence under the care of his virtuous parents. After finishing his studies he became professor in the University of Cracow, a position he occupied several years, endeavoring not only to train his pupils in science, but also to instill into their hearts the sentiments of piety with which he was himself animated.

Having been ordained to the priesthood, he distinguished himself by still greater zeal for the glory of God and his own perfection. The carelessness and indifference of so many Christians were for him a great source of affliction. As parish priest he became a true pastor of souls, severe toward himself and indulgent to others, showing himself the father of his people and their friend when they were in need. After some years he resumed his duties of professor, practicing at the same time prayer, love for the poor, and all Christian virtues.

Consumed by the desire of suffering martyrdom, he made a pilgrimage to Jerusalem and preached "Jesus Crucified" to the Turks. Four times he made a journey to Rome on foot. His sleep was short and taken on the floor; his food barely sufficed to keep him alive. By means of fasting and severe discipline he preserved his purity intact. During the last thirty years of his life he abstained entirely from meat. Finally, after distributing to the poor all he had in his house, he died in 1474. He was canonized in 1767 by Pope Clement XIII.

PRAYER Almighty God, help us to follow the example of Your Priest, St. John, in advancing in the science of the saints. May we show compassion to all who are in need so that we ourselves may obtain Your mercy. Amen.

ST. ADELE, Widow

December 24

A DAUGHTER of King Dagobert II of Germany, St. Adele became a nun upon the death of her husband, after making provision for her son, the future father of St. Gregory of Utrecht. She founded a convent at Palatiolum near Trier and became its first Abbess, ruling with holiness, prudence, and compassion.

St. Adele seems to have been among the disciples of St. Boniface, the Apostle of Germany, and a letter in his correspondence is addressed to her. After a devout life filled with good works and communion with God, she passed on to her heavenly reward in 730.

PRAYER God, You inspired St. Adele to strive for perfect charity and so attain Your Kingdom at the end of her pilgrimage on earth. Strengthen us through her intercession that we may advance rejoicing in the way of love. Amen.

CHRISTMAS DAY

December 25

MORE than nineteen hundred years ago, a decree went forth from the Roman Emperor, Caesar Augustus, commanding a general census in which all the people of the empire should be enrolled, "each in his own city," that is, in the place to which his tribe and family belonged.

Joseph and Mary went from Nazareth to Bethlehem, the city of David, because they were of the family of that king. Bethlehem is situated about five or six miles south of Jerusalem, and nearly seventy-five miles south of Nazareth. There, in a stable, Jesus Christ, the Son of God, the Redeemer of the world, was born, according to tradition, at midnight, or soon after, on December 25. And it came to pass that, when they were there, Mary "brought forth her first-born Son, and wrapped Him up in swaddling clothes, and laid Him in a manger, because there was no room for them in the inn."

The history of the first Christmas is made familiar to Catholics by the devotion of the "Christmas Crib." In the year 1226, St. Francis of Assisi, with the permission of the Pope, set up the first of these cribs for the purpose of instructing the people and increasing in their hearts love and devotion for the Infant Savior.

Christmas takes its name from the central and supreme act of Christian worship. Christmas means "Christ's Mass," the Mass offered in honor of the birth of Christ. Nearly all European languages, except English, use a word signifying nativity or birthday of Christ to designate the feast of Christmas: in Latin, *Dies Natalis*; in Italian, *Il Natale*; in French the Latin form is softened into *Noel.*

In all lands and languages the great fact commemorated is the birth of Christ, and the great action by which that fact is commemorated and renewed is the Mass. On Christmas priests may celebrate three Masses to honor the threefold birth of the Son of God: His birth in time and in our humanity in the stable of Bethlehem; His spiritual birth by faith and charity in the souls of the shepherds, and in our souls, and in the souls of all who earnestly seek Him; and lastly, His eternal generation in the bosom of the Father.

PRAYER God, in an admirable fashion You established the dignity of human nature and you reformed it in a more admirable manner. Grant that we may come to share in the Divinity of Your Son Who chose to share our humanity. Amen.

ST. STEPHEN, First Martyr

December 26—*Patron of Stonemasons*

ST. STEPHEN, a disciple of Christ, chosen after the Ascension as one of the seven deacons, and "full of grace and fortitude, was working great wonders and signs among the people." Many rose up against him, but they were not able to withstand the wisdom that spoke.

Accused of blasphemy against Moses and against God, he was brought before the Sanhedrin and condemned to be cast out of the city and stoned to death. Kneeling down before his murderers he cried out with a loud voice saying: "Lord, do not lay this sin against them." And when he had said this he fell asleep in the Lord, 35 A.D.

PRAYER God, grant that we may imitate the Saint we honor and learn to love our enemies. For today we celebrate the feast of St. Stephen who knew how to pray even for his persecutors. Amen.

ST. JOHN, Apostle and Evangelist

December 27—*Patron of Asia Minor*

ST. JOHN, the son of Zebedee, and the brother of St. James the Great, was called to be an Apostle by our Lord in the first year of His public ministry. He became the "beloved disciple" and the only one of the twelve who did not forsake the Savior in the hour of His Passion. He stood faithfully at the Cross, whence the Savior made him the guardian of His Mother.

His later life was passed chiefly in Jerusalem and at Ephesus. He founded many churches in Asia Minor. He wrote the fourth Gospel and three Epistles, and the Book of Revelation is also attributed to him. Brought to Rome, tradition relates that he was by order of Emperor Domitian cast into a caldron of boiling oil but came forth unhurt and was banished to the island of Patmos for a year. He lived to an extreme old age, sur-

viving all his fellow Apostles, and died at Ephesus about the year 100.

St. John is called the Apostle of Charity, a virtue he had learned from his Divine Master, and which he constantly inculcated by word and example. The "beloved disciple" died at Ephesus, where a stately church was erected over his tomb. It was afterward converted into a Mohammedan mosque.

PRAYER God, through St. John the Apostle You willed to unlock to us the secrets of Your Word. Grant that what he has so excellently poured into our ears, we may properly understand. Amen.

THE HOLY INNOCENTS, Martyrs

December 28—*Patrons of Choirboys*

TO THE male children of two years and under that were killed in Bethlehem and its environs by order of King Herod, Sts. Irenaeus, Augustine, and other early Fathers give the title of Martyrs, and as such they have been commemorated from the 1st century and honored in the liturgy of the Church. In the Western Church, the Mass of the Holy Innocents is celebrated like those of Advent and Lent, without festal chants.

These innocent victims gave testimony to the Messiah and Redeemer, not by words but by their blood. They triumphed over the world and won their crown without having experienced the evils of the world, the flesh, and the devil.

PRAYER God, today we recall that the Innocent Martyrs bore witness not by words but by their death. Grant that our way of life may give witness to our faith in You which our lips profess. Amen.

ST. THOMAS BECKET, Bishop and Martyr

December 29

ST. THOMAS was born in London in 1117, eight years after the death of St. Anselm, whose successor he was destined to become. He embraced the ecclesiastical state and attached himself to Theobald, Archbishop of Canterbury, by whose leave he went to Italy to study canon law at Bologna. On his return home he was ordained deacon and made archdeacon of Canterbury. In 1154, at the recommendation of Theobald, Henry II appointed him Lord Chancellor of England, a post which he filled with distinction.

On the death of Theobald, in 1160, the King forced upon him the dignity of Archbishop of Canterbury; but when St. Thomas refused to tolerate the existence of certain abuses, the King felt himself offended and finally matters came to an open rupture between Archbishop and King. After much persecution, to which he was subject, Thomas secretly left the kingdom and went to Pope Alexander III who was then in France and who received him kindly. Later he was able to return to England, but he went with the presentiment that he was going to his death. He was received with the greatest demonstrations of joy by his people, but the end was near. Henry, in a fit of passion, let slip some unguarded words which, however they may have been intended, were construed so as to place weapons in the hands of the Saint's assassins. The result was that St. Thomas was murdered in his church, at the foot of the altar, in 1170. Within three years after his death, he was canonized as a Martyr by Pope Alexander III.

PRAYER God, You enabled St. Thomas, Your Martyr, to sacrifice his life courageously in the cause of justice. Through his intercession, help us to give up our lives for Christ in this world so that we might find eternal life in heaven. Amen.

ST. ANYSIUS, Bishop of Thessalonica

December 30

WE KNOW very little about the life of this Saint who became Bishop of Thessalonica upon the death of Ascholius in 383. On this occasion, St. Ambrose wrote to the new Bishop and expressed the hope that since Anysius was a dedicated disciple of Ascholius he might prove to be "another Elisha to Elijah."

Pope St. Damasus made this saintly Bishop the patriarchal vicar of Illyricum and he was confirmed in his power by Sts. Siricius and Innocent I. When St. John Chrysostom was being harassed by the authorities, St. Anysius came strongly to his defense. In 404, he called upon Pope Innocent I to review the case whereby St. John had been exiled from his See, and he was joined in this by fifteen other Bishops of Macedonia. In return he received a letter from St. John thanking him for his efforts on his behalf.

St. Anysius was a dedicated shepherd who inspired his people by his life and teachings. Both St. Innocent I and St. Leo the Great had high praise for his virtues. He died about 410.

PRAYER God, Light and Shepherd of souls, You established St. Anysius as Bishop in Your Church to feed Your flock by his word and form it by his example. Help us through his intercession to keep the Faith he taught by his word and follow the way he showed by his example. Amen.

ST. SYLVESTER I, Pope

December 31

ST. SYLVESTER, born in Rome, was ordained by Pope St. Marcellinus during the peace that preceded the persecutions of Diocletian. He passed through those days of terror, witnessed the abdication of Diocletian and Maximian, and saw the triumph of Constantine in 312.

Two years later he succeeded St. Melchiades as Bishop of Rome. In the same year he sent four legates to represent him at the great Council of the Western Church, held at Arles. He confirmed its decisions and imparted them to the Church.

The Council of Nice was assembled during his reign, in 325, but not being able to assist at it in person, on account of his great age, he sent his legates, who headed the list of subscribers to its decrees, preceding the Patriarchs of Alexandria and Antioch. St. Sylvester occupied the chair of St. Peter for twenty-four years and eleven months. He died in 335.

PRAYER Lord, come to the aid of Your people who are supported by the intercession of St. Sylvester Your Pope. May they pass the present life under Your guidance so that they may have the happiness of attaining eternal life in heaven. Amen.

OTHER OUTSTANDING CATHOLIC BOOKS

ISBN 978-1-947070-67-7
90000
9 781947 070677